MATTHEW–REVELATION

Morning Conversations

on the New Testament

Your 260-day devotional journey through the New Testament with

JON R. ROEBUCK

Published in the United States by Nurturing Faith, Macon, GA.
Nurturing Faith is a book imprint of Good Faith Media (goodfaithmedia.org).
Library of Congress Cataloging-in-Publication Data is available.

Second Edition

ISBN: 978-1-63528-240-5

Dedication

This book is dedicated to Linda, my wife of four decades. She can sing with the best of the angels, laugh with ease in the company of family and friends, grandparent as well as anyone on the planet, and melt my heart with every smile.

Contents

Preface

It all started with a conversation. One Sunday, following the morning service, a member approached me and asked, "Got any good advice about a devotion guide?" He was looking for something that would help him to focus his thoughts each day. I mentioned that I had recently started the practice of journaling some thoughts each morning and wondered if he would like for me to email him a copy of my notes. He was excited about the suggestion and so, starting the following morning, I passed along a few thoughts. At the end of the week, I asked for some feedback. He indicated that not only had he found some good counsel and wisdom in what I had written, but that he had also forwarded a few of the email messages to his father. It made me wonder, "Would others like to be included on the email list of morning devotions?"

And so it started. For the next 460 days, I took on the discipline of writing a morning devotional thought. At first, the list of recipients contained only a handful of names. But word-of-mouth and a few "forwarded emails" soon caused the list to grow to well over 200 recipients. At first, I skipped around a bit… a few books in the Old Testament and then a few in the New Testament. Finally, I decided to pursue the writing of a devotional thought for each chapter in the New Testament. What you now hold in your hand represents a few thoughts from each day's conversation with God as I worked my way through the New Testament.

This book is not intended to be read cover-to-cover in a few short blocks of time. It is to be read like it was written, a thought for each day. It follows a very unoriginal format. Many believers across the country have been taught to use a Bible Study method, sometimes referred to as a "SOAP" study. The idea is to read a scripture passage, Observe what is being said, Apply the meaning, and Pray for wisdom to let the thought make a difference in one's life. You will notice that each day includes a single verse drawn from a chapter in the New Testament. I sincerely hope that you will take the time to read the entire chapter from God's word. Let the overall meaning begin to sink in. Then consider the focus verse, asking God to be revealed in a unique way through that particular verse. It is my prayerful hope that something I have written may help you to understand and apply God's word to the events of your everyday life.

Conversations are important. It's how relationships begin and grow. I encourage you to begin a conversation each morning with God, who has much to share as we read the scriptures. So explore. Dig deep. Reflect for a few moments. And when God speaks, listen, learn, and rejoice.

Morning Conversations Volumes 1-5

Morning Conversations on the Creation of a People and Place is the first volume of a set that follows the natural order of the Old Testament canon, and spans the Biblical narrative from the opening chapter of Genesis to the end of the book of Ruth.

Morning Conversations on the Rise and Fall of Kings and Kingdoms continues the orderly progression, spanning the books of 1 Samuel through Esther.

Morning Conversations on the Wisdom of the Ages covers all five books of wisdom literature from Job to the Song of Solomon.

Morning Conversations on the Prophetic Word wraps up the Old Testament with a look at the books of prophecy, covering both the Major and Minor prophets, Isaiah through Malachi.

Additionally, *Morning Conversations on the New Testament* is the final volume of this collection.

"And Joseph awoke from his sleep and did as the angel of the Lord commanded him, and took Mary as his wife." Matthew 1:24 NASB

Observation

Gospel writer Matthew begins his account of the story of Jesus by connecting Jesus to his Old Testament roots, carefully tracing the genealogy of Jesus all the way back to the time of Abraham. (Matthew was obviously an Old Testament scholar and links the story of Jesus to the events of the Old Testament more than the other Gospel writers. In fact, there are 53 references in Matthew's Gospel to the Old Testament.) In just eight verses Matthew tells the story of the birth of Jesus. In our focus verse, Matthew speaks of the remarkable obedience and faith of Joseph. After being told in a dream by an angel that Mary is pregnant by the Holy Spirit, that her child will be a son who is to be named Jesus, and that he should not be afraid to take her as his wife, Joseph wakes up and does exactly what the angel commanded him to do.

Application

Could any of us have displayed such obedience in the face of such mysterious, frightening, and life-change news? Surely that is why God chose him for such a task… complete obedience in the midst of an unclear future. There is something of our story mingled into this story of Joseph. It's called the "great unknown." Sometimes, if we have really placed our lives in God's hands, for God's purpose, we will find ourselves standing in the midst of the mysterious plan. We long to ask, "Now what is it that you really want me to do? Why is it that you want me to go in this direction? What is the action plan for my life?" You get it. We want all the details. We want the mystery explained. We want answers to the who, what, and why questions. The truth is that we seldom get those answers. We are simply called to obedience and compliance to the things God chooses for us. I can't fully explain the will of God for your life this day or any day. But I can remind you that complete obedience will lead to complete joy. Just do what you are told and see where the journey takes you.

Prayer

Father, teach us to do your will with great fervor and with a child-like trust. Remind us that it is about obedience and not always with a full understanding that we begin the journey. Amen.

"So Joseph got up and took the Child and His mother while it was still night, and left for Egypt." Matthew 2:14 NASB

Observation

Unlike the other Gospel writers, Matthew chooses to tell the story of the Magi who visit Mary and Joseph after the birth of Jesus. They bring him their gifts of gold, frankincense, and myrrh. As a result of their visit, King Herod is alerted to the fact that a new ruler, a possible threat to his leadership, has been born. This chapter speaks of the terrible slaughter of the male babies in the region surrounding Bethlehem. From the moment Jesus was born, one gets the sense that this will be no ordinary life. The chapter also tells of a series of dreams in which God speaks to both the Magi and Joseph, to give them clear direction. In today's focus verse, Joseph has been told to flee to Egypt because Herod is seeking to end the life of his son.

Application

What I want you to see in this verse is Joseph's remarkable faith and loyal obedience to the direction of God for his life. The key phrase in the verse is, "while it was still night." Did you catch that? God speaks to Joseph in a dream telling him to take the child and flee. Joseph then awakens from the dream and leaves before the new day even begins. He didn't take the time to question the dream, nor consider the details, nor hesitate as he determined if he should respond. He jumps up from his bed, grabs a few things, and leaves under the cover of darkness. God spoke and he responded... immediately.

What would most of us have done? Waited for more dreams? Put a packing list together? Consult a wise friend? Joseph clearly heard from God and he immediately responded. He takes leaps of faith because he was a person of faith. What slows down your faith steps? Why are you waiting to respond to God's direction for your life? Opportunities come and go. A vision for a new ministry might last for only a season. Your moment to make a difference might be this very day. Get up and go. If God reveals a plan, you better act.

Prayer

Father, we ask that you would give us both the wisdom to know your will and the urgency to chase after it this very day. Amen.

"And do not suppose that you can say to yourselves, 'We have Abraham for our father;' for I say to you that from these stones God is able to raise up children to Abraham." Matthew 3:9 NASB

Observation

These words are spoken by John the Baptist to the religious leaders who have come out to the wilderness where John has been baptizing people as they repent of their sins. These are strong words of rebuke. Religious leaders had come for baptism but John quickly sees through their false piety and their evil motives. Their purpose was not true repentance but rather to be seen by men. The intent of their hearts had remained unchanged. They still longed to promote their self-importance and not search for a genuine faith that would honor God. Specifically, John confronts their arrogance concerning their spiritual bloodlines. They boasted a moral superiority based on their lineage and not their relationship with God.

Application

We would do well to listen carefully to John's challenge to these religious men of his day. Sometimes, we mistakenly believe that we possess some sort of "favored status" before God based on our heritage, nationality, race, or religious affiliation. Sometimes, we even think that God must surely love us a little more because we are Baptist, or Catholic, or Methodist, etc. We even fall into the trap of believing that because our parents were people of strong faith that we get some sort of get-out-of-jail-free card. Faith is always an individual response to the wonder of God. We are saved, not by any other criteria except that of knowing Christ. Our lineage and heritage can offer only a false hope. True life-saving, destiny-altering faith is the result of genuine sorrow over the sins we have committed and an acceptance of the One who alone can grant us forgiveness. It's not about who we are... it's about what we believe and in whom we place our trust.

Prayer

Father, remind us that salvation is not an automatic right based on our heritage, but rather a gift based on our faith. Amen.

"And He said to them, 'Follow Me, and I will make you fishers of men.' Immediately they left their nets and followed Him."
Matthew 4:19-20 NASB

Observation

In Matthew's telling of the story of Jesus, Chapter 4 begins with the Temptation of Christ in the wilderness. After the time of temptation, Jesus' public ministry begins with the gathering of the disciples. As he walks along the shore of the Sea of Galilee, he calls two sets of brothers to come and follow—Peter and Andrew, then James and John. The words of our focus verses this morning are spoken just as Jesus begins to speak to Peter and Andrew. The invitation of Christ is to leave the ordinariness of their lives in order to begin a bold adventure with Jesus. No longer would they invest their lives in simple fishing, but instead, in the task of changing lives with the gospel story. "Immediately" they surrender their nets and begin to follow.

Application

Two ideas jump off the page this morning. The first, the invitation of Jesus to join him in the bold adventure of changing the world. As he did on the shore of Galilee, Jesus calls us away from the mundane, ordinariness of our lives to this amazing task of sharing his story. We are called to be disciples... followers... students of his life and teaching... ambassadors of his grace. When we accept the invitation to follow, nothing about our lives should stay the same. The outlook changes. The motivation changes. The spirit changes. The priority changes. The focus changes.

The second idea is that of our "immediate" discipleship. Notice these early men did not take the time to count costs, sell the business, say goodbyes, etc. They took off in wild abandonment, seeking to know fully the heart of Christ. Are we anywhere near that attitude? Can we even toy with the idea of dropping all of our old ways, our attitudes, our fears, and our securities for the sake of chasing after Jesus? We are invited to new life in Christ. Will we learn to "drop and go?"

Prayer

Father, teach us that the risk of following will bring the joy of faith. Thank you for the invitation to meaningful life. May we chase your purpose with wild abandonment. Amen.

"If your right eye makes you stumble, tear it out and throw it from you; for it is better for you to lose one of the parts of your body, than for your whole body to be thrown into hell." Matthew 5:29 NASB

Observation

The entire 5th chapter of Matthew consists of the words Christ offered about various topics in a teaching moment called, "The Sermon on the Mount." Our focus verse this morning is a very forceful and intentional word about the problem of sin. Jesus suggests radical steps to keep us from sinning. So much of the temptation that enters our minds does so through our eyes... what we see. Jesus' suggestion that we "pluck out an eye to keep from looking" may be an overstatement, but the message is clearly delivered. Remove from your life whatever it is that tempts you and keeps you from living a holy and pure life before God.

Application

Let's be careful with this verse. Jesus is not telling us to intentionally maim our bodies. He IS trying to get across the point that sin has such potential to disrupt our relationship with God and thus force us to miss the glories of heaven that we would do well to radically and completely remove those things from our lives that might lead us to sin. In other words, temptation is powerful. It is an ever-present force waiting to devour our lives. Can we confess its strength? Are we bold enough to take definitive steps that prevent its influence in our lives? Here are few suggestions. If you are struggling with Internet addiction (which could include pornography or simply excessive investments of time) then maybe you should consider living without a computer. If your television brings too much filth and violence into your home, maybe you should consider living without a TV. If your "friends" encourage you to do things that betray your convictions, then maybe you need to consider making new friends. If your casual reading causes you to think lustful thoughts, then maybe you should read better books. Get the point? As long as you are willing to let temptation have an inch, it will take a mile. Guard your life. Take radical steps. It's better to live without a few things than it is to live an eternity separated from your Heavenly Father.

Prayer

Father, may we be bold enough to "pluck" from our lives, anything that keeps us from living the life you intend for us to live. Amen.

"But if you do not forgive others, then your Father will not forgive your transgressions." Matthew 6:15 NASB

Observation

Again, these words come from the mouth of Christ, spoken as a part of the Sermon on the Mount. In the verses that precede these words, Jesus offered a model prayer, a pattern if you will, for the ways in which we should pray... not with meaningless repetition, but with simple, honest forethought and sincerity. Included in the prayer is the phrase, "and forgive us our trespasses, as we forgive those who have trespassed against us." A verse or so later he adds the caveat of forgiving others as a way that leads to the forgiveness of self. It is perhaps one of the hardest demands of the gospel. Do we really want God's grace in our lives dependent upon our measure of grace in the lives of others?

Application

If I had the right and the ability to edit scripture, this is one of the verses that I would try to delete. Its demands are overwhelming. Its implications too powerful. But there it is in black and white... a failure to forgive others will result in a lack of forgiveness from God. That's not the deal that I really would like to have. I want God to forgive me no matter what. I want God to offer limitless grace and continual second chances. It scares me to think that by my own pettiness and hardness of heart that I might limit the gift offered to me each day. So the answer is not easy. I have to live a lifestyle of forgiveness. I have to remove the will to seek revenge. I have to purposefully "practice a forgetfulness." I have to remove the barriers of relationship that keep me at odds with others. God's nature is that of creating peace. "Blessed are the peacemakers, for they shall be called the Sons of God." It must be said of God's children that they are willing to act like their Father. I encourage you to offer the gift of forgiveness this day and see how much that offer of grace will bless your own life.

Prayer

Father, teach us the ebb and flow of grace. May we be as willing to offer forgiveness as we are in our longing to receive it. Amen.

"And the rain fell, and the floods came, and the winds blew and slammed against that house; and yet it did not fall, for it had been founded on the rock." Matthew 7:25 NASB

Observation

Again these words of Jesus are taken from the Sermon on the Mount. In this passage, Jesus is addressing the need for a strong and sure foundation. He makes a comparison between the wise and the foolish. The wise man builds his house upon the rock and when the storms come, the house remains strong. The foolish man builds upon the shifting sand and when the winds howl, his house is destroyed. The foundation about which Jesus is speaking is his words... his truth. Built on the foundation of Jesus' teaching, our lives can know stability, strength, and security, even in the midst of the darkest storm.

Application

I want you to see something very clearly in this verse. It is the reality of the storm. Jesus does not say, "In case a storm ever comes," or, "If the winds should ever blow..." No. There is a sense of certainty that to each of our lives the rains and winds will come. It is not a case of "if," but "when." Jesus warns us to make preparation now for the storms that are sure to come. Knowing the reality of life-storms should push us into knowing the security that Christ can offer.

Yesterday, the Western World awakened to the news of a terrible earthquake in Japan. As I watched the news of the devastation, it became apparent that the buildings that seemed to weather the violent shaking of the earth were those that were constructed to do so... in other words, those with the right foundations. You get the point. If our lives are built simply on shallow platitudes and empty advice, the storms will quickly engulf each of us. But if we build our lives on Christian principles, a strong faith, and an enduring hope in Christ's daily provision, we can, not only survive, but even thrive in the midst of life's stormy weather. Work on the foundation. It will save your life.

Prayer

Father, may we have the wisdom to build that solid foundation of faith that can only come through those careful disciplines that connect us to Christ each day. Amen.

"And Jesus said to the centurion, "Go; it shall be done for you as you have believed." And the servant was healed that very moment."
Matthew 8:13 NASB

Observation

As Jesus entered the town of Capernaum, a Centurion approached him and asked that Jesus please heal a servant who was lying paralyzed and in great pain. Jesus offered to come and heal him but the Centurion protested saying that he was not worthy for Jesus to be under his roof, but that if Jesus would just give the command, his servant would be healed. He knew that Jesus had the authority to make him well, and as a Centurion he understood exactly what authority meant. Jesus was astounded at his faith and healed his servant. Notice the key phrase in the verse: "it shall be done for you as you have believed."

Application

There is always a direct correlation between belief and the works of Christ in our lives. The greater the belief, the greater extent to which Christ can work in us and through us. Little faith, little works. Great faith, great works. Jesus himself said that if we had the faith of even a mustard seed, that we could move mountains (Matt. 17:20). It is often our lack of real faith in what Jesus can do that keeps his power at bay in our lives. Paul acknowledges, "we can do all things through Christ that strengthens us" (Phil. 4:13). I wonder if we really believe that? Do we really accept the premise that God is all-powerful and that through faith, God's power can work in and through our lives? I am fearful that we often live lives of mediocrity and we settle for much less than our potential because we simply don't believe in the power of Christ. Maybe we see little evidence of Christ at work because we live with more doubt than we do faith. Understand that Christ is not limited by our lack of faith... what is limited is Christ's ability to work in and through our lives. His words ring true... "It is done for us as we have believed." As our faith increases, so will the evidence of Christ at work around us.

Prayer

Father, forgive the smallness of our faith. Forgive us when we thwart your plan for our lives by believing and risking very little. Amen.

Matthew 9: Our Faith Matters

"And they brought to Him a paralytic lying on a bed. Seeing their faith, Jesus said to the paralytic, 'Take courage, son; your sins are forgiven.'"
Matthew 9:2 NASB

Observation

As Jesus returned to his own region, he was met by a group of people who brought to him a paralytic lying on a bed. They brought him to Jesus in order for Jesus to heal him and allow him to walk again. The pronoun "they" could describe family, friends, or even believers who may not have known the man but knew of Jesus. Our focus verse states, "Seeing their faith," Jesus offered him the forgiveness of sins. Again, it is important to think about the antecedent to the word "their." It could refer to just the men who brought the paralytic, or it could refer to both the men and the paralytic. Either way, there is a remarkable element of faith that brings about the eventual healing of this lame man.

Application

A couple of thoughts... both wrapped around this idea of faith. First, it is important to remember that our faith can have an amazing affect in the lives of others. Most who read this verse assume that it is the faith of those who bring the lame man to Jesus that touched the heart of Christ. If so, is there not a lesson for us to learn, reminding us that our faith can make a difference in the lives of others? When we pray in faith for others, it matters. When we act in faith towards others, it matters. When we petition God for others, it matters. If our faith can move mountains, a promise from Christ, then it can certainly focus the attention of God on the needs of someone we know.

The second thought swirls around the suggestion that both his friends and the paralyzed man came to Jesus in faith. What a powerful force is the faith of those who "agree in the Lord." God is moved by our hearts and prayers. Whenever we collectively move out in faith, seeking the will and purpose of God, great things can be accomplished. Our lack of collective faith only lessens the blessings of God in our lives. Our unity of faith changes lives and brings healing to those crippled by life. May God grant us a strong, life-changing belief.

Prayer

Father, remind us of how important our faith can be in the lives of others. Amen.

"And whatever city or village you enter, inquire who is worthy in it, and stay at his house until you leave that city." Matthew 10:11 NASB

Observation

In this passage Jesus is sending the disciples out into the surrounding regions to proclaim the Kingdom of God. He has given them the ability to heal the sick, raise the dead, cleanse the lepers, and cast out demons. They are not to take many provisions for their journey, but instead, they are to receive the hospitality of the homes in which they will stay as they do their work. Notice the careful phrasing of our focus verse, "and whatever city or village you enter, inquire who is worthy in it...." The disciples were encouraged by Jesus to seek out those with good reputation among the families of each town and stay in that place.

Application

If strangers were to walk into our town and inquire about those "who are worthy," would our names be brought to mind? This verse speaks about the importance of reputation. We earn our reputation in the eyes of others over a long period of time. People look for consistency, honesty, fairness, graciousness, and dedication to faith. Others will regard us as being people of faith or as being pretenders, based on how well and how consistently we have lived out the faith before them. That means that our "professed faith" and our "lived-out" faith have to match. In other words, there has to be consistency between "walk" and "talk." Consider your reputation for a moment. Do others see Christ in you? Do they see you as a person of integrity and honesty? Will they seek out your counsel in a time of crisis? It is not impossible to turn a bad reputation into a solid one. It does take a lot of intentionality and hard work. It takes a fidelity to the vision of walking in the footsteps of Christ every day. Set your mind to that task. Be a person who is worthy of a good reputation.

Prayer

Father, teach us the importance of a good reputation. May ours be built on the relationship we have with Christ. Amen.

Day 11 Matthew 11: The Proof of Your Faith

"Jesus answered and said to them, 'Go and report to John what you hear and see: the blind receive sight and the lame walk, the lepers are cleansed and the deaf hear, the dead are raised up, and the poor have the Gospel preached to them.'" Matthew 11:4-5 NASB

Observation

In this passage, John the Baptist, who is in prison, sends some of his disciples to ask Jesus if he is in fact the "Coming One." John wants to know if he is the long-awaited Messiah. Notice how Jesus responds to his question. He offers the fruit of his labor as a testimony. He tells the disciples of John to go back and report what they themselves have seen and heard. Blind people are now seeing again. The lame can now walk. Lepers are cleansed of their skin disease. Deaf people can now hear. The dead are raised and the poor have received the message of the gospel. The "proof" of Jesus' Messiahship was evident by the deeds of his life. The fruit his life was producing validated who he professed to be.

Application

If someone were to ask us, "Are you a Christian?" we would reply with such words as these, "Yes, I invited Christ into my heart when I was a child." Or, "Certainly! I walked the aisle in the Baptist Church." Or, "Of course I am, I read my Bible each day, pray every morning, and go to church on Sundays." The truth of the matter is that we can "say" just about anything to justify our faith. We can "profess" all day long that we belong to Jesus. The real proof is proclaimed by our lifestyle, our actions, and our deeds. Understand that I am not advocating a "salvation by works" theology. I am suggesting, however, that true faith always has resulting action. James reminds us that, "faith without works is dead." So take a close look, not at your "profession" of faith, but at the fruit your life produces. Are lives being changed because of your faith? Are people being encouraged? Are friends finding hope because of your actions? Are your priorities different than those around you because you are a Christian? Our faith is validated by our fruit and not merely by our words.

Prayer

Father, remind us today that if our faith is real and vibrant, that we should leave a trail of lives influenced and hope offered. Amen.

"But I tell you that every careless word that people speak, they shall give an accounting for it in the Day of Judgment." Matthew 12:36 NASB

Observation

These words are actually words of warning given to a group of Pharisees who had spoken maliciously against Jesus. He was warning them how important words can be in the revealing of one's character. Jesus told them that, "the mouth speaks out of that which fills the heart." His reminder was that words that come from someone's mouth are extremely important for they reveal much about the character and heart of that person. His warning is also quite strong. How frightening to think that our careless words can be used against us in the Day of Judgment.

Application

I wonder if we are as careful with our words as we should be. I am not simply talking about our use of expletives, or "cuss words." Jesus is not just speaking about the crude words we sometimes say in anger or fear that suddenly jump out from our mouths. (Although even one misspoken word at the wrong time can certainly damage both our witness and our Christian reputation.) His warning goes even deeper. We need to think about the malicious nature of our words. Our words can hurt, inflict pain, destroy a sense of someone's worth, belittle, or mislead. We sometimes say things carelessly without considering the damage those words will cause. The old adage of childhood is wrong when it says, "Sticks and stones can break my bones but words can never hurt me." The truth is that our words can hurt. They can cripple someone emotionally for life. They can wound and cut beyond anyone's ability to restore. So guard the words you choose in every context. Season them with grace. Offer them with compassion. Speak as though Christ is using your mouth to communicate. Jesus promises that we will be accountable for every careless word we say. So, think before you speak. Use the filter of Christ's love before you release your words into the hearts of others.

Prayer

Father, may we choose silence over conversation if our words do not reflect the grace, compassion, and affirmation of our Lord. Amen.

"The Kingdom of Heaven is like a treasure hidden in the field, which a man found and hid again; and from joy over it he goes and sells all that he has and buys that field." Matthew 13:44 NASB

Observation

In this 13th chapter of Matthew, Jesus is teaching the crowds many things in parables concerning the Kingdom of God. In our focus verse for this morning, an entire parable is recorded. Jesus compares the Kingdom of Heaven to a "treasure hidden in a field," which is worth any price to obtain. Notice the action of the traveler who happens upon the field with its treasure. There is a point of discovery in which he realizes that something of great worth is hidden in this portion of land. The discovery brings him such joy that he realizes he must claim the land at any cost. He sells "all that he has" and buys the field. It's the image of a life that both claims a treasure and is claimed by that treasure.

Application

The Kingdom of God is certainly a treasure to be claimed at any price. The problem is that many never discover its worth. Many seem to aimlessly stumble their way through life trying to find meaning and purpose from many different sources. But their quest always comes up empty. Their marriages are without passion, their jobs offer no satisfaction, and their hobbies are nothing more than temporary distractions that help them to forget the emptiness for a while. There is a deep longing for which many have yet to find an answer.

And then suddenly and unexpectedly, the weary pilgrim stumbles across the messages of grace and purpose that are found in Jesus Christ. Suddenly, life makes sense. And with joy that person begins to lay hold of that which has suddenly laid hold of him/her... the love of God. My question for you this morning is one of passion and pursuit. How dedicated are you to finding the "treasure of great worth" in your life? Are you willing to sell all to know Christ in his fullness? In other words, is there a passion and resolve to pay the price of honest and sincere dedication so that the treasure is revealed and the joy becomes uncontainable? I pray that you will stumble across something new in the story of Jesus this day and that it will change your life forever.

Prayer

Father, may we be willing to invest all that we have into this life of discipleship so that we may claim the treasure of the Kingdom and know the joy it offers. Amen.

"And He said, 'Come!' And Peter got out of the boat, and walked on the water and came toward Jesus. But seeing the wind, he became frightened, and beginning to sink, he cried out, 'Lord, save me!'"
Matthew 14:29-30 NASB

Observation

This story takes place on the day that Jesus fed the 5000. When the meal is over and the day is complete, the disciples are sent by boat to the other side of the sea. Jesus takes a moment to be alone with God on the mountain to reflect and pray. He sees from a great distance that the boat in which the disciples are traveling is being beaten by the waves for the wind was strong. Jesus goes out to them to comfort them and he does so by walking on the water. When they first see him, they are fearful. Jesus identifies himself and tells them to "take courage." It is at that point that Peter asks Jesus for the ability to come to him on the water. And for a moment it happens... Peter walks across the surface of the sea! The walk is cut short by his fear and doubt and suddenly he begins to sink.

Application

We all have those great faith moments when we feel as though we can conquer the world. Our resolve is strong, our commitments are rock solid, and our faith is secure. And then it happens... something raises a momentary doubt, a sudden fear, or a life-sinking distraction. In an instant our resolve weakens, our hearts melt, and suddenly our "once strong" faith turns soft again. One moment we walk on the water with Jesus... the next we sink in the mire of doubt and fear. It's a pattern in our faith-life that most of us have known for a very long time.

What's the answer? Maybe it is as simple as owning up to our smallness of faith. Once, when a man asked Jesus to heal his son, Jesus said, "All things are possible to him who believes." In response the man says, "I do believe; help my unbelief" (Mark 9:24). Maybe the point for us this morning is to honestly admit that sometimes our faith is not as strong as it needs to be. Somewhere in the honesty of that confession we may find the strength to trust God even more. Our occasional doubts do nothing to lessen God's power. It was not Jesus who began to sink, but Peter. Let's pray for a great faith based on the power of the greatness of God.

Prayer

Father, forgive our faith-stumbles and the moments when our resolve is very weak. May we find a strong and resilient faith as we pursue Christ this day. Amen.

Day 15 — Matthew 15: Tough Question

"So the crowd marveled as they saw the mute speaking, the crippled restored, and the lame walking, and the blind seeing; and they glorified the God of Israel." Matthew 15:31 NASB

Observation

These words describe a day in the life of Jesus when he was teaching the multitudes on the hillside near the Sea of Galilee. People brought to Jesus those who were lame, crippled, and blind. They brought them to his feet and he began to heal them all. The crowd marveled at what they saw. They saw the power of God at work through the healing acts of Jesus. As they saw the result of each miracle, they glorified the God of Israel. Did you catch that? When the people saw what Christ had done, they glorified his Father.

Application

My question today is this... When people see what we have done, is it their natural tendency to glorify God? Or, is it more likely they will shake their heads and condemn us for acting in ways that don't glorify God? We were created to bring God glory, and our desire to do so reflected in our actions, our thoughts, our words, and our attitudes. We have to live with the burden of knowing that others are always watching and that it becomes our duty to help them discover who God is, not repel them from faith considerations. We may not possess the power to make speechless men talk again, or set the lame to walking, or heal blind eyes so they can see again. But we can let God work through us in the ways that he chooses. We can season our words with grace. We can share from our abundance. We can encourage a feeble spirit. And we can offer friendship to the lonely. Our purpose for doing such things is never about self-glorification. It's always about bringing glory to God. So again the question is, "When people see what we have done, is it their natural tendency to glorify God?" I challenge you to live by a higher standard and a nobler calling. It is not about us. It's about the God who longs to be glorified in us.

Prayer

Father, may we in some small way bring glory to you this day as we seek to live in ways that please you and will testify to others. Amen.

Day 16 — Matthew 16: Whose Agenda?

"But He turned and said to Peter, 'Get behind Me, Satan! You are a stumbling block to Me; for you are not setting your mind on God's interests, but man's.'" Matthew 16:23 NASB

Observation

Just a few verses earlier in this chapter, Simon Peter had answered correctly when Jesus asked, "Who do men say that I am?" He had replied, "You are the Christ, the Son of the Living God." Jesus had praised him for his astute answer. In fact, Jesus called him "The Rock" and vowed to build the church upon his confession. But notice how quickly Peter goes from receiving a pat on the back to a very powerful rebuke. Jesus had just told the disciples that he must go to Jerusalem, suffer many things, be killed, and then raised up on the third day. Peter strongly protested saying, "God forbid!" And so in our focus verse, Jesus has to correct Peter's way of thinking. The key is not to think in terms of one's own self-interests, but in the greater work of God's Kingdom.

Application

What a struggle for most of us. Like Peter, we too are often torn between self-will and Godly sacrifice. So many of our decisions are based on our agendas, our desires, our opinions, and our attitudes as though our preferences are of greatest worth. When God speaks of sacrifice, service, and dedication, we long to stop up our ears so that we can't hear such demands. We care about pushing our own agendas and not those of the Kingdom. We often ask, "How does this course of action benefit my life? How does it serve my needs? What do I get out of it?" Maybe those are the wrong questions. From an "obedient follower" perspective, we should instead ask, "How can this course of action help the Kingdom to move forward? What is required of me? What sacrifice must I make? What attitude or opinion must I surrender so that I can be used of God?" We are not on the planet to serve ourselves. We are here to serve the God who has called us into being. What motivates your thoughts today... selfish interests or Kingdom pursuits?

Prayer

Father, forgive us when we allow our self-interests to overrule your Kingdom plans. Teach us servanthood, not selfishness. Amen.

Matthew 17: The Mystery of God

"However, so that we do not offend them, go to the sea and throw in a hook, and take the first fish that comes up; and when you open its mouth, you will find a shekel. Take that and give it to them for you and Me." Matthew 17:27 NASB

Observation

The Temple tax was a tax given annually by every adult Jewish male over 20 years of age for maintaining the Temple. Evidently, Jesus had not yet paid the tax and he along with Peter was approached about doing so. Jesus made the point to Peter that the kings of the earth do not require a tax from their own children and thus, the real King of the Temple would not either. (In effect Jesus was saying that he was exempt from the tax.) However, not to offend anyone, Jesus agrees to pay the tax, but uses a very unusual method for obtaining the needed coin. Apparently some days it really does pay to fish!

Application

As I read this passage I am again reminded of the power and the authority of Christ over all things. Jesus needed a coin to pay the tax. He ordained that Peter catch a fish that happened to have a shekel in its mouth. Some would argue that the whole event was just a really weird coincidence, while others would argue the providential hand of God was at work. Let's be honest, people of faith view things differently than those who have no faith. The world often sees the unexplainable mysteries of God and can offer no explanation other than that of saying, "It's just a coincidence... just dumb luck." But people of faith know better and believe differently. What may seem to some as a coincidence is really the miraculous hand of God at work. Because God is intimately acquainted with all our ways and desires what is best for us, the people, places, and events of our lives are arranged for God's purposes. What joy there is when we experience one of those moments when there is no other explanation other than a "movement of God." It is in the unexplained mysterious moments of life that we can see that there really is a bigger picture... and that picture is being painted by a very purposeful God.

Prayer

Father, allow us to see you at work today in even the smallest details of our lives. Thank you for those special moments of mystery that remind us of your presence. Amen.

"See that you do not despise one of these little ones, for I say to you that their angels in Heaven continually see the face of My Father Who is in Heaven." Matthew 18:10 NASB

Observation

Read this verse again... slowly. There is a little weird twist to it. It's the pronoun "their." In this passage Jesus is giving strict warnings about not being a stumbling block to "little ones." He set a child in their midst and taught his followers about having such an innocent and pure heart reminding them that such a faith is what God desires from each of us. Jesus goes on to speak about the value of little ones and of their importance to God. Some Bible scholars argue that Jesus was referring not just to children, but also to those who are very young and impressionable in the faith. Either way the warnings are valid... don't corrupt the innocence and faith of those still tender.

But jump back to the focus verse. Jesus says that "their" angels in heaven continually see the face of God. He seems to imply that people here on earth, even children, have angels who apparently represent them in some way in heaven.

Application

So what if that is true? What if all of us really do have those "guardian angels" that we mention from time to time? A couple of thoughts... First, I find Jesus' warning to those who try to cause little ones to stumble even more powerful. If their angels continually see the face of God, doesn't that mean that our sinful actions are told in that realm? Do we think for a moment that we will go unpunished if we cause them to stumble? Second, I like the thought that all of us may have angels who represent us in someway in heaven. It gives me an added assurance that God does know my needs, my fears, and my troubles. It helps me to know that my life is not lived out in some lonely solitude, but that there are others who walk with me each day. This day, your life might be guarded and protected from some danger of which you will never be aware. I am grateful for all of God's provision in my life... even those I cannot see.

Prayer

Father thank you for your provision in ways seen and unseen. Amen.

Matthew 19: It's Not Rocket Science

"And someone came to Him and said, 'Teacher, what good thing shall I do that I may obtain eternal life?'" Matthew 19:16 NASB

Observation

This verse is lifted from the passage usually known as "The story of the Rich Young Ruler." A wealthy man comes to Jesus to ask how he might obtain eternal life... what is required? And Jesus will, of course, confront him about his wealth because it is his wealth that becomes the one thing he is unwilling to surrender for the sake of following Jesus. But notice again, his initial question... "What good thing shall I do that I may obtain eternal life?" It's the wrong question. The wealthy inquisitor was asking a salvation-by-works kind of question. "What is the one thing that I need to do? What's the good deed? What's the key to unlock the gates of heaven?" Jesus reminded him (and us) that salvation is not an earned commodity, but the result of a faith declaration.

Application

Admittedly, most of us still ask the same question in terms of our own salvation. We tend to think in terms of "doing" things to make God like us and accept us. We reason that if we do enough good works, pray enough prayers, attend enough churches, and read enough verses, that somehow God will have to look favorably on us. And so we try to earn our way into Glory. "What must we DO to inherit eternal life?" Eternal life is not granted by what we do, but instead by what Christ has already done. The Good Deed has been done. The price has been paid. The sacrifice has been made. The redemptive act has been accomplished... not by us, but by him. So the question is not "What must I do?" but simply, "What must I accept?" You can spend your whole life trying to buy your way into heaven and you won't be one step closer at the end of your struggle. Or... you can confess your need, admit your sins, and accept the grace of God offered to you through Jesus Christ. May God help us to see the simplicity of salvation and accept grace with joyful and willing hearts.

Prayer

Father we thank you today for the sacrifice of Christ through which we find salvation. Remind us that grace is not an object to purchase, but a gift to receive. Amen.

> "Moved with compassion, Jesus touched their eyes; and immediately they regained their sight and followed Him." Matthew 20:34 NASB

Observation

This verse is drawn from the end of chapter 20 when Jesus is leaving the city of Jericho, headed toward Jerusalem where both the crowds and the cross await him. As Matthew relates the story, two blind men are sitting by the road and when Jesus passes by, they beg for mercy. Jesus asks the men what they want from him and they simply say, "Lord, we want our eyes to be opened." And then, "moved with compassion," Jesus heals their eyes and they immediately begin to follow him. (They will become some of the last to declare discipleship, which is interesting in light of the parable Jesus told only moments earlier about the 11th hour workers.)

Application

A few thoughts... First, there is honesty and depth in their request of Jesus, "we want our eyes to be opened." Certainly the thought of seeing again was their greatest need. It is interesting that Jesus grants them physical sight and in that healing event they also gain the wisdom to see through spiritual eyes as well. They become instant followers... ready to chase after Christ wherever the journey will take them. As I read of their experience, I wonder if each of us should not echo their prayer. Surely the dust of daily living clouds our vision to the point that we can no longer see Jesus clearly. Our vision becomes impaired by prejudice, greed, lust, anger, etc. We begin to see the world through the corrupt lens of our humanity and thus, at times, we should pray, "We want our eyes to be opened again." For example, what if we could see the world through the innocent eyes of a child?

My second thought swirls around the actions of Jesus. He was moved with compassion. He always is. It is the compassion of Christ that heals the sick, gives sight to the blind, strength to the weak, and life to the dead. It is because of his compassion that he willingly makes the journey to the cross so that he can offer his life to pay the price of our sin debt. How grateful we should be for the compassion of Christ that gives life to even blind sinners like us.

Prayer

Father give us fresh eyes today to see clearly the compassion of Christ and to see those around us who need for us to extend to them, the same compassion. Amen.

Day 21 — Matthew 21: Bearing Fruit

"Seeing a lone fig tree by the road, He came to it and found nothing on it except leaves only; and He said to it, 'No longer shall there ever be any fruit from you.' And at once the fig tree withered."
Matthew 21:19 NASB

Observation

Matthew records this very brief incident on the first day of the week following Palm Sunday. Jesus is on the way to the Temple to continue his teaching concerning the Kingdom of God. He obviously goes to the fig tree in the hope of finding fruit to eat. When he finds none, he pronounces a judgment on the tree, declaring that it will never produce fruit again. Matthew tells the story as a foreshadowing of the condemnation that Jesus continues to give towards the religious rulers of his day who, because of corruption and misplaced priorities, have long since stopped producing fruit for the Kingdom. It is a reminder that in Christ, the Kingdom is about to unfold in the lives and hearts of people in ways unimaginable to the religious establishment of his day. The old system will no longer produce Kingdom fruit.

Application

I find in these words, a warning for the church of today and in fact, a warning for this generation of believers. We are called by God to bear fruit for the Kingdom. That means we are to lead people to experience faith in Christ, sow seeds of kindness, role-model grace in our forgiveness, and love all in his name. When we look at our faith journey and consider the places we have had the opportunities to "live as Christ," there should be evidence of our walk. Something of our faith should be fruit-producing. We are not called to simply consume the resources of the Kingdom as gluttons of self-indulging Christianity. Instead, we are called to take those resources and produce results. Because of our faith, lives should be influenced, hearts changed, and relationships mended. In very real ways, the lame should walk, the blind should see, and the dead should be raised to life again because of the lived-out expressions of our faith. When Christ stares at the branches of your spiritual limbs, will he rejoice in the bountiful harvest that he finds?

Prayer

Father may each of us be reminded today, that we are called to be "fruit-bearers" of the Kingdom and not merely hoarders of the faith placed within us. Amen.

"'Teacher, which is the great commandment in the Law?' And He said to him, 'YOU SHALL LOVE THE LORD YOUR GOD WITH ALL YOUR HEART, AND WITH ALL YOUR SOUL, AND WITH ALL YOUR MIND.'" Matthew 22:36-37 NASB

Observation

An expert in Mosaic Law comes to Jesus in an attempt to test Jesus' knowledge and to examine his teachings. He asks Jesus to evaluate the law and give the greatest of the commandments, perhaps thinking that Jesus would focus on some fine point and would neglect some other important teaching. But Jesus responds by quoting the "Shema." This phrase from Deuteronomy was spoken by the Jews everyday as being the very essence of their faith. Jesus' response told of true devotion to God... a devotion that many of the Jews claimed but failed to live out each day. In the eyes of the lawyer, Jesus spoke with such truth that no one dared to ask other questions.

Application

I think that there is often a "disconnect" in our faith between our spoken confessions and our lived-out actions. Surely we would echo the words of Jesus and quickly profess to any and all that ask that to love God supremely is the greatest of all commands. But do the actions of our lives prove the validity of our confession? If we love God supremely, then there are certain parameters and guidelines that have to govern our thoughts and behavior each day. In other words, we can't declare an allegiance to God and then live according to selfish motivations. We have to exchange our "ways" for God's ways. We have to love, forgive, show compassion for the poor, love justice, walk humbly, strive for peace, speak truthfully, respect others, give sacrificially... and the list goes on and on. To declare a love for God requires that the very lifestyles we live will be dramatically altered. We are forced to consider each day if our actions and motivations truly reflect that confession we long to make. So, which is it? Do you SAY you love God, or do you REALLY love God? We'll see...

Prayer

Father, remind us that mere confession is worthless apart from dedicated obedience. Amen.

"So you, too, outwardly appear righteous to men, but inwardly you are full of hypocrisy and lawlessness." Matthew 23:28 NASB

Observation

For much of the entire 23rd Chapter, Jesus lashes out against the false faith and erroneous practices of the Pharisees. As if their opposition to Jesus was not strong enough already, these words of teaching and challenge would have sent them over the top. He continues to expose their inconsistent teachings, their lack of piety, and their inability to lead men into the presence of God. Our focus verse this morning is a word of rebuke given in the midst of seven "woes" of judgment that Jesus proclaims before them. In this verse, Jesus speaks of the hypocrisy of their lives. They long to give the appearance of righteousness before others, but on the inside, they are full of corruption and evil.

Application

It's called "putting up a false front," and most of us are pretty good at doing it. For the sake of appearance, we dress ourselves in the robes of righteousness. We put on a happy face, we speak kindly to our fellow church members, we offer pearls of wisdom at a Bible study, and give regularly to every important cause. We want to give the appearance that all is right with our spirituality. We do and say all the right things. But if others could only see on the inside... they would see our selfish thoughts, our evil motivations, and our inconsistent character. If others had "spiritual x-ray vision," they would see through much of our false front. Here's the real danger... we can certainly fool a lot of people, but not our God. Remember that God "looks not at the outward appearance, but judges the heart instead." Part of the call of the Christian faith is a call to a consistency of lifestyle, an honesty of conduct, and a purity of heart. There really should be an authenticity about who we are. Let it become our challenge to really living on the inside that which we are so adapt at portraying on the outside.

Prayer

Father, may we be fully invested in our pursuit of you. May we be pure without and within so that what we profess to be outwardly, can truly be found inwardly. Amen.

""Therefore be on the alert, for you do not know which day your Lord is coming." Matthew 24:42 NASB

Observation

Matthew 24 is filled with language and mystery that even the greatest Bible scholar would love to fully understand. In this chapter Jesus talks about the signs of his return, the perilous times that will come upon the earth, his glorious return, and even how to get ready for his return. Throughout the ages, men have sought to interpret all the meaning of this chapter, decipher the timetables, and predict the moment of Christ's return. Much of it still remains mysterious and open for much interpretation. A few things, however, are very certain. One is the certainty of Christ's return. There is never even a notion in these words that it will not happen. Jesus clearly proclaims that he WILL come again. A second certainty contained in these verses is our need to stand ready whenever that day comes. In our focus verse Jesus warns us to "be on the alert, for you do not know which day your Lord is coming."

Application

We prepare for the uncertainties of life by making prior preparation for the possibility that some difficult day could come. For example, each time the weatherman speaks of snow in the forecast, we rush to the store for milk and bread just in case we get stranded for a few days. We buy insurance policies just in case we are ever in an accident. We stockpile firewood to burn when the days are cold. We take extra pencils to a test, just in case one doesn't stay sharp enough to complete the exam. You get the point... we plan ahead in order to relieve the pressure and stress of what could happen.

Jesus is not speaking of something that "could" one day happen. He speaks of that which "will" occur. He is coming again to judge the world and to redeem the faithful. Because we know that day is coming, is it not prudent for us to stand ready? We prepare ourselves by consistent Christian living. Each day we pray. Each day we forgive. Each day we seek God's purpose. Each day we care for the poor and needy. Each day we look to the needs of others. Each day we dig deeply into scripture. The day is coming. Let us live with a sense of anticipation and celebration as we welcome the day of his appearing.

Prayer

Father, make us ready for the day of Christ's return. May we live each day in ways that bring you glory and ways that prepare our hearts. Amen.

"To one he gave five talents, to another, two, and to another, one, each according to his own ability; and he went on his journey."
Matthew 25:15 NASB

Observation

These words are taken from a parable of Jesus titled, "The Parable of the Talents." In this parable, a man who is "preparing to take a journey," leaves behind talents of silver that he entrusts into the hands of his servants. Each receives a varying amount and from each something will be expected upon the master's return. The day of accounting arrives and each offers a report. The man with 5 talents is able to return 5 additional talents. The man with 3 talents is able to return 3 additional talents. The servant who is punished is the one who received only 1 talent initially. He is scolded for not investing the single talent that he was given.

Application

Read the focus verse carefully and you will discover that the master gave talents to each of his servants, "according to his own ability." Did you catch that? Not all of the servants receive the same amount of talents to invest. They are given a level of responsibility equal to their ability to manage that responsibility. It is, of course, a parable of the Kingdom, which reminds us that we too are gifted according to our ability to manage our gifts. Yes, there are some who have the ability to do amazing things with the talents that God provides. There are some among us who seem to do a lot of things really well. Others of us seem to have less variety in our gifts and abilities. According to the parable, we are gifted according to our potential ability. In other words, God doesn't expect all of us to be talented in every way, but does expect our willingness to use what we have been given to God's glory. God is angered by those who take a talent and squander it. So ask yourself, "What is it that I do well? What talent do I believe God has given me?" You may be multi-talented or you may possess but one. The point is not to bemoan what you lack in the light of what others possess, but to take your gift and invest it well. When you do, you will find a joy and peace because you will find yourself in the center of God's purpose for your life. Go and make careful investments.

Prayer

Father, give us the eyes with which to see our God-given talents and the courage to use those talents fully. Amen.

Day 26 Matthew 26: Name Your Price

"Then one of the twelve, named Judas Iscariot, went to the chief priests and said, 'What are you willing to give me to betray Him to you?' And they weighed out thirty pieces of silver to him." Matthew 26:14-15 NASB

Observation

Judas had his price. He goes to the chief priests with a willingness to betray Jesus into their hands. Apparently his loyalty has limits and for 30 pieces of silver he sells Jesus out. Later, within this fast-paced chapter, Judas brings the Temple guard with him to the Garden of Gethsemane and there he betrays Jesus with a kiss. Within moments, Jesus is led away to be tried, beaten, and crucified. He does so with the knowledge that one of his trusted followers... one that had been with him from the start... betrayed him for a few measly coins. Is there any cup more bitter to drink than that of betrayal?

Application

So what's your price? Would you sell your soul if the price were right? I hope the question bothers and even angers you. It should. Surely our faith means more than anything else... or so we say. Surely it is the pearl of greatest worth. Surely there is not a single person named among us who is willing to betray Jesus at any price. Or then again, maybe we are willing to do it almost anytime.

Let's be honest... there is a little selling of our faith that happens nearly every day. Whenever we allow our faith to be compromised, our resolve to weaken, or have our absolutes turn soft, are we not betraying our Lord? Don't we betray Jesus with every harsh word spoken, every prejudicial attitude offered, every crude website visited, and every lust-filled thought allowed? There is an old adage that states, "Jesus is Lord of all, or he is not Lord at all." So what's your price? Are you willing to compromise your faith for the cost of a momentary outburst, or a flash of fantasy, or maybe an insensitive remark? How it must hurt the heart of Christ when he sees his faithful act in ways that betray him again and again. There is no cup more bitter to drink. Why do you keep insisting that he drink the bitter brew that you keep serving up?

Prayer

Father, we do not desire to wound the heart of Christ. Forgive us when our acts of betrayal come too often and our dedicated acts of obedience come too infrequently. Make us consistently and thoroughly yours. Amen.

Day 27 Matthew 27: Make It Stop?

"He saved others; He cannot save Himself. He is the King of Israel; let Him now come down from the cross, and we will believe in Him."
Matthew 27:42 NASB

Observation

On the day of his crucifixion, Jesus had to endure many indignities and insults. Our focus verse is drawn from the words of abuse thrown at Jesus while he dies on the cross. These words come from the chief priests, scribes, and elders of Israel who take delight in the fact that they have finally accomplished their goal of eliminating Jesus. They mock him by saying that he "cannot save himself." They think to themselves, "If he really was the King of Israel, the Son of God, then shouldn't he have the power to take himself down from the cross?" Verse 44 indicates that even the "robbers also who had been crucified with him were casting the same insult at him."

Application

As believers, we know that Jesus had the power to take himself off of the cross. By his authority, he could have called down from the heavens, a thousand angels to rush to his side. He could have stopped it all. He could have ended the agony, stopped the pain, and forever silenced his accusers, but he didn't. He let the scene play out in its horrific fashion. He let the evil of men scourge his body, smash thorns on his head, and nail spikes into his hands. He had the power to declare, "Enough!" and make it all go away. But he didn't. Why did Jesus not save himself? Simple. He could have saved himself, but then he could not have saved you and me. His death on the cross was not to atone for his sins, but ours. It was not to pay the price of his transgressions, but those we committed. It was not to give himself eternal life, but to offer it to us. It was his desire, his love, and his passion to die so that we can live. I would hope that in light of such love, such sacrifice, and such grace, that we would be thankful enough to live transformed lives... lives of grace, courage, and service.

Prayer

Father, remind each of us again this morning, of the passion of the Christ, who, though he had the power to stop it, took on the disgrace of death so that we might live. Amen.

"And when they had assembled with the elders and consulted together, they gave a large sum of money to the soldiers, and said, 'You are to say, 'His disciples came by night and stole Him away while we were asleep.'"
Matthew 28:12-13 NASB

Observation

Matthew 28 includes the amazing story of the Resurrection of Jesus. It opens with Mary Magdalene and the "other Mary" making their way to the tomb. Matthew tells the reader that an earthquake had occurred and the stone in front of the tomb was rolled away by an angel of God, whom the women find sitting on top of the stone. The angel tells the glorious news that Jesus is risen and the women rush to tell the disciples. The Temple guards, who had been entrusted with keeping the grave secure, report to the chief priests all that they had witnessed. Not wanting to promote the news of Jesus' resurrection, the priests pay the guards money and give them a fictitious story to tell... "The disciples came at night and stole the body."

Application

Since that first Easter Sunday, there have been those who deny the resurrection of Jesus, dismissing the story as "non-sense" or a myth kept alive through the ages by brainwashed followers. The lies and doubts of men do not change the truth of the risen Lord. The early priests and leaders of the people thought that by simply paying off a few guards they could silence the news of the resurrection. In like fashion, modern day Bible critics and faith-scoffers think that their dismissal of the truth of God's word will somehow lessen the power of the resurrection.

The story is not going away. Truth never changes. God's eternal plan will not change. So the only question is whether or not we will choose to believe in the story and through our belief gain eternal life. Not only are we to believe the story, but also, according to the last few verses of Matthew's Gospel, we are to make it our life's calling to make sure others have at least heard it. "Go therefore and make disciples of all the nations..." What will you do with the story of Jesus? Suppress it? Deny it? Dismiss it? Or... will you choose to believe it, tell it, and share it? The truth of the story will not change. What can change is your life with each telling of the story.

Prayer

Father, thank you for the glorious story of Easter. May it so change our lives that we feel the desire to change others with it. Amen.

"The time is fulfilled, and the Kingdom of God is at hand; repent and believe in the Gospel." Mark 1:15 NASB

Observation

The Gospel of Mark begins very differently from that of Matthew or Luke. There is no birth story, no angels to announce the birth, no shepherds on the hillside, and no baby in a manger. Instead Mark simply begins with the preaching of John the Baptist and the baptism of Jesus. In fact, the action moves so quickly that by the end of the first chapter, the crowds become so large that Jesus cannot enter a city without drawing a huge audience. Our focus verse this morning reveals the very first words of public ministry from the mouth of Jesus… "Repent and believe." With those words the gospel took flight and the world began to change.

Application

Sometimes we tend to overcomplicate the story of Jesus. We get sidetracked by various discussions about fine points of theology, various worship practices, and various interpretations of key passages and concepts. We take eager and hungry individuals who desire to enter a relationship with Christ and try to force them to understand everything from ethics to politics, evangelism to ecology, in order to become a good Christian. Aren't we getting the cart a little before the horse? When Jesus began calling men and women to faith, it just wasn't all that complicated. He used two words... "Repent and believe." Repentance simply means, "to completely turn around... to make a 180 degree change." It means to stop doing the things that displease God and start doing the things that honor God. In other words... change your ways. Step away from your human nature and start seeking Godly leadership.

The second word used by Jesus was the word, "believe." The Bible is pretty clear on this point... "I assure you: Anyone who believes has eternal life" (John 6:47). Our salvation is not granted based on works, or on a correct world-view, nor even a perfect life. It's based simply on belief. When we believe in the story of Jesus, confessing that he is the Son of God, suddenly our hearts are transformed and our lives are changed. We don't go through radical change in order to become Christians... we repent and believe. The changes come as the Lordship of Christ begins to fashion us into his image.

Prayer

Father, forgive us when we make the gospel too complicated and too shackled with difficult doctrine. Remind us that it's all about new direction and new belief. Amen.

"As He passed by, He saw Levi the son of Alphaeus sitting in the tax booth, and He said to him, 'Follow Me!' And he got up and followed Him." Mark 2:14 NASB

Observation

As the story of Jesus begins to unfold in Mark's Gospel, Jesus continues to collect followers. In this case, as he is walking along the sea, he spots Matthew (Levi) sitting in the tax booth. He is a tax collector, known to all as a notorious sinner. Where others would view him with disdain, Jesus sees him through the eyes of potential. He extends the invitation to follow and Matthew does just that. In fact, so strong would be the draw to discipleship, that Matthew would later become one of the writers of the New Testament. Jesus invited him to leave his past in order to discover a new life that following Jesus would offer.

Application

Odd, is it not, how Jesus can take the most unlikely person and transform him/her for use in his Kingdom. People just like us. Think about Matthew for a moment. He was well educated, smart, organized, but misguided. He had wonderful and useful skills, but was misguided in how he chose to use them. Jesus understood how his gifts could be channeled differently, and how his gifts could be useful to God's work. That's how the call of Christ works. Jesus sees us through the lens of faith and potential. He notices, not what we once were, but how we can be used to further the Kingdom. Jesus is a very "forward-thinking" Savior. It is not about our past, but our potential... not about our failures, but our future... not about our transgressions, but our transformation.

Admittedly, most of us seem to be very unlikely candidates to become world-changers. We never see ourselves in the same way that Jesus does. We keep looking over our shoulders back to our imperfect past. Jesus keeps looking ahead to the distant horizon when everything about us changes. Don't be surprised if you feel God tap on your shoulder, picking you and calling you into deeper discipleship. God made you for a reason. It's time to embrace that call and figure out your place.

Prayer

Father, thank you for seeing the potential in us that we cannot see in ourselves. Call us and use us to your glory. Amen.

Day 31 — Mark 3: Family Affair

"For whoever does the Will of God, he is My brother and sister and mother." Mark 3:35 NASB

Observation

This verse is spoken by Jesus at a moment when his own family had come looking for him. The news of Jesus' preaching and healing ministry had become so widespread that enormous crowds were rushing to see him, touch him, and hear him. Verse 20 indicates that, "the multitude gathered again, to such an extent that they could not even at a meal." At a certain moment, Jesus' mother and brothers arrived at the place where he was staying and they sent word to him that they were there. He responded by looking around at all who were gathered and declared that they too were his family, adding, "For whoever does the will of God, he is My brother and sister and mother."

Application

There are always perks for being in a family. When you're young, your needs are met. Food is provided. Clothing is placed on your back. And if you are lucky, you even get to drive the family car! Because you are in the family, you enjoy the safety and protection of home. You get added to the will. You live with the confidence of belonging. As you age, the privileges of family only increase. You gain of sense of inclusion that cannot be taken from you. You know the joy of children. You know the protection and security of belonging. And as good as it is to be a part of an earthly family, image the joy that comes through our inclusion into God's family. Peace. Joy. Protection. Provision. Inclusion. The list of such privileges is lengthy.

But notice what Jesus indicates as being the glue that cements the relationship of being his brother or sister. Obedience. Those who do the will of God find the greatest joy of inclusion. I don't know about you, but I want to be in a family with Christ. I want to have that sense of inclusion and know the joy of his eternal blessings. We are connected with him in a close and personal way each time we attempt to do the will of God. In other words, each time we strive to live out the purposes for which we were created, we are connected to Jesus. We find ourselves acting just like our brother.

Prayer

Father, thank you for including us in your family. May we live with gratitude that finds expression through serving others. Amen.

"As he was sowing, some seed fell beside the road, and the birds came and ate it up." Mark 4:4 NASB

Observation

This verse is drawn from Jesus' parable of the Sower and the Seed. In the story, the sower broadcasts seed upon the ground. Some of it will find fertile soil, grow deeply, and produce much fruit. But the first of the seed that is cast falls beside the road and the birds quickly come and eat it. In explaining the parable a few verses later Jesus says, "And these are the ones who are beside the road where the word is sown; and when they hear, immediately Satan comes and takes away the word that has been sown in them" (v. 15). It is the image of people whose minds are so closed to the gospel, that the words of hope, grace, and love it offers simply fall on deaf ears. They have been so calloused by life that Satan prevents even a seed to sprout.

Application

This image resonates with me. On my back deck, we have a couple of bird feeders. Linda and I enjoy watching the wrens, the blue jays, and the chickadees that come our way. At certain seasons of the year we have to fill the feeders every day. The birds all but attack the feeders. They swarm in and quickly devour all that we have provided. So in my mind's eye, I see the birds of Jesus' parable, quickly devouring the loose seed that has been scattered.

We know the parable to be correct. We know people who are seemingly outside the scope of the gospel. They seem too far gone... too calloused... too unconcerned about spiritual matters. And yet we share the call to cast the seed. Our task is never to sit in judgment over those we think will never receive the grace of the gospel. Our task is to be faithful in casting the seed. Our task is not to doubt what God can do in the life of any person... our task again, is to cast the seed. Though there are some we might want to quickly write-off, we must never underestimate the power of God's Spirit. Sometimes hard hearts just need more ounces of seed. Who do you know that is living without the hope of the gospel? Go cast some more seed, and then some more, and then some more.

Prayer

Father, may we be as stubborn about our resolve to cast the seeds of the gospel as you are about loving each of us. Amen.

Day 33 Mark 5: Reach Out and Touch

"For she thought, 'If I just touch His garments, I will get well.'"
Mark 5:28 NASB

Observation

This scene in Mark 5 begins with Jesus traveling to the home of Jairus in order to heal his daughter. As Jesus and his followers walk through the community, the crowds rush to Jesus and press in all around him. A woman who as been suffering an illness for the past 12 years dares to push her way towards Jesus in order to touch him. It is said in scripture, that there is "healing in the wings of the Savior" (Malachi 4:2), meaning that for her, touching the tassels on Jesus' robe will impart healing. Her belief is that if she can just touch him that she will be made well. She believes that Jesus is sent from God and she also believes that to touch him will bring wholeness to her life. It is her faithful act that eventually brings the healing event.

Application

Notice the faith step... "If I just touch His garments, I will get well." It's the idea that if a person gets close enough to touch Jesus, healing will come. I suggest that our willingness to touch Christ would bring a renewed sense of wholeness to our lives. How is that done? We can't physically touch Jesus, so how can we draw close enough to make contact? It's a faith step. We draw close to him through our relationship with him. Like the suffering woman of Mark 5, we must have a deeply held conviction about the identity of Jesus. We must acknowledge that he is the Son of God and that he comes to offer healing and wholeness to each of us. We must then find ways to connect with him, knowing that as we do, we will find grace. We connect to him through faithful and consistent reading of his story. We connect to him through obedience to his teaching. We connect to him through prayerful conversation. If we will dare to risk moments of connection, we will discover how his power can make us whole. What do you bring to the table? Skepticism or faith... doubt or belief... despair or hope? When your faith teaches you that Jesus is Lord, then your connection to him will bring you wholeness.

Prayer

Father, give to each of us a simple faith in the Son of God. May our connection to him bring us healing in all the ways we need his touch. Amen.

"And he swore to her, 'Whatever you ask of me, I will give it to you; up to half of my kingdom.'" Mark 6:23 NASB

Observation

Mark Chapter 6 tells the story of the death of John the Baptist. King Herod kept John in prison and on occasion, would speak to him with a certain fascination at his teaching. Because of John's popularity with the people, Herod was afraid to execute him, although the pressure to do so from his wife was great. The moment came when her daughter danced at a party in a way that pleased the king greatly. Caught up in the moment, he swears to give her anything she wants. With her mother's counsel, she asks for the head of John the Baptist on a platter and the king is forced to have him executed.

Application

Ever get caught up in the moment and make a foolish choice? Sometimes we let peer pressure, financial pressure, or job pressure keep us from thinking rationally. We get squeezed by circumstance and end up making some really foolish decisions. In fact, there are those moments of impulse that return to haunt us for a lifetime. We are all victims of our hastily and foolishly made choices. At times, a moment's pleasure results in a lifetime of remorse. So how can we make better decisions? How can we live with less regret?

New Testament writer James writes, "If any of you lack wisdom, he should ask God, who gives generously to all without finding fault, and it will be given to him" (James 1:5). Let's acknowledge that our wisdom is limited at best. All of us need the counsel of our Heavenly Father. We need the wisdom that only God can offer. We have to learn how to retrain our minds to make better choices. The old "What Would Jesus Do?" question is still valid. What if we stopped long enough at the intersection of any decision to really ask, "What's the better choice? What brings honor to God? What choice provides the best long-term result?" May God help us all to slow the impulses that lead to poor decisions in exchange for Godly wisdom that leads to success.

Prayer

Father, may we be mindful of the danger of poorly made decisions. Grant us wisdom for the facing of each hour. Amen.

Day 35

Mark 7: Real Faith

"And He said to them, 'Rightly did Isaiah prophesy of you hypocrites, as it is written: 'THIS PEOPLE HONORS ME WITH THEIR LIPS, BUT THEIR HEART IS FAR AWAY FROM ME.'"
Mark 7:6 NASB

Observation

As chapter 7 opens, Scribes and Pharisees travel from Jerusalem to observe Jesus and to listen to his teaching. They noticed that Jesus and his disciples were eating bread with "unwashed" hands. They questioned such a practice because they were always careful to ritually and ceremonially wash their hands before eating. They were critical of Jesus and his disciples for not observing the traditions passed down to them from their elders. They became so caught up in the rituals of their faith that they failed to understand the importance of relationship with God that should be at the heart of worship. Jesus pointed to their false-piety with the words of Isaiah, which reminded them that anyone can "claim" to honor God with mere words (and traditions). It is those whose hearts yearn for God that honor God best.

Application

Which do you offer to God... lip service or a compassionate and pliable heart? There are many among us who "claim" to have a valid faith. Many claim to be religious. Many say that they love God. Many say that they are very spiritual. Anyone can "say" just about anything. The real demonstration of our faith is not simply found in our confessional words. It's found in the compassion of our hearts. James wrote a lot about the connection between faith and works. He knew that real faith always resulted in tangible works. There has to be a connection. Our faith is validated, not by words, but through actions driven by a heart of compassion.

With which are you honoring God... your words, or your heart? Need some stats to think about? Less than 20% of all professing Christians attend church regularly. 95% of those who claim the Christian faith will never personally lead someone to experience faith in Christ. Charitable giving among evangelicals is at all-time low (about 3% of income). There are plenty who "claim" to love God. Why not become one who really does?

Prayer

Father, teach us that unless we honor you with our hearts, our words will carry no truth. Amen.

Mark 8: How's Your Vision?

"And he looked up and said, 'I see men, for I see them like trees, walking around.' Then again He laid His hands on his eyes; and he looked intently and was restored, and began to see everything clearly."
Mark 8:24-25 NASB

Observation

Of all of the stories of Jesus and his miracles, this one has a little twist not found in any other story. A blind man is brought to Jesus in order to be healed. Jesus spit on the man's eyes to heal him and asked, "Do you see anything?" The man had received partial sight and told Jesus that he could see men, but they "looked like trees walking around." So Jesus laid his hands on the man's eyes for the second time and suddenly he was able to see everything clearly. Did you catch the twist? It took a double dose of Jesus to heal the man completely. It's the only time when Jesus had to touch a man twice to completely heal him.

Application

I can't explain the "double dose." Why was he not healed completely at the first touch? Why did his vision only partially return until Jesus touched him again? Though I don't have those answers, I do find an important faith lesson in the story. Sometimes our vision of Christ is not made clear in a single moment of time. There are moments when we see only dimly, but as we spend time in his presence, our vision continues to clear. So don't think that all you need to know of Jesus, all that you need to experience, all that you need to learn, or even all that you need to see, will become clear at the first encounter. Our pursuit of Christ takes a lifetime to fully experience. I've been a believer for nearly 50 years. I understand more about Jesus than I did on the July morning in '68 when I first put my trust in him. The exciting thing is to know that years from now I will see him even more clearly. My faith was not completed the moment I prayed to invite him into my heart. My salvation was complete... but not my knowledge of Jesus. It continues to clear with each encounter that I have with him.

Prayer

Father, give us special moments with Jesus so that we might see him and our faith more clearly. Amen.

"Elijah appeared to them along with Moses; and they were talking with Jesus." Mark 9:4 NASB

Observation

At a very unusual moment in the life of Jesus, Jesus was transfigured on a mountaintop. His clothing became radiantly white. Peter, James, and John were there to see the moment, but what they saw next really caught their attention. Suddenly, standing with Jesus, were both Elijah and Moses! Talk about some of the heavyweights of faith... it doesn't get much bigger than those two. Jesus stood in the presence of God, surrounded by Elijah and Moses, with his closest followers only a few feet away. What a glorious moment for Christ to experience. Sometimes the people surrounding your life make all the difference.

Application

Today's verse begs the question, "Who are the important people in your life? Who are the ones who stand faithfully with you in moments of both crisis and victory?" The right people can make all the difference. Most of us tend to collect a few friends along the way. We connect with key people and they tend to become very influential in our lives. If we have chosen well, our friends push and prod us to become our best. If we choose poorly, our friends can pull us down to the point we live well beneath God's intended purpose for our lives. So who are the people who most influence your life? Who gets to be a part of your inner circle?

Let me offer you a suggestion for connecting with the kind of people who will challenge you in positive ways... go to church. That's right. Go to church. You and I need to experience life surrounded by the people of God. That's not to say that everyone at church is perfect, or that they will never let you down. They're just human and at times they will disappoint. But most of the time they will lift you, pray with you, care for you, and inspire you. People of genuine faith and piety are just the types we need in our lives. Invest your life with theirs and see where the journey takes you.

Prayer

Father, lead us to faithful friends who will make a difference in our lives. May we be careful to surround ourselves with people who challenge us to grow. Amen.

"And He took them in His arms and began blessing them, laying His hands on them." Mark 10:16 NASB

Observation

During a moment of travel and teaching, people brought children to Jesus in order that he might bless them. The disciples tried to discourage such action, thinking that the children were a distraction to Jesus. But Jesus rebukes the disciples and uses the moment to teach a faith lesson about receiving the Kingdom as a child with innocence, trust and belief. And then he does a really shocking thing... at least to the culture of that day... he begins picking them up and blessing them.

Here's why such an action would have been shocking to his audience. Imagine a number of street children running all around the disciples. What if some who brought the children to Jesus were not parents, but just concerned followers who felt compassion for orphans and longed for Jesus to simply offer them a blessing in order to give them the chance for a better life? What if the children belonged to no one, but only to a city where they survived on their own? In the culture of the day, adoption had no formalized process. A Jewish man could gather any homeless child in his arms and declare publicly, "This child is mine!" and the child would be forever joined to his family. It was a rare thing for a Jewish man, especially a rabbi, to ever pick up a child. In this scene, Jesus joyfully and gladly picks up a number of children, holding them and blessing them, in the posture of adoption, as though he was declaring, "These children are mine!" The image of grace—that of loving the unloved, accepting the unacceptable, and including the unwanted—would have been clearly communicated.

Application

In the same way, Jesus lifts us and holds us and declares, "This child is mine!" Who are we that we should be loved, accepted, forgiven, and welcomed into his family? It's not that we first had the wisdom to choose him... it's that he first had the love to choose us. Let that thought run through your mind today and feel the joy of inclusion.

Prayer

Father, we thank you that we have been claimed by Christ. Thank you for our inclusion into your forever family. Amen.

"Therefore I say to you, all things for which you pray and ask, believe that you have received them, and they will be granted you." Mark 11:24 NASB

Observation

Jesus spoke these words in the early days of that first Holy Week. One morning, as Jesus entered the city, he saw a fig tree and hoping for something to eat, he approached the tree. Discovering no fruit, for it was out of season, he cursed the tree. The next morning, when Jesus and the disciples passed the same spot, they discovered that the tree had withered from the roots up. The disciples were amazed. In response, Jesus offered the words of our focus verse. It was a momentary lesson on prayer and what makes for effective prayer. Jesus was joining the idea of faith to prayer. "Believe in the things for which you pray, and they will be granted." (The cursing of the fig tree is seen by many as mirroring the cursing of the religious leaders of the Temple who failed to produce the fruit of the Kingdom.)

Application

Jesus promised that, "all things for which you pray and ask, believe that you have received them, and they will be granted." Obviously there is a connection between our level of faith and the effectiveness of our prayers. The lesson seems to be, "If your faith is strong enough, you will receive the things for which you ask in prayer." That raises some issues, doesn't it? There seems to be no limit on this promise of Jesus. Ask away in faith, and the answer will come. So does that mean if our prayers are not answered that our faith was simply not strong enough? Is the effectiveness of our prayers totally dependent on our level of faith? Do we control the power of prayer regardless of the Father's wishes? Are there qualifiers to our prayers, like having to pray according to God's will, or praying with a formula and by a certain criteria?

I don't have all the answers to why some prayers are quickly answered and some are not. There is still a level of mystery to it all. But I am convinced of this... God hears our prayers and something about the level of our faith stirs the heart of God. While it is true that not all of our prayers are answered in the ways we have prayed them, it is also true that few of us really pray with the kind of boldness and faith of which Jesus speaks. God's response is not limited... our asking is.

Prayer

Father, like the disciples of old, we would ask you to teach us how to pray. Invest in us a strong faith that we might pray bold prayers. Amen.

"And they were seeking to seize Him, and yet they feared the people, for they understood that He spoke the parable against them. And so they left Him and went away." Mark 12:12 NASB

Observation

Jesus had just told a parable about a landowner who left his vineyard in the care of vine-growers. When the time of the harvest had come, the owner sent slaves to gather his portion of the produce. One by one the slaves were mistreated and even killed by the wicked vine-growers. Eventually, the owner sent his own son and he too was killed. The parable ends with the owner destroying the evil vine-growers and giving the vineyard to others. The religious leaders of the day were angered at his teaching. They understood that he was clearly speaking about them and their rejection by God because they had not received his Messiahship.

Application

It is no small thing to come under the scrutiny of God's word. In this passage, it is the Pharisees who are confronted by the claims of scripture. God's truth exposed their falsehood and sinfulness, and out of shame, they direct their anger towards Jesus. Scripture, if taken seriously, always has the power to expose our hypocrisy and our sinfulness. It continually offers correction, insight, challenge, and truth. And yes, at times, it speaks very directly and forthrightly in our direction. Ever read a passage of scripture and have it leave you a bit uncomfortable because it seemingly is directed straight at your life? Hebrews 4:12 reminds us "The Word of God is living and active and sharper than any two-edged sword, and piercing as far as the division of soul and spirit, of both joints and marrow, and able to judge the thoughts and the intentions of the heart." Supplying you with comfort is only one of the roles that scripture is to play in your life. It is also to expose your sins, challenge your prejudices, and correct your thinking. I challenge you this morning, to read the Bible faithfully and consistently, keeping an open mind as you do, to all that it longs to reveal to you.

Prayer

Father, we thank you for the word of God. May it become a lamp unto our feet and a light unto our path and may we hide its words in our hearts that we may not sin against you. Amen.

"But of that day or hour no one knows, not even the angels in heaven, nor the Son, but the Father alone." Mark 13:32 NASB

Observation

In this passage Jesus is speaking to his closest disciples about the Day of the Lord when God will bring final judgment upon the earth. The disciples asked for a sign. They wanted an indication as to when such an event would come to pass. The response of Jesus provides both uncertainty and clarity. The uncertainty lies with a timetable indicating at which moment the day will arrive. Jesus clearly teaches that such knowledge is beyond any mere mortal... that only God knows the moment. The clarity provided has to do with the reality of the event. Standing just as forcefully as all the other promises of scripture is the promise that such a moment will surely come. Such knowledge should bring both intentionality to our mission zeal and assurance that our destinies are secure in Christ.

Application

Certainly this verse was well quoted during the past few years as a California pastor garnered world-wide headlines with his prediction of the end of the world was to have occurred on some particular recent Saturday. When the moment failed to arrive, he stated that he was "dumbfounded" at the results. Most pointed to our focus verse reasoning that, "if even Christ was not made aware of the actual date, how could one man seem to have such clarity?" Let's be honest, there are always a few ministers out there who love to claim a superior knowledge they simply do not possess. It's not my purpose nor place to judge the reasons for his prediction. But I do want to offer a brief comment. Though he was wrong about the date, he was right about the coming day. There is a moment at which the world and all who dwell within it will be held accountable for the actions committed. Scripture is crystal clear. Those who will escape judgment and find themselves living in the splendor of God's forever Kingdom are those who have joined their lives to Jesus Christ and who have proclaimed him as Lord and Savior. It's that simple and that hard. Know Jesus and know life. So if the day should come like a thief in the night, are you ready? Why live with uncertainty? Instead, choose to live in faith.

Prayer

Father, we thank you for the assurances of your word that remind us of the eternal life we have in Christ Jesus. Amen.

"Truly I say to you, wherever the Gospel is preached in the whole world, what this woman has done will also be spoken of in memory of her."
Mark 14:9 NASB

Observation

Spoken during Holy Week, Jesus offers a prophetic word about a woman and her extraordinary act of compassion. Jesus is with his disciples, staying in the home of Simon the Leper, whom he had apparently healed of his leprosy. As Jesus reclines at the table, an unnamed woman breaks open a very costly bottle of perfume and pours the fragrant oil over his head. It is an extremely costly moment of grace. Worth nearly a year's wages, this perfume was without question the most valuable possession that she had, and she anoints the head of Jesus in the way that Heads of State are crowned. It is an act of worship, dedication, and sacrifice. Jesus' response to her extravagant act is to proclaim that her sacrifice will be forever remembered wherever the gospel is proclaimed.

Application

Talk about leaving a legacy... though Mark did not give us her name, her compassionate act has never been forgotten. For the past 2000 years, believers have read about her story and talked about her dedication and commitment to Christ. It was a quick moment in time, but one that may have been years in the making. How would she have possessed such a valuable vial? Through years of hard work? Had she guarded this heirloom, perhaps given to her by her family, for years? Had she sold much of what she possessed in order to buy it? You can bet that it was not a "spur of the moment" kind of thing. With great thought and intentionality she brings it to the place where Jesus is dining, and she anoints his head.

Leaving a legacy remembered for generations is rarely the result of one simple "spur of the moment" action. Though our children and grandchildren may well remember a single gift given, or a day spent at the park, or even a carefully timed word of advice, what truly endures is the consistency of lifestyle that we live before them. The legacy we leave is lived out in their presence over a long period of years. The grace of our words, the commitments of our hearts, and the dedication of our lives must be displayed both constantly and consistently if our legacy is to make a difference. I challenge you to be thoroughly Christian. Live in such a way that in the generations to follow, people will talk of your faith and your dedication to Jesus.

Prayer

Father, may we live the kind of life that will glorify you and that will teach our children. Amen.

Day 43 Mark 15: A Little Backbone, Please

"Wishing to satisfy the crowd, Pilate released Barabbas for them, and after having Jesus scourged, he handed Him over to be crucified."
Mark 15:15 NASB

Observation

Pilate had it within his authority to release Jesus or to bind him away to be crucified. The crowd, of course, wanted his death. So intent were they for his crucifixion that when given a choice, they shouted for the release of Barabbas who was a known murderer. Pilate, in an act of political expediency, decided to bend to their wishes and pronounced the sentence of death. Notice again the opening phrase of our focus verse... "Wishing to satisfy the crowd..." Often doing the right thing is not the popular choice. Appeasing the crowd is not always the best decision to make.

Application

Most politicians of our day seem to follow the pattern of Pilate. They quickly gauge the flow of public opinion and base their decisions on what seems to be the majority voice. Don't we all wish for government leaders who will vote their convictions and do the right thing no matter what the winds of popularity dictate? But before we judge our leaders too harshly, let's take a moment to do a little self-assessment. Are we not often driven by a desire to "satisfy the crowd?" Let's be honest... who among us doesn't want to be popular? Who among us wants to rock the boat? Who really wants to stand up to peer pressure? When faced with a decision, most of us cower to the pressure to do what everyone else is doing. Is that a good practice? Is that even a Jesus ethic? Sometimes doing the right thing is far from the popular thing. Sometimes making the right choice can create a lot of enemies. Sometimes our faith should demand a greater integrity. So you'd better put a stake in the ground and decide... should I do what is right, or should I do what is popular? One choice will make you a friend to many; the other will make you a friend to self. Doing the right thing is not always popular. I pray that you will have the courage to do what is right according to your Christian faith, and not bend to the whims of society's opinion.

Prayer

Father, may we live courageous Christian lives that force us to do the right things, not simply the popular things. Amen.

Day 44 — Mark 16: One and Only One Task

"And He said to them, 'Go into all the world and preach the Gospel to all creation.'" Mark 16:15 NASB

Observation

Sometimes the last words are the most important words. These words spoken by Jesus at the end of Mark's Gospel are among the last that he would speak to his disciples. Obviously, they carry enormous weight and are meant to be taken quite seriously. Notice these words are spoken with the imperative voice... "Go and preach." There is no conditional clause... "Go if you want to..." or "Go if you have time..." or "Go when you think it is convenient to do so..." or "Go if you are a member of the clergy." Nope. It's a word spoken to every believer. The responsibility to spread the message of salvation is placed upon all of our shoulders. It is not an optional calling. It is a commandment from our Lord.

Application

Follow this line of thought for a moment. If Jesus is King of all Kings and Lord of all Lords, and if all authority has been given to him in heaven and on earth, then shouldn't his words direct our actions and govern our thoughts? It is a little weird that we would claim him as Lord and not do the things he commands us to do. And yet, most of us are a little uncomfortable about sharing our faith. We feel a little awkward when it comes to spiritual conversation. Does that excuse our responsibility or take away the commandment of Christ? Never. A slave doesn't question a master's command. A soldier doesn't balk at the orders from his General. How can we dare to think that when Christ left us with this one single, great commission, that he never really intended for us to obey?

There is a mentality that seems to be creeping its way into the mindset of modern-day American Christianity. It's the mindset that says, "Live and let live. Let people believe whatever they feel is right for them. There are many ways to experience God." You've heard that, right? It's still a lie. Christ never intended for us to be silent or to be lazy. He intended for us to preach the gospel to all the world. May God give us a bold faith and a strong belief that will compel us to actually tell someone about Jesus.

Prayer

Father, may we be so burdened with the responsibility of preaching the gospel that we actually find ways to share the message faithfully and consistently. Amen.

Day 45 Luke 1: Better Than You Think

> "They were both righteous in the sight of God, walking blamelessly in all the commandments and requirements of the Lord." Luke 1:6 NASB

Observation

The Gospel of Luke begins with the story of the birth of John the Baptist. John's father was named Zacharias and his mother was named Elizabeth. Zacharias served as a priest before God. His wife, Elizabeth was barren. The angel Gabriel appeared to Zacharias and announced that Elizabeth would have a son. Because of his initial lack of belief in the words of Gabriel, Zacharias was unable to speak until the birth of his son.

Application

What I want you to notice this morning, is the description given concerning Zacharias and Elizabeth. "They were both righteous in the sight of God, walking blamelessly in all the commandments and requirements of the Lord." Wow. What a testimony to their faith commitments before the Lord. Would any of us have such noble words said of us? Are any of us "righteous in the sight of God?" The truth is that we are anything but righteous. From birth we have been shackled with a sin nature that pushes us toward disobedience. We fail. We sin. We are tragically flawed. Even on our best days we still miss the mark of God's intention for our lives. Who could ever dream of our being righteous in the eyes of God? Who but Jesus?

Check out 2 Corinthians 5:21, "He made Him who knew no sin to be sin on our behalf, so that we might become the righteousness of God in Him." Read it again... slowly so that its impact can soak in. Christ became as sin for us, so that we could stand forgiven in the presence of God. As strange as it may seem, by the sacrifice of Christ, we are righteous in the sight of God. As we start out on a whole new day, let us be reminded that through the blood of Jesus Christ, we are cleansed, forgiven, and made perfect in the eyes of God. God chooses to forgive our sins and forget our deeds. All of which places us in a position to be used today for God's glory. You may not be told by an angel today that your son will be the forerunner for the Messiah, but you may well be called to influence someone so that they can discover the love of Christ. Someone might one day talk of your faith and the difference you made.

Prayer

Father, thank you for your grace that forgives and forgets and causes us to stand righteous in your presence. Amen.

"And then as a widow to the age of eighty-four. She never left the temple, serving night and day with fastings and prayers."
Luke 2:37 NASB

Observation

When Jesus was 40 days old, his parents took him to the temple to present him to the Lord according to the Law of Moses. While in the Temple, the young family encountered an older priest named Simeon who immediately recognized that Jesus was the Messiah. He praised God and blessed the young family. They also met an 84-year-old woman named Anna. She was a "prophetess" who came daily to the Temple. It is likely that she addressed all who would listen to her, though she had no official function in the running of the Temple. Notice from our focus verse that she served night and day with fastings and prayers. What strikes me is the way in which she found a place of service by fasting and praying each day.

Application

I like that this woman chose a life of service before God. The culture and customs of the day did not allow her to serve as a priest, but she found a way to serve God. There is something to be said for offering ourselves in any way we can to further the Kingdom. Many crave the limelight or seek a position in the church and if not offered such they feel their lives are wasted. Not so with Anna. She practiced the spiritual disciplines of prayer and fasting daily as a way to further God's Kingdom. She found a way to "plug-in" where her life would make a difference.

It begs the question... "How are you helping the Kingdom of God move forward?" Are you exercising your gifts and using your talents? Are you dedicated to the practice of spiritual disciplines? Or... are you waiting on the sidelines pouting until someone asks you to do something? Become a prayer warrior. If you really want to help the church, or help the ministry of the Kingdom, or encourage those in positions of leadership, start praying night and day for God to work in your world. Anna is remembered for all of time, not because she was called to some great and noble position, but because she was faithful to play her part consistently before God. Don't wait to be asked. Take your gift from God and create a way to use it in God's service. Your name may not appear in the bulletin, but your Father in Heaven will know it. Nothing about your effort will go unnoticed.

Prayer

Father, may we be faithful to use our gifts in great and small ways. Reveal opportunities and then grant us the courage to serve. Amen.

"Therefore bear fruits in keeping with repentance, and do not begin to say to yourselves, 'We have Abraham for our father,' for I say to you that from these stones God is able to raise up children to Abraham."
Luke 3:8 NASB

Observation

When John the Baptist appeared in the wilderness preaching a message of repentance, many of the religious leaders of his day came to him to hear his preaching. To them, his preaching was radical, challenging, offensive, and heart piercing. He challenged them to live lives that reflected a genuine obedience to God. He called them to repent and turn from their false piety and selfish practices. Their argument was bound up in their heritage. Because they could trace their roots to Abraham, they argued that God would surely bless them. John attempted to teach them that faith is not based on family ties but on a genuine desire to be obedient before God.

Application

There are many among us who believe in "faith by association." There are some who think that as long as they hang around people of faith, live in a household of dedicated Christians, or even go to church most Sundays that surely God will accept them and bless them. It's the idea of riding someone's coattails into the Kingdom. The Pharisees of Jesus' day believed their bloodlines were all that was needed to prove their acceptance before God. In the same way, many of us believe that somehow the faith of our parents or close friends someway gets us a pass on the whole "religion thing." Go to church on occasion, maybe drop a few coins in the plate and surely God's favor will rest on us, or so we think. It is never about our lineage, or the faith of our families. Our acceptance in the eyes of God is based solely on one thing... our faith in Jesus Christ. John's message was to "bear fruit in keeping with repentance." I hope you hear that message carefully. Your faith should produce "Kingdom Fruit." Your faith should produce results in your life and in the lives of those around you whom you influence each day. If there is little fruit, that is probably an indication of little faith. Don't think that you are accepted in the eyes of God because of who you are. You are made acceptable by what you believe and how well you live out that belief.

Prayer

Father, may we not talk of the faith of our fathers as though it brings a saving grace to our lives. Teach us to be obedient and faithful and in those challenges to find our hope. Amen.

"Jesus, full of the Holy Spirit, returned from the Jordan and was led around by the Spirit in the wilderness for forty days, being tempted by the devil. And He ate nothing during those days, and when they had ended, He became hungry." Luke 4:1-2 NASB

Observation

John had just baptized Jesus. His baptism and the descending of the Holy Spirit in the form of a dove marked the official start to his public ministry. No sooner had his ministry begun, than the Spirit led him out into the wilderness. Did the Spirit lead him there to fortify him? Give him rest? Strengthen his resolve? While in the wilderness the devil appears. He knew that Jesus was famished after 40 days of fasting, and tempted him to turn stones into bread. The devil saw his greatest weakness at the moment, his physical body, and threw out the powerful temptation to satisfy his physical needs. Pretty clever. Attack when and where a person is most vulnerable.

Application

Don't think that you are less vulnerable than Jesus or that the devil is less interested in controlling your life. The purpose of temptation is to destroy your relationship with God. The devil longs to disrupt, separate, and destroy. His purpose has always been to keep you from knowing the love of God and enjoying a life lived in his presence. And so he comes to us... repeatedly, relentlessly, cunningly, creatively, and powerfully. In the areas of our lives where we are weak, he offers his best shots. Are we without hope? Is it a forgone conclusion that we will fall victim to his pursuit? Check out 1 Corinthians 10:13, "No temptation has overtaken you except what is common to mankind. And God is faithful; He will not let you be tempted beyond what you can bear. But when you are tempted, He will also provide a way out so that you can endure it." Do you see the promise in that verse? When you are tempted, and you will be, God will provide you with enough strength to endure. The key is to ask for help. Often we don't include God in the battle and try to handle things on our own. If we were strong enough to defeat temptation ourselves, would we be claimed as easy victims? You need help... God-sized help. Temptation is coming... it always does. From where will your help come?

Prayer

Father, remind us that our help comes from the Lord. May we be humble enough to seek your aid and courageous enough to fight well our battles with temptation. Amen.

Day 49 — Luke 5: Make It Happen

"But Jesus often withdrew to lonely places and prayed." Luke 5:16 NASB

Observation

By the time that chapter 5 begins, Jesus' ministry is well underway. In this chapter he begins calling his first disciples, there is the great catch of fish, there is the healing of a leper, and there is the dinner at the home of Matthew. People are starting to notice and crowds are starting to gather. In the midst of miracles, multitudes, and messages, notice that Jesus continues to slip away to the places of solitude to pray. He recognizes that his strength comes from God and so he is careful to keep the relationship in focus. Jesus knows that there is nothing more important than time with the Father.

Application

Are we willing to withdraw often, to the lonely places to pray? In the midst of our hectic and chaotic lives, we need both solitude and moments with the Father. It seems increasingly difficult to find both. Jesus taught in the Sermon on the Mount about the importance of finding the inner room, closing the door, and praying in secret (Matt. 6:6). Jesus knew that all of us would need the quiet in the midst of chaos, the solitude in the midst of the storm. What a refreshing moment can occur, whenever we shut out the world long enough to spend some quiet time in the presence of God. It's the "still water" that David writes about in the 23rd Psalm. Here's the point... we will never experience the solitude if we do not carve out the time from other less important involvements. Let's be honest... we all live very busy lives. Our time is precious and it is often over-scheduled and frantically spent. None of us have time to pray. We have to make the time. That's why we call prayer a spiritual "discipline." We have to discipline ourselves to take the time to do it. If it was important enough for Jesus to practice the discipline of prayer, how much more for us? Carve out a little time today in a place of solitude and spend a few moments with your Father.

Prayer

Father, teach us to value the discipline of prayer. Remind us that consistent conversations in your presence bring peace, insight, and joy. Amen.

"Each tree is recognized by its own fruit. People do not pick figs from thorn bushes, or grapes from briers." Luke 6:44 NASB

Observation

Jesus was teaching his disciples about the fruit that would be produced from their lives. The results of who they were and how they lived would be evident to all. A good heart produces good fruit. An evil heart produces evil. There is always consistent fruit produced in each man's life. Fig bushes produce figs. Grape vines produce grapes. A man's true heart can only produce one kind of fruit, ultimately good or evil, but never both.

Application

So take a look around and consider the kind of fruit that you are producing in your life. Look back over the past few years and examine the kind of results your life has produced... the kind of legacy that marks your passage. Jesus said that, we would all be recognized by our fruit. Either we produce the fruit of peace, harmony, joy, and grace, or we produce the fruit of anger, discord, jealousy, or strife. It all comes from the heart. What's on the inside has to eventually show-up on the outside.

Here's the deal... when we live according to mere human instinct and emotion, we will produce fruit that only reveals what is the worse in all of us. We have to replace selfish motivation by allowing the Spirit of God to dwell fully within us. Galatians reminds us that, "the fruit of the Spirit is love, joy, peace, patience, kindness, goodness, faithfulness, gentleness, and self-control." Doesn't that sound like the kind of fruit you'd like to produce... the kind of legacy you'd like to leave? Let me suggest that you start this day a little differently. Pray this morning that God will fill you completely with the Holy Spirit. Ask that your life might glorify God this day through your words, actions, and even attitudes. You are capable of living a better life. Ask God to prune the vine of your heart in a way that selfishness will give way to the Spirit.

Prayer

Father, this morning we want to offer you an open door to our hearts. Rid from our lives the anger, the bitterness, and the hatred that can so easily produce the wrong kind of fruit in our lives. Fill us with your Spirit so that you will be glorified in us. Amen.

Day 51 Luke 7: How Can We Be Silent?

"The dead man sat up and began to talk, and Jesus gave him back to his mother." Luke 7:15 NIV

Observation

Jesus was traveling with his disciples and as they approached the small village of Nain, they encountered a funeral procession. The body of a young man was being carried away for burial. He was the only son of a widow. Consider her plight for a moment. Not only had she lost her husband, but now her son. Those two events would forever define her life and alter her status. Often to be widowed was to lose one's life, at least socially. Widows often were forced to live the life of a servant in the household of their former husbands. Sometimes they were cast aside by society and considered "used goods." Therefore, many had to resort to prostitution to survive. This widow of Nain was a bit better off. Because she had a son, she had some status and some hope. Her son would provide for her and keep her from living a life that many widows were forced to live. But when he died, everything about her world changed. Her hope was gone. Her future, forever banished. And so when Jesus restored the life of the son, he in fact, also restored her life.

Application

I sometimes wonder about the story of this young family. Where would life take them from this moment forward? Having been rescued from the grave, surely this young man went on to tell his story a thousand times and was able to convince many that Jesus was the Messiah. And what of her testimony? Surely she lived out her days as a loyal follower of Christ. How could she not tell of the great things that Jesus had done for her? And yet, nowhere else in scripture is their story told. There is no mention of either of them again as the Ministry of Jesus continues to be written. Find that odd? I do. How can someone with such a radical life change and such a testimony to offer, go without mention? Surely they didn't fail to tell the story a thousand times... or did they... or do we? I find it odd that we as believers, who have been saved from sin, rescued from our former lives, and given everlasting life could ever fail to tell the story of Jesus. Shouldn't his praises be forever on our lips? Shouldn't we tell the story of being lost and found over and over again with each day's conversation? It is no small thing being brought to life again. Let's make sure we tell the story of Christ's resurrecting love to all we encounter.

Prayer

Father, we praise you and thank you for raising us to life through Jesus Christ. May we become grateful enough that we tell his story for as long as we live. Amen.

> "And He said to them, 'Where is your faith?' They were fearful and amazed, saying to one another, 'Who then is this, that He commands even the winds and the water, and they obey Him?'" Luke 8:25 NASB

Observation

Our focus verse is from the story of the crossing of the sea. Jesus and the disciples are in a boat crossing the Sea of Galilee. Exhausted from the day's activities, Jesus falls asleep while resting in the stern of the boat. A fierce gale blows up and the disciples fear for their lives. They awaken Jesus who stands in the face of the storm and commands the storm to become calm. Jesus then turns to the very bewildered disciples and asks about the status of their faith. How could they have thought for even a moment that the storms would overcome their lives?

Application

How we respond to the storms is always an indication of the strength of our faith. When panicked, Jesus asked his followers, "Where is your faith?" They had momentarily substituted faith for fear, hope for hopelessness, peace for anxiety. They had allowed their insecurities to overrule the assurances that Christ longed for them to know. We could learn a lot from this story. We often fall into the same pattern. Let the first raindrop of a storm fall in our direction and we begin to panic. All that we know of faith, all that we understand of God's promises seem to blow away with the approaching wind. We forget God's presence and provision. We forget God's power and protection. And so again the question echoes in our minds, "Where is your faith?" Understand that faith doesn't prevent storms from coming our way. It does provide what we need most in the midst of the swirling winds... hope. In fact, faith is what connects us to the reassuring power of Christ when the winds howl and the waves assail. I can't pretend to know all of the storms that might be gathering on the horizon of your life, but I can offer you this... Christ stands with you and if you will but call on him with faith and assurance, he will respond. You will be amazed at how differently you react to the swirling winds.

Prayer

Father, though we never welcome the storms in our lives, how we do thank you that in the midst of the storms we see you at work. Give us hope for the living of each day. May we find calm through the strength of your love. Amen.

"For whoever is ashamed of Me and My words, the Son of Man will be ashamed of him when He comes in His glory, and the glory of the Father and of the holy angels." Luke 9:26 NASB

Observation

Jesus spoke these words to the disciples at the end of a conversation about discipleship. Jesus had just taught them that to be a follower they must take up their cross. It was a reminder to them, and to us, that the road to discipleship is not necessarily easy. Some of the most rewarding journeys we take are filled with struggle. To be a Christ-follower, at least for the 1st century believers, was a call to persecution, danger, hardship, and maybe even death. The conversation ends with our focus verse. Christ reminded his disciples that those who distance themselves from Christ might find themselves distanced by Christ on the day that he returns. It was a call to loyal, obedient, and enduring discipleship.

Application

Tough verse, right? It really does say that our denial of Jesus in this present age will mean a denial by Christ of us in the age that is to come. To be honest, such a verse scares me to death, especially when I consider the number of times I act as though I am ashamed to be associated with Christ. Oh, it's not in the bigger moments of my life. I don't stand on a street corner and swear off my faith. I don't take out ads in the paper and denounce my Christianity. Nothing like that. It is in the smaller choices of my daily life when I deny his Lordship that are the moments that trouble me. Sometimes I make choices based on my will, my attitudes, and my desires that have nothing to do with Jesus. In fact, many of those choices are the exact opposite of what I know Jesus would have me choose, but I make them anyway. Is that not a denial of his Lordship? Is that not an indication that I am "ashamed" of Jesus because I don't want him to lead me at those moments? I suspect that I am not alone in my behavior. Most of us practice the same type behavior, repeatedly. The old adage states, "Jesus is Lord of all, or he is not Lord at all." Think about it. Are you really willing to claim his authority for your life? Is your goal to honor him and bring him glory? Until you make such a claim as the motivation for your life, you will struggle to do the right thing. I challenge you to fully embrace the life of a disciple. Live consistently, thoughtfully, and obediently.

Prayer

Father, forgive us when we make choices that deny the Lordship of Christ. Make us faithful. Make us loyal. Make us yours. Amen.

Luke 10: Open Your Eyes, Open Your Heart

"Likewise a Levite also, when he came to the place and saw him, passed by on the other side." Luke 10:32 NASB

Observation

This verse is part of the parable told by Jesus commonly known as "The Good Samaritan." As the story unfolds, a man is robbed on his way from Jerusalem to Jericho. Left for dead on the side of the road, both a priest and a Levite pass by, unwilling to offer aid. Finally, it is a Samaritan who comes to the rescue. The story was shocking to the listeners of Jesus because Jesus chose a Samaritan to be the hero of the story. The young lawyer, whose question prompted the telling of the story, is forced to confess that his definition of who can be a neighbor must be broadened dramatically. Let's focus for a moment on the Levite. A Levite was descended from the tribe of Levi and as such had been given duties as a priest. Levites were particularly charged with the reading of the Torah scrolls in both the Temple and synagogues. Here was a man who would have known the intention of God's "law and purpose" better than most, and yet he refuses to help the man in need. We can offer many suggestions as to why he may have refused, but the truth remains... he had the ability to offer help and chose not to act.

Application

It is easy for us to point to his moral failure. He knew God... the word of God... the love of God. And yet, he refused to help. He failed to recognize the stranger as a "neighbor" who was worthy of his attention. We tell ourselves that certainly, if interjected into the story, we would have done better. But would we? How often do we fail to act with the love of God when we see hurting people around us? Not only the homeless or hungry, but also those who need a listening ear, an encouraging word, a warm smile, and an affirmation of worth. You have seen them... the lady who sits alone at lunch, the new student who seems alone in a room filled with other students, the man who is ignored as he sits at church. They are all our neighbors and we are charged with offering the gift of simple hospitality. Surely the lonely, the left out, and the so-called "losers" are worthy of our attention. Can we not offer the simple gift of eye contact, a friendly word, or a handshake? These people are found daily on the roadsides of our journeys. Do we help? Or are we too filled with false piety to even notice them?

Prayer

Father, may we see opportunities for ministry in the lives of lonely people. Give us grace and love for those who are hurting. Amen.

"I tell you, even though he will not get up and give him anything because he is his friend, yet because of his persistence he will get up and give him as much as he needs." Luke 11:8 NASB

Observation

Jesus was once asked by his disciples to teach them to pray. He offered the words of the Lord's Prayer and then told them a parable about a man who goes to a neighbor at night to seek provisions. A guest has come and the man does not have what he needs to welcome his guest. The neighbor refuses to get up to offer help because the hour is late. But because of the persistent pleading of the desperate man, the neighbor finally gets up and offers the man all that he needs. Remember the parable is told in the context of Jesus' teaching on prayer. The lesson is that of persistence when praying.

Application

Like the early disciples, we too struggle at times in knowing what to pray or how to pray or even when to pray. The simple lesson of Jesus' parable is to be persistent in the discipline. In other words, we are reminded to pray and to pray often. Understand that we do not pray for the same need over and over again to get the attention of God. (God already knows what we need long before we ask.) We pray with persistence to teach ourselves of our dependency upon God to bless. It is as we keep on asking, and keep on knocking, and keep on seeking that our prayers become effective. It is not that God needs to be awakened or reminded of our needs; it is that we need to be reminded to bring our needs before God. I think the lesson here is not that if we pester God long enough we will get an answer. Instead, I think the lesson is that in our persistent conversation with God, we build both a relationship and a sense of dependency on our Heavenly Father. God responds to the persistent pleading of our desperate hearts, so do we. So even if you are praying about a need for the one-hundredth time, don't stop. Each time you pray, you will remind yourself of your own inability to fix the need, and of your reliance upon God who alone can work miracles.

Prayer

Father, teach us to pray, and to pray, and to pray. May we learn the lesson that each conversation deepens the relationship and unburdens our lives. Amen.

"And which of you by worrying can add a single hour to his life's span?"
Luke 12:25 NASB

Observation

On this occasion, Jesus was attempting to teach the disciples about God's provision for their lives. He reminded them of God's care for the birds of the sky and the lilies of the field. He reminded the disciples that each of them was worth more than many sparrows. His point was that if God cares for even the smallest details of the smallest creatures, then surely God will care for the affairs of men. And so to spend one's life in needless worry is indicative of having little faith in God's ability to provide. Jesus' counsel is to trust more and worry less.

Application

Let's be honest... worry swirls through most of our lives like an afternoon breeze. We stress over many things. We worry about our health, our wealth, our kids, our jobs, and our futures. We wring our hands and play the "what if?" game in our minds a dozen times a day. "What if I get a bad report? What if I can't pay that bill? What if my business downsizes? What if I can't pass that test?" Sound familiar? So much of our life energy is spent worrying about things we can't control. We fear the unknown and worry about the "what if." In response to our worry, Jesus teaches us to trust. His simple reminder makes sense..."Which of you by worrying can add a single hour to his life's span?" In fact, we know that the stress of worry can actually shorten our lives. So why do we do it? Is there a lack of trust on our part? Do we really doubt that God will provide for our needs? Jesus is not calling us to a frivolous lifestyle that throws all caution and concern to the wind. Certainly, we are called to live rationally and act wisely. There are many wise choices to make that will protect us from a lot of the stress that fills our days. But the point of Jesus' teaching is that of learning to lean on the wisdom and counsel of God more than we do. Go back to the "what if" phrases I listed above. Notice how many times the word "I," or "my" appears in those phrases. Maybe a word from the Proverbs can offer some insight this morning... "Trust in the Lord with all your heart and do not lean on your own understanding. In all your ways acknowledge Him, And He will make your paths straight" (Pr. 3:5-6). It's up to you... worry more or trust more. Which is the better choice?

Prayer

Father, teach us to trust you each day for both the great and small needs of our lives. Forgive our foolish worry. Give us a greater faith. Amen.

Day 57 — Luke 13: A Welcoming Community?

"And this woman, a daughter of Abraham as she is, whom Satan has bound for eighteen long years, should she not have been released from this bond on the Sabbath day?" Luke 13:16 NASB

Observation

Jesus was teaching in one of the local synagogues on a Sabbath day when he saw a poor woman who had been suffering from an illness for 18 years. He called her over, laid His hands on her, and immediately she was well. She rejoiced. The religious leaders grumbled. They took offense that a miracle had been performed on the Sabbath day. Rather than acknowledge a miracle of God, they offered condemnation because their religious rules had been violated. Jesus questioned their motivation. Was it not right to free a woman from illness on God's Holy day?

Application

Is it possible that religion can limit the growth of our faith? Is it possible that we can become too rigid, too judgmental, and too overbearing to allow the Kingdom to grow? When I read the gospels carefully, I find joy in the hearts of those who encountered Jesus. Burdens were lifted, eyes were opened, and broken bodies were healed. Those touched by Jesus rejoiced, some skipping along on legs that hadn't worked in years. In those moments of grace all that mattered was the joy of being made well and having been welcomed into the presence of Christ. My fear is that sometimes we limit the joy of the Kingdom. When someone wants to claim faith for the first time, we talk about orthodoxy and doctrine. When a struggling sinner wants to be forgiven, we talk about the depth of his/her sin and the shame they should harbor. When a family wants to join the church, we talk about whether or not they have been baptized in a proper manner. When a new girl starts coming to the youth group, we talk about the length of her skirt. Rather than throw open wide the doors of the Kingdom, we tend to set out hoops through which people must jump. What if we gave the impression of welcome and acceptance long before we ever talked about the boundaries of acceptable religious practice? What if we celebrated newfound faith, long before we spoke of doctrinal issues? What if we dared to love, forgive, heal, and touch like Jesus? Could our churches even hold those who would rush to experience Jesus?

Prayer

Father, forgive us when we put up barriers that repel rather than offer open arms that accept and rejoice. May we never limit the Kingdom because of the boundaries imposed by our religious practice. Amen.

"And you will be blessed, since they do not have the means to repay you; for you will be repaid at the resurrection of the righteous."
Luke 14:14 NASB

Observation

These words were spoken to a man, presumably a Pharisee, who had invited Jesus to a dinner on a Sabbath day. At the dinner, Jesus healed a man, which caused more than a little discussion. Next, he told a parable about picking the places of honor at a banquet. And finally, he offered a few words to his host about the guest list for the event. Jesus' instruction was that of inviting the poor, the crippled, the lame, and the blind... in other words those who would never expect to be invited, and those who could never return the favor. Jesus reminded him that such a noble and generous act would be repaid at the resurrection of the righteous. Simple truth… some acts of kindness and grace will never be repaid in this life, but they will also never be forgotten, not by the beneficiaries, and not by God. God will reward our acts of grace.

Application

There is something bound up in the Christian ethic that calls us to generosity. Over and over, Jesus reminds us that we have an obligation to care for the poor, to feed the hungry, to include the disenfranchised, and to give to those in need. We are to do such acts, not for the fame and notoriety such generosity can bring, but simply out of a sense of compassion. We bless from the abundance of our blessings. We give from the storehouse of grace given to us. Such noble deeds never go unnoticed. The recipient welcomes the generosity, and our Father remembers the deed. I hope that you do some acts of kindness that never get noticed. I hope that you give generously in ways that will never find your name in print in some boring list of donors. You will discover that there is great joy in the anonymous gift. There is both a deep satisfaction and a lasting contentment that comes when we allow the compassion of Christ to be exhibited through us, without any hint of notice in this life. The Father will see and you will know the blessing both now and later.

Prayer

Father, teach us the joy of giving and the contentment that is offered through our acts of compassion. Amen.

"So he got up and came to his father. But while he was still a long way off, his father saw him and felt compassion for him, and ran and embraced him and kissed him." Luke 15:20 NASB

Observation

This verse from the parable of the Prodigal Son is one of the greatest lessons in all of scripture. The parable focuses on a wayward son and his loving father. The son takes his inheritance, moves out, and squanders both his money and reputation in a foreign country. When he finally comes to his senses, he longs to return home and hopes beyond hope to make things right with his father. He expects his father's anger, wrath, and retribution. Instead he discovers grace, acceptance, and love. Notice that it is the father who runs out to embrace the son. The son limps along... the father races forward. It's a lesson for the ages. Jesus uses the story to remind us of the attitude God harbors towards all of us who sometimes walk away from the blessings of God's presence. It's always about grace and not condemnation.

Application

So where do you find yourself right now? Not geographically, but spiritually? Have you wandered from the presence of God? How far have you drifted from the place you need to be? It's easy to do. Oh, we don't mean to run away from God. We don't intend to fall into disobedience. We just slowly drift away. It's a slow fade for most of us. It begins with one simple choice and then another and then another. Soon we find ourselves walking in the "distant land" out of sync with God and even with ourselves. We squander the blessings of God by using our gifts and abilities in ways God never intended. And one day it will come... the moment when we realize that we are not in the place we really need to be. We start to wonder how we can "fix" things. The truth is we can't. It's not about our ability to make things right, it's about God's will to restore that which is broken. As soon as we turn toward home and take the first step toward reconciliation, we will discover that God is running in our direction. The scene is never one of chastisement or anger or even disappointment. It's one of glad reunion, welcome, and renewal. This morning, if you discover that you have drifted to the distant country, take one step toward home and discover what grace is all about.

Prayer

Father, thank you for loving us even when we least deserve it. May we understand this day, the joy of forgiveness and the depth of grace. Amen.

"He who is faithful in a very little thing is faithful also in much; and he who is unrighteous in a very little thing is unrighteous also in much."
Luke 16:10 NASB

Observation

Jesus spoke this verse in the context of teaching the disciples about the power of wealth to control and dominate a person's life. Just prior to this verse, Jesus told the parable of the unrighteous steward who losses his job because he has squandered the Master's possessions. Being shrewd about business and being worried about losing his status, he quickly "cooks the books" by erasing some of the debt owed by many, in order to be received well by those people once he is no longer steward. Jesus uses the parable to talk about being faithful and honest in both the great and small things of our lives.

Application

It's in the details. Jesus reminds us that those who are faithful in the small things are trustworthy in the larger things of life. Conversely, those who are unrighteous in the little things are unrighteous in the big things. We can't get away from our nature. Either we are honest in all things or we are not. Our character, our integrity, and our honesty are demonstrated one decision at a time. Find someone who is willing to fudge a little with even a small decision, and you will find a person who is willing to compromise with the greater decisions. It comes down to trustworthiness. Are we people of character or not? Do we do what we say that we are going to do? Do we keep our word? Can people trust us when we make even a small commitment? It is important to pay attention to even the smallest of promises we make... "I will call you tomorrow... I will be home by 6:00... I will take you to the park on Saturday... I will return that book in a week." We make dozens of little commitments each week. And how well we keep our word in the "little things" will be an indication of how well we will keep our word in the greater things. Let's prove ourselves to be people of character. Let's leave a trail of kept promises. If our words are inconsistent and our promises are flippantly made, how will people believe us when we tell them about the gospel message? Let's be people of integrity in both the great and small.

Prayer

Father, remind us today that you have called us to live a life of integrity. May we live consistently and honestly, knowing that each commitment kept is a reflection of our character. Amen.

Day 61 Luke 17: A Dedicated and Deliberate Walk

"He said to His disciples, 'It is inevitable that stumbling blocks come, but woe to him through whom they come! It would be better for him if a millstone were hung around his neck and he were thrown into the sea, than that he would cause one of these little ones to stumble.'"
Luke 17:2 NASB

Observation

Jesus first offered this instruction to his disciples on a day that he also taught them about forgiveness, servanthood, and the coming Kingdom of God. In this teaching, Jesus stresses the importance of authentic faith and honest living. He reminds his followers of the great importance of vigilantly keeping the faith at all times. To stumble even once, to act out of character, to say or do the wrong thing even for a moment, can bring horrible consequences. His teaching was a reminder that our actions always produce rippling effects in the lives of those around us.

Application

One of the toughest aspects of the Christian faith is understanding that when we join ourselves to Jesus Christ, we are from that moment expected to imitate his life in every way possible. We take on the challenge of representing him. That means our words are governed by his grace, our actions are tempered by his example, our thoughts are held captive by his words. We must live with the realization that our declared faith must be consistently and constantly lived-out before the world. When people see our actions, hear our words, listen to our attitudes, and see our response to whatever life throws our way, we must be careful to demonstrate the heart and passion of our Lord. The reason our faith is so critical at such moments is because of our influence. People are watching. When we act out of character and compromise our faith, we may well cause another to stumble... especially those who are still very young in their faith. Such a moment can have disastrous results. Rather than draw someone to faith in Christ, we may repel him or her from belief. Ghandi wrote, "I would have become a Christian had I not met so many of them first." Today's challenge is to live-out your Christian faith. Walk the walk. Talk the talk. The world is watching. You have the opportunity to lead others to faith or to keep them from ever finding Jesus. Be careful. Be faithful.

Prayer

Father, remind us of how important our faith can be in the lives of others. May we never allow even a single moment of compromise to destroy the faith of another. Amen.

"Two men went up into the temple to pray, one a Pharisee and the other a tax collector. The Pharisee stood and was praying this to himself: 'God, I thank You that I am not like other people: swindlers, unjust, adulterers, or even like this tax collector.'" Luke 18:11 NASB

Observation

These two verses are drawn from a parable that Jesus offered in response to those who praised themselves for their sense of self-righteousness and who judged others with contempt. Jesus was careful to point out that it is not the haughty and proud that stand justified before God, but those who come before God with a sense of humility and honesty.

Application

It's a game that most of us play, most of the time. We measure our sense of righteousness not by the standard of Christ but by the standard of comparative religion. We look to those around us with an attitude that states, "I may not be as good as I should be, but I am a whole lot better than 'those' people." Sound familiar? We attempt to make ourselves look righteous by comparing ourselves to those around us whom we deem to be unrighteous. Who do we think that we are kidding? First, we are not in a position to judge what or who is righteous, and second, such a standard of measurement is not ours to invent. As Christians, our role model is always the person of Jesus Christ. He sets the standard. His grace, his compassion, and his attitudes set the pattern that we are to follow. The question is not "Are we better than others?" It is always, "Can I become more like Christ?" The truth is that all of us have room to grow. Rather than worry how well we are doing in comparison to those around us, let us concern ourselves with how well we are role-modeling the Christian faith. Let this be a day when our actions glorify God, our thoughts honor God's Spirit, and our words bring joy to God's ears. The comparison will come at the end of the day... Am I better than I was yesterday? Am I more like Christ than I have been before? Let's become a little more honest in self-evaluation, and a little more gracious when we speak of others.

Prayer

Father, teach us today that we are not to look at the faith of others to validate our own faith experience. May Christ remain the only standard we raise. Amen.

Day 63 — Luke 19: What Faith Demands

"If anyone asks you, 'Why are you untying it?' you shall say, 'The Lord has need of it.'" Luke 19:31 NASB

Observation

Jesus was traveling from Jericho to Jerusalem where he would live out his final week of ministry prior to the crucifixion. As he entered the small villages of Bethany and Bethpage, he gave instructions to his disciples about obtaining a colt on which he would ride into Jerusalem, in a processional that is often referred to as "The Triumphant Entry." The disciples were to go to a certain spot to find a colt. They were to untie it and bring it to Jesus. He told them, if asked about why they were taking the colt, to simply say, "The Lord has need of it." It happened just as Jesus had said. The owners did inquire and the disciples offered the words Jesus had given to them. The owners quickly released the animal for Jesus' use.

Application

It is interesting that the owners of the colt quickly, obediently, and willingly gave up their animal as soon as they knew that "The Lord had need of it." The gift of the colt obviously meant some sacrifice, if not some inconvenience, on the part of the owners. Knowing that Jesus wanted the use of their animal brought immediate obedience. I wonder if we are so ready, willing, and able to offer whatever possessions we have, if Christ demands their use. Are we willing to sacrifice and even put ourselves in a position of hardship all for the sake of the Kingdom? Would we give up our cars, our homes, our books, or our tools if Christ demanded that we do so? Would we willingly empty out our bank accounts if impressed with the need to help someone who is struggling? We claim the Lordship of Christ, but we still cling tightly to our stuff. Remember how the rich, young, ruler once went away from the presence of Jesus saddened, because of his unwillingness to "turn loose" of his stuff in order to "grab hold" of the Kingdom? What is it that you possess of which the Lord has need? Is there a talent you haven't offered to his glory? A skill that you could use in ministry? Is there a check you could write to help the poor? If we are truly his disciples our hearts must become obedient, our attitudes compassionate, and our "stuff" must become His. More than anything, the Lord has need of your life. Are you willing to offer it quickly, obediently, and willingly?

Prayer

Father, give us such a spirit of discipleship that whenever Christ demands something of us, that we quickly and gladly respond. Amen.

"For they cannot even die anymore, because they are like angels, and are sons of God, being sons of the resurrection." Luke 20:36 NASB

Observation

As Jesus was teaching in the Temple courts a group of Sadducees, who did not believe in life after death, came to him to pose a question about the resurrection. Their question was about a woman was married to several brothers while here on earth. Their question was, "Whose wife will she be in heaven?" In response, Jesus basically says that things are different in heaven. The relationships that are so important here take on a different quality there. He teaches that the everlasting life of a resurrected person makes that person something like an angel. Paul explains further that in the resurrection we will be given resurrection bodies similar to Christ's (1 Cor. 15:25-58). Heaven will be a new experience that will not necessarily parallel experiences on earth, such as marriage.

Application

When we read this passage we get hung up on the marriage question and ignore the greater teaching. Will we be married in heaven? Will we know our spouse and will we exist in some type of eternal bond to one another? I do believe that we will certainly know and be known in heaven. I believe that we will recognize those we have known and loved on earth. I also believe that the joy and love and grace that we experience here is only a hint of what we will know there. In other words, there will be no disappointments in heaven. Things are only going to get better. The God who formed your heart and gave you a spouse and taught you to experience love, is not going to rip that away from you when you get to heaven. He is only going to make things better.

The greater part of the teaching is the news about our resurrected bodies. We will be changed. We become like angels, beings sons and daughters of the resurrection. Jesus promises that we will not die but that we will take on a miraculous new form. The things of this earth—illness, stress, worry, pain, heartache, and suffering—will all be erased. We will experience life in ways we can only begin to dream about.

Prayer

Father, thank you for the promise of eternal life and a place called Heaven. As we look to that which is to come, may we do so with great hope and the promise of life, not yet even imaginable to all of us. Amen.

Day 65 Luke 21: Obstacles or Opportunities

"It will lead to an opportunity for your testimony." Luke 21:13 NASB

Observation

By this point in Luke's Gospel, the moments of teaching from Jesus are quickly drawing to a close. It is in the midst of Holy Week that these words are spoken. Jesus is teaching that perilous times are coming. He speaks very clearly to the disciples reminding them that persecution and destruction are headed their way... that they will be brought before various authorities and made to defend themselves in the presence of kings and governors. But notice what he says will be the result... "It will lead to an opportunity for your testimony." Jesus knew that those moments that seemed as obstacles to some, would serve as opportunities for others. Sometimes our brightest and best moments of testimony occur when the times seem darkest.

Application

Sometimes, it's all about perspective. We all face those moments in life when a sudden crisis will raise its ugly head. In those moments, we have the choice to react in fear, or to move forward with resolve. As my former assistant, Lil, often pointed out to those going through a difficult time, "This could be your finest hour." She's right. Sometimes it is in the difficult moments that our faith shines most brightly. Sometimes, the moments that seem dark and troublesome are the God-ordained moments when our testimony will become most effective. In fact, it is often the difficult moments that define our faith more than the easy ones. So as you consider the obstacles that currently block your path towards a stress-free and easy life, just know that there may well be opportunities for your faith to grow and for your witness to affect others. The world is always watching the way we respond while dressed in the robes of Christianity. Our faith can have ripple effects. Our best prayer is not always for an easy life, but for God to be glorified even in the midst of the struggles we face.

Prayer

Father, thank you for your grace, your provision, and your presence that doggedly pursue us each day. Make us mindful that our obstacles can become opportunities and that our weaknesses can become moments for your glory. Amen.

"But behold, the hand of the one betraying Me is with Mine on the table." Luke 22:21 NASB

Observation

This verse is drawn from the context of the Passover meal that Jesus ate with his disciples in the Upper Room on the night he would later be arrested. As they shared the meal, Jesus spoke of many things. He spoke of his broken body and spilt blood. He spoke of the new covenant with God that would be established by his sacrifice. And then he offered these words about betrayal. It must have been a shocking thing for the disciples to suddenly know that one of their own would be the one to betray their Lord.

Application

It had to hurt, right? Even though Jesus knew the Father's plan, and even though he knew the sacrifice demanded, and even though he knew the coming of the resurrection, still it had to hurt. Who wants to be betrayed, especially by someone so close? We tend to count on the key relationships in our lives. We depend on our friends, our family, and our co-workers. We love knowing that they "have our backs" in any situation. In fact, if someone close has ever betrayed you, you know how intense the pain can be. The sting can linger for years.

And yet, most of us tend to become the betrayers more than we would care to mention. Oh, it's not our friends and family that we betray so easily, it's our Lord. We betray him each time that we deny his Lordship. Each time we act as though his authority doesn't matter, is that not a clear betrayal? We betray him with our impure thoughts. We betray him with our selfish actions. We betray him with our bursts of anger and our lack of self-control. Whenever we do not choose to act as his ambassadors, his hands and feet, nor as his servants, surely he feels the sting. Let's remember that Jesus is counting on us to help him change the world. Let's vow to live authentically, honestly, and consistently. Let's strive with all our might to honor him, obey him, and represent him. To do anything less, is to betray him.

Prayer

Father, forgive us when we make choices that fail to bring you honor. Forgive us when we harbor the impure thought. Forgive us when we live selfishly and sinfully. Forgive our betrayals. Make us yours. Make us Holy once again. Amen.

Day 67 Luke 23: Prevailing Voices

"But they were insistent, with loud voices asking that He be crucified. And their voices began to prevail." Luke 23:23 NASB

Observation

This verse is drawn from the dialogue between Pilate and the angry Jewish mob that clamored for the death of Jesus. Pilate, in trying to decide the case, had already turned Jesus over to Herod for his opinion. Herod had sent Jesus back to Pilate, and after further speculation, Pilate was prepared to release Jesus saying that he had found no guilt deserving of a death sentence. The crowd only grew angrier and demanded the death of Jesus. As our focus verse indicates, "they were insistent... and their voices began to prevail." Pilate knew the right thing to do, but allowed the voices of popular opinion to overrule his better judgment.

Application

There are a lot of competing voices out there. Most of us get pulled and stretched between the voices of truth, culture, peer pressure, etc. We have all heard them. We know the right thing to do, but other "insistent voices" try to lure us into doing other things and if we are not careful, we will let the other voices "begin to prevail." The voices come at us through the words of a business associate. Sometimes it's a friend at school that tries to lead us down a dark path. Sometimes the constant bombardment of the media world tries to lure and tempt us to think differently. The question is whether or not we will let the prevalent voices control our actions. Surely they will unless we fortify our hearts and minds with better, stronger voices. In a world filled with a thousand voices of temptation and compromise, we must fill our hearts with a greater truth. That truth, of course, is the word of God. It alone must become the voice that we allow to penetrate our minds and govern our days. To help us hear that voice clearly, we must commit ourselves to some important disciplines. Reading the scriptures is, of course, fundamental. But we must also commit ourselves to fellowship with other Christians, and to the faithful discipline of weekly worship. In the midst of all the various competing voices, let's make sure that the voice that prevails, is that of Our Father.

Prayer

Father, may we have enough wisdom to carefully sift through the voices that reach our hearing each day. May we discard those that are false, so that we might hear your voice in a clear and powerful way. Amen.

"And they, after worshiping Him, returned to Jerusalem with great joy, and were continually in the temple praising God."
Luke 24:52-53 NASB

Observation

In these final two verses from the book of Luke, we gain insight into what the disciples first chose to do after Jesus had ascended into heaven. At first the disciples were skeptical of the resurrection. It seemed too amazing... too good to be true... too unbelievable. In fact, when the women reported about their experience at the tomb, the disciples thought their words to be nonsense. But soon afterwards, Jesus appeared to the entire group. He continued to teach them and share his glory with them. He led them out as far as Bethany, and then was taken up into the heavens. Notice that their skepticism had long since vanished. They returned to Jerusalem with great joy and continually made their way to the Temple to praise God.

Application

Why would they not? Where else would people of faith go to celebrate the miraculous work of God in their midst? They needed a sense of community. They desired a sense of fellowship. They found both strength in numbers, and exuberance in their collective spirits. They quickly learned the value of assembling together. Nothing has changed in the 2000 years since that first Easter morning. People of faith should still celebrate the Good News of the Resurrection. People of faith should still feel the need to gather together. One of the great gifts to the world from God is the creation of the Church. Because God created a place that offers us a sense of community to meet our needs: that heals when we hurt and celebrates when victories are claimed. God created a place where the joy of the Christian faith can be reinforced daily.

I encourage you to become a great person of the church. Make the investment. Pour your life into the place that God has created just for you. Find the sense of community, the sense of belonging, the sense of camaraderie that is found when you faithfully join your heart to the hearts of fellow Christians. What to do with the news of the resurrection? Gather with the people of God to celebrate, and then go in the strength of that fellowship to share the news with others.

Prayer

Father, we thank you today for the Church. Thank you for creating a place of acceptance, growth, and community for each of us. Amen.

Day 69 — John 1: Inclusion

"But as many as received Him, to them He gave the right to become children of God, even to those who believe in His name"
John 1:12 NASB

Observation

Gospel writer John wants his reading audience to be aware of the divinity of Christ from the very first page. John asserts very plainly in his opening sentences that Jesus is the Christ, the promised Messiah, the One who brings light (truth) into the world. Notice that his account of the life of Jesus does not begin with the story of Mary and Joseph, or any account of the Virgin Birth, not even a mention of shepherds or wise men. John writes from a different perspective. He begins with the ministry of John the Baptist and from the start introduces Jesus as the Divine Son of God. From the first page forward, the reader quickly learns that this is no ordinary man, and this is no ordinary life.

Application

Our focus verse for the day is such a powerful verse of assurance and simplicity. Read it again slowly. It offers both the fundamental step and the overwhelming reward of finding faith in Christ. It reminds us that we receive him by believing in his name. Such a simple and powerful step... it's called faith. With simple trust and an open heart, we acknowledge that Jesus is the Son of God. We "receive" him. We welcome him. We invite him. We trust him. We walk with him. And notice the reward of doing so... we are given the right to become children of God. What a powerful message that is. To be a child of God means that we are loved by God, protected by God, nurtured by God, and welcomed by God. What loving father does not long to spend time each day with his child? Being a child of God also means that we become heirs to all that the Father owns. We will inherit God's eternal life. We will inherit the riches of God's eternal Kingdom. We will inherit the joy that God alone can offer.

At times we make coming to faith a difficult thing, with so many conditions to be met. But the word of God offers a simpler path. Believe and become. Believe in Jesus Christ and become a child of the Father. Pretty simple. Pretty amazing.

Prayer

Father, thank you for claiming us as your children through our simple belief in and confession of Christ as Lord. May we live today in the sheer joy of knowing that we have been included in your forever Kingdom. Amen.

"His mother said to the servants, 'Whatever He says to you, do it.'"
John 2:5 NASB

Observation

This verse is drawn from the first miracle that Jesus performed once his public ministry began. He was at a wedding feast in Cana where his disciples and most of his family were in attendance. An embarrassing moment is averted when Jesus' mother informs him that the wine has run out. Though he protests for a moment that, "His time had not yet come," Mary simply tells the servants to do whatever Jesus instructs them to do. As a result, pots once filled with water become miraculously filled with wine. This is the first of seven signs in the Gospel of John that point to the divinity of Christ.

Application

The instructions given to the servants by Mary are good instructions for us... "Whatever he says to you, do it." The Christian faith thrives on obedience. The more we are willing to do the things of Christ, the greater the impact of our faith. What exactly is it that we are called to do by Christ? The answers are plain, yet quite demanding. We are called to love our enemies, pray for those who persecute us, forgive, love, share sacrificially, pray fervently, heal, preach, teach, feed, clothe, and rescue. So why are we not giving each of those demands our best attention? Is it not a question of obedience? The problem comes with our definition of Lordship. If Christ is truly Lord, then all we live for is to obediently act as his ambassadors each day. But if we have given him only temporary authority, keeping the bulk of our days reserved for our own agendas, then how can we practice obedience? Either we live as his followers, or we demand that he somehow follow us.

I wonder if we can get to the place in our lives when we say, "I will do whatever you tell me to do"? Can we offer ourselves that freely? Are we ready to forsake all other pursuits other than those of the Kingdom? Probably not. Truthfully, most of us will struggle as long as we have breath to surrender Lordship to him. But our failure to do so readily can never negate his calling to that level of commitment. May Jesus somehow take the imperfection of our lives... the little obedience that we reluctantly offer each day, and do miraculous things. If he can turn ordinary water into wine, then surely he can turn our ordinariness into his glory.

Prayer

Father, forgive us. Transform us. Use us. Amen.

> "For God did not send the Son into the world to judge the world, but that the world might be saved through Him." John 3:17 NASB

Observation

This verse is taken from the conversation between Jesus and Nicodemus as they discuss the Kingdom of God and what it is to be "born again." Having just offered the timeless promise of John 3:16, Jesus offers these words about the intention of God for the world. Notice that Jesus teaches that God's purpose in sending the Son was not punitive, not judgmental, not for wrath, but for life. God longs to redeem the world. God longs to rescue creation. God is compelled by love to reach towards humanity with compassion and grace, not threats and punishment.

Application

A lot of people seem to have the wrong impression of God. They seem to think that God is "out to get them." They see God as a wrathful Being, bent on zapping into oblivion all those who don't live a perfect life. That's not the message spoken from the lips of Jesus. Check it out again. God's desire is for our salvation. God is on our side. God offers passion not punishment. So why do so many get it wrong? Why does most of the world have the wrong impression about God? Could it be that most of us have given them that impression? Is it not true that sometimes, those of us who have experienced grace seem to be the very ones who are the least likely to extend it towards others? As believers, have we not offered a lot of judgment? Do we not offer a lot of condescension toward the sinners of the world? It becomes very easy for us to forget that God loves the world and all the people of the world and longs to bring us all into the family. We, on the other hand, would rather dismiss those different from ourselves. We see people languish in their guilt and sins and offer little hope in helping them to find a better way. It's no wonder why most mainline denominations are in such decline. We have found a way to condemn, but very few ways to redeem.

God's hope is for the world to be saved. If we are truly God's children then our hope must become God's hope. What if we offered more grace than guilt? More hope than hype? More passion than punishment? More inclusion than exclusion? What if we discovered ways to love the lost, rather than finding ways of ignoring them? Could the Church hold the people?

Prayer

Father, we pray today that our intentions would begin to match yours. Amen.

"Jesus answered and said to her, 'Everyone who drinks of this water will thirst again; but whoever drinks of the water that I will give him shall never thirst; but the water that I will give him will become in him a well of water springing up to eternal life.'" John 4:13-14 NASB

Observation

In a conversation with a Samaritan woman at Jacob's well, Jesus describes the "Living Water" that he offers to those who come to him in faith. Jesus discovered this woman as she was drawing water to quench her thirst. He also knows that she was trying to quench an even deeper thirst in her life. She longed for a sense of satisfaction and hope. She had experienced 5 broken marriages and even at the time of this conversation was in another relationship. She was attempting to fill the void in her life with one relationship after another. It is obvious that she had yet to find real meaning, real contentment, and real life. Jesus offered her a different kind of life... a life of faith through which all of her deepest longings would be met.

Application

How many of us look for satisfaction in things that will never really satisfy? Like her, some try to meet the great longing of their hearts by jumping from one relationship to another. "If I can just meet the right guy...." Others try to fill the void with "stuff." They try to possess enough things that make them happy in the hope that their things will bring them a lasting sense of joy. Buy the latest car, the newest cell phone, the widest screen, or the biggest house and surely satisfaction will come. Still others try to fill the void with hobbies, or clubs, or involvements... again hoping to stay one step ahead of the ever encroaching disappointment of dissatisfaction. The problem is that most of us continue to satisfy our souls with temporary things. The answer is never in temporal things. The real life for which we hunger is found only in a relationship with Jesus Christ. And until we figure that out, our lives will be empty and our searches will result in futility.

Christ invites us to real life... meaningful life... satisfying life. As the great Church Father Augustine once wrote, "Our souls are restless until they find their rest in Thee." Aren't you tired of looking? Aren't you weary of chasing after the next "big thing" in the hope that you will find meaning and purpose? Place your life energy into a pursuit of Jesus Christ and in him alone will you find your true joy.

Prayer

Father, remind us today that real life is only found in Christ. Amen.

> "Truly, truly, I say to you, he who hears My word, and believes Him Who has sent Me, has eternal life, and does not come into judgment, but has passed out of death into life." John 5:24 NASB

Observation

In chapter 5, Jesus was having a discussion with various Jewish leaders. They were angry with him because he healed a man on a Sabbath day, which they saw as a violation of Mosaic Law. The occasion of their conversation allowed Jesus a moment to teach them more completely about the ways of God. Read the verse carefully and notice the promises that Jesus makes. He promises that eternal life comes to those who believe in God and who hear the testimony Jesus offers. He reminds believers that they will not come into judgment, but will pass into life.

Application

I have done a few things in my life that deserve a little punishment. I confess that I have rolled through a few stop signs, exceeded the speed limit, and even said a few things that I regret. Actually it gets even worse, at least in the eyes of God. I have not always forgiven those who have wronged me. I sometimes fail to pray for my enemies. I don't always think pure thoughts. And far too many times I seek to follow my own will rather than the will of God. We are all in the same boat, right? All of us have missed the mark. As Romans 3:23 states, "For all have sinned and fall short of the Glory of God." We have all committed punishable crimes. We have all committed deeds worthy of wrath. But hear again what Jesus offers each of us in the way of a promise. Because he has claimed us and offered us eternal life, we do not come into judgment! We are pardoned. Forgiven. Set free. Liberated. It is not that we have no guilt... it is that we have been claimed by grace. I know... it sounds to good to be true. That's why we call it, "Amazing Grace."

What if you were to take the time this morning to make a list of your ten greatest sins? What if you wrote them on a sheet a paper? And then, what if you dared to mark through each one of them as though they are no longer counted against you? Why labor under the guilt of sin and the remorse of so many mistakes? If the Son sets you free, you are free indeed. Congratulations. You just dodged a really big bullet.

Prayer

Father, we thank you this day, for the wonderful, compassionate love of Christ that offers us freedom though we deserve punishment. Set us free to live in the afterglow of grace. Amen.

Simon Peter answered Him, "Lord, to whom shall we go? You have the words of eternal life." John 6:68 NASB

Observation

During a long teaching session in which Jesus taught about being the Bread of Life and what it would mean for followers to "eat His flesh and drink His blood," many of his disciples "withdrew, and were not walking with Him anymore" (v. 66). At that moment Jesus confronted the twelve about their level of discipleship. Simon Peter offered the correct response... "To whom shall we go? You have the words of eternal life." There are many demands of the gospel that are difficult to obey. The life of a disciple is not always easy. But following Christ is the path that leads to life.

Application

There are a lot of people who are searching for answers... answers to the bigger questions of life. "Why are we here? What is our purpose? What is the meaning of life? Is there more than just the living of these days? Why was I created?" Admit it... you too have pondered such questions at some point on your journey. And because of such questions, we tend to search for answers in a lot of places. We look to philosophies, ideologies, various theories and explanations. But here, Simon Peter gets it right. Where else are we to go? Jesus alone has the words of eternal life.

In Christ alone are our hope, our answer, and our salvation. Until we finally figure that out, we will spend our lives in futility and confusion. According to the "Divinely Inspired word of God," there is but one path to salvation, one method, one way. We have life in Christ alone. Only through putting our faith and trust in him, and claiming him as Savior and Lord do we discover the joy of God's forever Kingdom. So let me invite you this morning to redirect your energies. Rather than seek various ways to find God, accept the fact that you come to know God through the personality of Jesus Christ. Use your energies to grow deeper in your knowledge of Jesus and discover the joys that a relationship with him will bring.

Prayer

Father, teach us again this day, that our hope, our joy, and our answers are found in Christ alone. Give us a simple faith and trust that we might know the blessings of your Kingdom. Amen.

"So Jesus said to them, 'My time is not yet here, but your time is always opportune.'" John 7:6 NASB

Observation

At this point in John's Gospel, Jesus and his disciples are in the northern region of Galilee. It was the time of the year for the Festival of Booths, one of the three great feasts of the Jewish year. Typically, all who were able would travel to Jerusalem to join in the celebration. The Jews in Jerusalem were seeking Jesus' death and so Jesus does not plan to travel to Jerusalem, because he knew that the time of his redemptive actions were not yet ready to be fulfilled. He speaks about timing in our focus verse. He mentions that his "time" (*kairos*, a moment in time) had not yet come, but that the disciples would certainly have opportunity to act in the present moment.

Application

"Timing is everything," or so they say. There is something to be said for knowing when just the right moment presents itself for some action. We sometimes wait for a difficult conversation when the "time is right." We sometimes wait on a making a large purchase when the "time is right" based on both the cost and our ability to afford such an item. Timing. We look for the right moment to do the right thing. Notice what Jesus says to his followers... "Your time is always opportune." There is a sense of immediacy in his voice. There is a sense of action to his command. I think that sometimes we put off doing the things we know we really should do, because we are waiting on "just the right time..." (Maybe hoping that such a time will never present itself.) We delay doing the things of God's prompting by making excuses about time, situation, and money. We keep thinking that a perfect moment will one day present itself, when maybe the best moment is now.

Today is an opportune moment for you to do something to further the Kingdom. Because God has awakened you, there must be things that God intends for you to be doing. So why delay? Make the phone call you have been putting off. Visit the friend you know that needs a word of correction or encouragement. Write the check that will help the cause. Sign up for the ministry that needs your help. "Your time is always opportune..." Today requires your involvement.

Prayer

Father, teach us to value our time. May we never delay in our quest to do the things you ask of us. Help us to see the opportunity that today will afford. Amen.

"Therefore I said to you that you will die in your sins; for unless you believe that I am He, you will die in your sins." John 8:24 NASB

Observation

Chapter 8 of John's Gospel begins with the marvelous story of grace where Jesus is able to rescue, forgive, and restore a woman caught in adultery. His treatment of her sinfulness initiates an extended dialogue between Jesus and some Pharisees. They are doubtful of his claims. They reject his teaching. They cling to their tradition rather than hearing the truth he attempts to teach them. Our focus verse is a rather poignant verse that surely pierced their hearts. In fact, as the conversation eventually ends, they become so enraged that they pick up stones... maybe the same ones they intended to use to kill the woman in adultery... to throw at Jesus. Truth can always anger those who refuse to hear it.

Application

Let's not shy away from the truth that our focus verse reveals to us. Though spoken to the Pharisees of Jesus' day, it is a timeless truth that must be embraced by the people of our generation. It should quicken the pulse and fuel our evangelistic zeal. We need to be reminded over and over that apart from a relationship with Jesus Christ, people will die in their sins. Everyone on the planet has a sin problem. As Roman 3:23 states, "For all have sinned and fall short of the glory of God." The word "all" is very inclusive. Because of our humanity and bent toward disobedience, none of us can earn our way into the presence of God. None. Zilch. Zero. Our only hope of escape, our only way to gain salvation, is through our confession of and belief in Jesus Christ. As he plainly states, "You will die in your sins unless you believe..." In many ways, that message becomes the "marching orders" of the church. We are duty bound to proclaim that message. Without a knowledge of Jesus Christ, people will die in the midst of their sins. Though we may want to water down the threat of such a message, though we may want to believe some kind of universalism that somehow gathers everyone into Glory, the crystal clear, unalterable truth of God's word is that salvation comes through Christ alone. Once we finally believe that message, how can we sit idle while the world perishes? God help us to find ways of sharing Christ... deliberately, powerfully, gracefully.

Prayer

Father, quicken us to the task of gospel-sharing. May we feel a restlessness in our souls until we have done all that we can to share the hope of the gospel. Amen.

> "He then answered, 'Whether He is a sinner, I do not know; one thing I do know, that though I was blind, now I see.'" John 9:25 NASB

Observation

The entire ninth chapter of John is devoted to the story of a blind man who is given the ability to see by the healing power of Jesus. Blind from birth, his sudden ability to see certainly causes a stir within the community. The Pharisees suggest that Jesus is a sinner because the day on which the miracle occurred was a Sabbath day. Their interpretation of the Law of Moses forbade any kind of work on the Sabbath. And so they accuse Jesus of disobedience to the Law of Moses. When asked about his opinion, the formerly blind man simply answers that he has no judgment to offer, but simply the proof that he can now see.

Application

Sometimes, actions really do speak louder than words, or even theological debate. The Pharisees of Jesus' day tried to argue religious decorum, while Jesus offered genuine healing. They attempted to argue that his actions were inappropriate, but counter to their argument came the declaration, "I was blind, now I see." There are moments when modern day believers get caught-up in a game of spiritual one-up-man-ship. We all attempt to prove we are a little more spiritual than the next guy. We try to rank our piety above those around us. The truth is this... it really doesn't matter what we say we believe, or how well we articulate our theological arguments. All that matters is the fruit that our faith bears. Are people being led to Christ? Are the lost being found? Are the broken-hearted finding hope? Do the hungry get fed? Do the lonely find friends? The authenticity of our faith is proven by our actions. We demonstrate the fact that we belong to him when we do the things that are demanded by him. Your faith journey should always leave a trail. Genuine faith always finds practical expression. I challenge you to go out and truly live your faith this morning. Don't just wear a cross around your neck or hang the 10 Commandments on your wall... do something that makes a difference in the life of someone else.

Prayer

Father, may our acts of charity, devotion, and compassion speak so loudly that even when our words are silent, the gospel is still proclaimed. Amen.

"My sheep hear My voice, and I know them, and they follow Me; and I give eternal life to them, and they will never perish; and no one will snatch them out of My hand." John 10:27-28 NASB

Observation

Throughout the 10th Chapter of John's Gospel, Jesus teaches both the disciples and the Jewish leaders through the use of an extended metaphor. He compares himself to a shepherd who carefully and lovingly cares for his sheep. The metaphor communicates well. A good shepherd guides lovingly, corrects gently, defends fiercely, leads passionately, and feeds abundantly. As our Good Shepherd, Jesus always acts on our behalf. Not only does he offer us abundant life, he gives us eternal life as well. He defends, protects, nurtures, leads, and provides. We find ourselves safe in his care.

Application

Need a little assurance today? Here's some. In his role as our Good Shepherd, Jesus radically and fiercely protects us. Notice that once we find ourselves in the grip of his grace, that there are none who can snatch us away. We become joined to him with an eternal bond that cannot be severed. There is no foe strong enough, no enemy powerful enough, and no assailant crafty enough to ever remove us from his hand. So here's the assurance for today. If we join our lives to his through faith, we will remain safe and secure in his hands. No matter what life may throw in our direction, we are his and he is ours. As Paul rhetorically asks, "What can separate us from the love of Christ? Shall tribulation, or distress, or persecution, or famine, or nakedness, or peril, or sword?" (Rom. 8:35) He goes further a couple of verses later... "For I am convinced that neither death, nor life, nor angels, nor principalities, nor things present, nor things to come, nor powers, nor height, nor depth, nor any other created thing, shall be able to separate us from the love of God, which is in Christ Jesus our Lord" (Rom. 8:38-39). Do you get it? The Great One is guarding our lives. We are joined to Christ with bonds that can never be broken or cut. You're safe if you are in his hands.

Prayer

Father, we thank you for the eternal love of Jesus Christ. We thank you for the promise that in his hands we are safe and secure, and loved beyond measure. Amen.

"Therefore Thomas, who is called Didymus, said to his fellow disciples, 'Let us also go, so that we may die with Him.'" John 11:16 NASB

Observation

The central great event in John 11 is the raising of Lazarus to life. Jesus and the disciples are in another region, several days' journey away from Bethany when Lazarus dies. Jesus indicates that the delay is in order to reveal the glory of God. Jesus declares that they must return to Judea to be with Mary and Martha. The disciples protest because of the threats of violence directed against Jesus by the Jewish leaders. When he insists on going it is Thomas, the "doubter," who offers this courageous word. Thomas is prepared to die if that is what is required of him as a follower of Christ.

Application

What will be required of you this day as a follower of Christ? If today happens to be a Sunday, for most of us, it's a pretty easy demand. We will put on our Sunday clothes, drive to church, worship a while, and then head to dinner. For most of us, there is not a lot of sacrifice demanded. It's easy to summons up enough courage to go to church. There is little threat to health or safety in attending. But what it that was not the case? What if we lived in a place where a profession of Christ could mean real persecution or even death? Would we be so flippant about worship? Would we have enough boldness to declare Christ in the face of such hostility? There are two prayers we should pray this morning. The first is a prayer of thankfulness to Almighty God for allowing us to know the freedom of worship and the joy of holding a Bible, singing hymns of faith, and hearing the word proclaimed in an unhindered way. What freedoms we often take for granted. The second prayer is a prayer for our fellow believers for whom today brings great fear. We should pray for the persecuted church. We should pray for those who are literally risking life and limb in order to be God-followers. We should pray that we would dare be as bold as they in the living of our faith. Let us be courageous as believers. Let us boldly live out our faith, regardless of the ramifications that such a discipleship will bring.

Prayer

Father, we thank you for the joy of knowing Jesus and for the privilege that is ours this day to worship in freedom, to live without persecution, and to openly express our faith. We remember those who know none of those joys, but who follow Christ devotedly. Amen.

"Nevertheless many even of the rulers believed in Him, but because of the Pharisees they were not confessing Him, for fear that they would be put out of the synagogue; for they loved the approval of men rather than the approval of God." John 12:42-43 NASB

Observation

In the 12th Chapter of John, the tension between the Pharisees and Jesus begins to escalate sharply. Chapter 12 tells the story of the Triumphant Entry into Jerusalem just before the feast of Passover. As Jesus arrives in the city, there is a great deal of excitement and talk about his teachings and miracles. Many continue to come to faith, among whom are some of the religious rulers. But notice from our focus verse that they remain "secret" believers. They fear that their association with Jesus will lose them both prestige and privilege. Not wanting to be put out of the synagogue (place of assembly) they keep their faith a secret. They were more concerned about having the favor of men than gaining the favor of God.

Application

There have always been those who long to practice a convenient Christianity. There are many who treat their faith in Christ as though it is some "ace" card hidden up their sleeves, only to be played when the situation demands. In other words, there are many who live a "situational faith." If they are around other believers and it seems advantageous to act and speak as a Christian, then count them in. At other moments however, if the situation demands that they keep their faith a secret, they are glad to do so. What they lack is consistency and commitment. Surely our faith must demand more from us. Either we live the faith that we claim each moment, or we have no faith to claim. In a time when Christian values seem to wane, when morality fades to grey, and when the absolutes are challenged daily, those who belong to the faith must stand up and be counted. Jesus has already felt the sting of betrayal... he doesn't need to feel it again from us. It's time to be known for our faith. Let's be bold, courageous, and authentic. May the world see very clearly on whose side we stand.

Prayer

Father, forgive us when we have exchanged the demands of our faith for the popularity of men. May our goal be this day, to live a life that honors and glorifies you regardless of what such commitments will mean to our approval rating. Amen.

"By this all men will know that you are My disciples, if you have love for one another." John 13:35 NASB

Observation

Chapter 13 of John's Gospel tells of the experience in the Upper Room where Jesus shares the Passover meal with his disciples. He speaks of many things during the course of the meal. He speaks of the example of washing the feet of others. He speaks of sacrificial love. He speaks of betrayal. He speaks of the promise of life after death. He also challenges them to love one another. He goes on to indicate that love will become the distinguishing mark of the Christian faith. People will know we follow Jesus when our love for each other is evident.

Application

I was reading some rather frightening statistics yesterday about the state of the Church here in America. People are leaving the faith in droves. In fact, one statistic indicated that over 4000 churches close their doors each year. And in response to that alarming statistic, only 1000 new churches are started each year. There are other startling numbers. Did you know that only 51% of all Americans claim any type of connection to protestant churches? And of those claiming some connection, less than 17% actually attend church on any given Sunday. Why are people not going to church the way they once did? Why are so many churches losing ground to other involvements? Why is the Islamic faith growing at a faster pace than Christianity here in America? There are many reasons and many explanations, but perhaps the greatest factor may be our lack of genuine love and compassion for one another.

Think about it. Real love forces us to do many things. It forces us to forgive those who have made mistakes. It forces us to accept those different from ourselves. It forces us to embrace those whose opinions don't always match ours. It forces us to share our possessions, offer friendship, and care for the poor. Maybe the reason that people don't rush to our churches is because they see very little of Christ in our actions, attitudes, and thoughts. Maybe it's not always about bigger buildings, slick advertising, or a plethora of programs designed to meet every need. Maybe it's as simple as learning to love authentically and offer ourselves sacrificially.

Prayer

Father, may we be known by our love. May people see clearly that we belong to Christ because of the ways in which we demonstrate compassion towards each other and towards those in need. Amen.

Day 82 John 14: Dumbing Down Our Abilities

"Truly, truly, I say to you, he who believes in Me, the works that I do, he will do also; and greater works than these he will do; because I go to the Father." John 14:12 NASB

Observation

In the table conversation that Jesus has with his disciples as they share the Passover meal, Jesus offers a promise of power to his followers. The promise is that his followers will be able to do even greater works than he has done. Because he is going to the Father, the disciples will have the resources of the Kingdom available through him. All that Jesus has done, the disciples will be able to do.

Application

That's quite some promise. Do we believe that we can do even a tiny fraction of the things that Christ did? Consider all the miraculous things that Christ did while here on earth. He caused the blind to see, the lame to walk, the mute to speak, and the deaf to hear. He cast demons from bodies and even raised the dead. He broke small loaves and with them fed 5000 people. He walked on water, calmed raging seas, and turned water into wine. And he tells us that we will do even greater works? That's seems a little hard to believe. I can't even balance a checkbook or fix my hot water heater... how can I even think of doing miraculous things?

It's all about connection. In my own strength, in my own body, in my own wisdom, I really can't do a whole lot. But because I am connected to Christ through faith, I can do all things. I am joined to the One who can conquer all. Because his love, grace, and power flow through me, fantastic things can happen. I become a conduit for his power to work. And so, if I really want to do miraculous things, then I must also connect the power of Christ in me to the needs of the world around me. You see, it is not just about connecting to Christ; it is also about connecting the power of Christ to those around me. That's when the miracles start to unfold. If I dare to introduce someone to Jesus Christ, have I not performed a miracle in that life? Will hearts not change, brokenness become mended, and eternal life granted? And the exciting news becomes that I can repeat that miracle as many times as I choose to tell the story. So why sell ourselves short? We have the power to do great things if we will but make the connections needed.

Prayer

Father, inspire us today to tell the story of Jesus. May we in some way, connect the power of the Risen Lord to the needs of human life. Amen.

Day 83 — John 15: Feast or Famine?

"My Father is glorified by this, that you bear much fruit, and so prove to be My disciples." John 15:8 NASB

Observation

Jesus offered his disciples a litmus test in regard to true discipleship. Those who sincerely practice their faith will bear much fruit. By "fruit" Jesus is referring to tangible results that are produced when faith is lived out deliberately and intentionally. "Fruit" could refer to the making of new converts. It could refer to forgiving transgressions. It could refer to mending relationships. It could refer to selfless acts of compassion. It could refer to taking the right stand based on a Jesus ethic. It could refer to changed attitudes toward former enemies. The fruit that is produced is borne from a life that is transformed daily by the power of Jesus Christ. And notice that when disciples produce fruit, God receives the glory. We bring honor to God when we produce the fruit of the Kingdom.

Application

So take stock of your vineyard this morning... how much fruit has been produced by your walk of faith? Is the harvest plentiful or are the clusters non-existent? Jesus states that the validity of our faith is proven by our fruit. No fruit = No Faith. Much fruit = Much Faith. Christ intends for us to live lives that make a difference. We are called as salt and light. We are called to change the world. The only way we can make such a difference and produce any fruit is by actively living out our faith each day. That means that the love of Christ controls, compels, governs, and frees us all at the same time. Our daily prayer should not be a simple request asking God to bless us yet again... it should be a heartfelt request asking God to fully use us to God's glory. We need to think consciously about the fruit. Are we seeking to live in ways that bring honor to God, or honor only to ourselves? Why not start this day with the questions, "What can I do today to move the Kingdom a little farther along? What life can I touch? What word can I offer? What gift can I give? What standard can I raise?" It's time to make a difference. Live intentionally, devotedly, and authentically.

Prayer

Father, give us a bold faith and an active Christian walk. May we bear fruit this day, that both brings you glory while pointing someone to a greater curiosity about the Christian faith. Amen.

Day 84 John 16: Courage or Compromise?

"These things I have spoken to you, so that in Me you may have peace. In the world you have tribulation, but take courage; I have overcome the world." John 16:33 NASB

Observation

Just moments before he leads the procession toward the Garden of Gethsemane, Jesus offers final words of teaching and encouragement to the disciples. He has taught them again about the coming of the Holy Spirit and the role the Spirit will play in their lives. He has also taught them again about his death and resurrection. Quite plainly, he has reminded them that the moments before them will result in great sorrow, yet joy will overcome their hearts in but a few days. He leaves them with a final word of encouragement. Reminding them that they will have tribulation because they are a part of the physical world, he also reminds them to take courage, for he will overcome the world.

Application

Last summer, during our Youth Retreat experience, I told our students that they had the choice to either live a courageous life or a compromise life. The temptation to compromise is so strong in each of us. We can compromise our character, our morality, our convictions, our values, and even our hope. It is so easy to give-in through subtle and simple ways. Oh, we never mean to drift apart from God, we just compromise a bit each day to the point we awaken one day to discover we have drifted far from God's plan for our lives. Rather than compromise, Christ calls us to courage. He invites us to live emboldened lives that are bolstered by his presence in our hearts. He reminds us to draw courage from the fact that he has overcome the world and all the things of the world. He has conquered death and sin and temptation and evil. When we feel the temptation to compromise, all we need to do is to remember that he has overcome the world. He never promises that the struggle to do the right things will be easy. He just promises victory in his name. So expect some tribulation, but claim victory. Remind yourself that the One who has overcome the world, is the same One who walks with you each hour.

Prayer

Father, we thank you for the courage that we can claim through the strong name of Jesus Christ. May we become more than conquerors in his name. May we live lives of courage and not compromise. Amen.

Day 85 John 17: Home to a Place We've Never Been Before

"They are not of the world, even as I am not of the world."
John 17:16 NASB

Observation

Chapter 17 of John's Gospel records Jesus' prayer on behalf of his followers. He petitions God to protect, gather, and redeem his followers. With very lofty language, Jesus prays about his coming glorification and how he longs for his followers to one day share in his glory. The transcendent nature of Christ is also displayed throughout this prayer as he describes his eternal existence with the Father, long before the world was created. In our focus verse Jesus teaches us that just as he is transcendent, and not a part of this world, that we too, as his followers, share an eternal life that transports us well beyond the living of these days.

Application

"Where's home for you?" When we Southerners ask that question, we mean, "Where did you come from? Where did you grow up? Where do your folks live?" Perhaps a better question is, "Where do you really feel at home?" I grew up in Georgia and even after some 40 years of being away there is something about crossing the state line that still feels right. Sometimes we travel to Gatlinburg, where we lived for five years before moving to Nashville, and we still feel a connection to the place. For more than two decades now, our home and hearts have been in Nashville. Maybe the old adage is right and "home is where the heart is." It just feels right when we're where we belong.

I think heaven is like that. Though we have yet to claim that land, I think that when we do, it will just feel right. It's where we belong. It is where we were created to live. It is our ultimate home where we will experience grace, acceptance, and love. Jesus teaches that this world is not our home. It's not the place where we have been created to live forever. We look to a better day and better place. Currently, we live as though in temporary housing... we look forward to being at home. So, if middle Tennessee, or North Georgia, or central Alabama "feels right" to you, just wait till you get to the place where God has created you to live forever.

Prayer

Father, we thank you for a place called heaven and for our welcome to that place. We thank you that even now, Christ is making provision for all of us. Give us hope while we wait and grant us joy in the meantime. Amen.

John 18: A Place of Respite

"When Jesus had spoken these words, He went forth with His disciples over the ravine of the Kidron, where there was a garden, in which He entered with His disciples. Now Judas also, who was betraying Him, knew the place, for Jesus had often met there with His disciples."
John 18:1-2 NASB

Observation

Chapter 18 records the events and movements of Jesus and the Disciples from the moment they leave the Upper Room and walk to the Garden of Gethsemane. John adds details not found in the other gospels and leaves out others. John does not record Jesus' prayer in the Garden, but he does tell us that the place was well known to the disciples because Jesus had often met with them there.

Application

Jesus used the Garden often for several reasons. First, it was a secluded place that provided a good meeting place near the city of Jerusalem. Second, it was a place where the disciple group could meet with relative privacy for prayer and teaching with Jesus. Third, it was a place of solitude that provided Jesus and the others with a place to pray and reflect.

My question for you is this, "Where is your place of solitude? Where is the spot you consistently go in order to spend time alone with God?" When teaching about prayer, Jesus mentions the importance of going "into your closet" to pray in secret to The Father who hears in secret. "Place" can be of great importance. One of the essentials that brings consistency in our prayer life is not only the establishment of a time for prayer but also a place for prayer. Where is your place? Do you have a place of respite where you can close out the world long enough to spend a few peaceful moments with God? It may be at your bedside, or in your study. It could be on your porch, or in your den. It could even be a quiet spot where you linger on your morning walk. I don't need to define the place for you; I just want to encourage you to find it. Find a place where you can consistently place yourself in the presence of God. Find a place of solitude and silence where you can find strength for each day and hope in the midst of all that life throws in your direction.

Prayer

Father, help each of us to find a private place where we may consistently find you present. Amen.

"Nicodemus, who had first come to Him by night, also came, bringing a mixture of myrrh and aloes, about a hundred pounds weight."
John 19:39 NASB

Observation

Let me set the context of our focus verse... after the death of Jesus on the cross, once his body was removed, Joseph of Arimathea asked for the body and placed it in a tomb. Gospel writer John adds the detail that Nicodemus, whose story started almost 20 chapters ago, is also involved. He shows up to bring various perfumes and spices to use in the burial process, almost a hundred pounds. Together, Joseph and Nicodemus prepared the body for burial. I find it interesting that Jesus once prepared Nicodemus for death, by offering him the promise of eternal life (John 3:16). Now, it is Nicodemus who helps to prepare Jesus for death by offering him the dignity of a proper burial.

Application

Sometimes we really do "pay it forward." Our acts of compassion and grace have a way of boomeranging back on us when we least expect it. Our deeds of kindness are never forgotten by the Father. When we act out of a pure heart to meet the needs of someone who is struggling, we discover blessings in our own lives. We often gain more joy and satisfaction through our act of compassion than even the recipient of our deed. Understand that we don't do good deeds in order to be rewarded. We do good deeds because it is the right thing to do. But noble deeds do reward both the giver and the recipient. As Shakespeare once wrote, "The quality of mercy is not strain'd. It droppeth as the gentle rain from heaven upon the place beneath. It is twice blest: it blesseth him that gives and him that takes" (*Merchant of Venice*, Act 4, scene 1). (Wow... who knew that my high school English classes would still pay off?)

Here's my point... we are to be compassionate because our Father in heaven is compassionate. Our compassionate deeds strike a chord with The Father and they are not forgotten. God will use our acts of service to both build the Kingdom and meet a need. So keep your eyes open today. God may present you with an opportunity to do something extraordinary. Don't miss the blessing.

Prayer

Father, may we see clearly this day, the lives that you long for us to touch in your name. Thank you in advance for giving us the joy of Christian service. Amen.

"But Mary was standing outside the tomb weeping; and so, as she wept, she stooped and looked into the tomb" John 20:11 NASB

Observation

Do you remember this scene? Mary had gone early to the tomb of Jesus only to discover that the stone had been rolled away. She assumed that the body of Jesus had been moved and so she ran to tell the disciples. Peter and John race to the tomb and they discover that her claims were true. They return home to ponder all that they have witnessed. Mary is understandably quite upset. She finds herself at the entrance of the tomb, distraught, confused, and fearful. Within moments, the Risen Lord will appear and everything about her world will make sense again. But for this brief moment, she weeps alone while the disciples abandon her to her grief.

Application

It seems a bit calloused, does it not? Two of the closest disciples fail to offer a compassionate word or comforting embrace in the midst of Mary's worst moment. They leave her to fend for herself. In their own confusion and bewilderment, they fail to see the opportunity they have to be Christ-like and offer genuine care. We might be quick to condemn their actions, but are we much better? Do we take the time to both see the needs around us and respond in appropriate ways? It is my experience that we don't see ministry opportunities because we are in too great a rush to see them. We become so caught up in our own little worlds of worry and stress that we quickly bypass the hurting in order to fix our own problems. What we fail to see is the potential joy and satisfaction that awaits us if we but dare to become involved. We need to pray for slower steps and less encumbered days. If we are too busy to recognize the cries of the hurting, then we have become too busy to respond in Christ-like fashion. May God give us the eyes with which to see the hurting and the compassion with which to act. One small word of hope, one touch of compassion, one simple prayer and another's life could be radically altered. Let us never become so busy pursuing the Kingdom that we miss the meaningful moments that are sprinkled along the way.

Prayer

Father, slow us down, open our eyes, and fill us with compassion. May we be more concerned with offering hope and help than we are in submitting to our agendas for the day. Amen.

> "And He said to them, 'Cast the net on the right-hand side of the boat and you will find a catch.' So they cast, and then they were not able to haul it in because of the great number of fish." John 21:6 NASB

Observation

In this final chapter of John's Gospel, the Risen Lord once again appears to the disciples. According to what is recorded, about half of the disciple group has chosen to spend an evening on Galilee fishing. Their efforts prove futile and there is nothing to show for their night of toil. As the dawn appears, always a symbol in John's Gospel that the presence of God is about to be revealed, Jesus stands on the seashore and instructs them to let down their nets again. This time, the nets are filled with a huge number of fish. As they experience the miracle, they realize that the One calling to them from the shore is in fact, the Risen Lord.

Application

Notice that at the end of a very long and unproductive night, the disciples are told to fish a bit longer and the results are incredible. I wonder if sometimes we just don't fish long enough. Sometimes the call to ministry can be frustrating. There are some lives in whom we invest much, only to see little result. Maybe you have had a friend for whom you have prayed for years for a change of heart and life. Maybe you have invited that person to church, or even attempted to share a word of the gospel, but with little success. The long nights of futility can rob us all of our zeal and desire to push on. And yet, Jesus bids us to keep fishing... to continue to do those things that would open a door for the gospel message. There is always mystery to this Kingdom-building task. I can't explain why some seem so receptive to the gospel while others seem so reluctant to respond. I just know that we are called to keep fishing. Let me encourage you this morning if you are weary of trying to help a friend or family member come to know the love of Christ, don't give up. Don't take your foot off the gas. Keep praying. Keep looking for opportunities to speak hope. Keep fishing. The great catch may be waiting for the next casting of your net.

Prayer

Father, may we never tire, nor grow weary of sharing the love of Christ. Keep us at the task of fishing for men. Amen.

"These all with one mind were continually devoting themselves to prayer, along with the women, and Mary the mother of Jesus, and with His brothers." Acts 1:14 NASB

Observation

These words are from the opening verses of the Book of Acts, which was written by Gospel-writer Luke and is a continuation of the story of Jesus and the growth of the early church. The pronoun "these" used at the beginning of the verse refers to the 11 disciples that are mentioned as "being together in the Upper Room" following the ascension of Christ into Heaven. There are two important things to note about these believers finding their way into the unchartered seas of doing the Kingdom's work: they were "of one mind," and they were "continually devoting themselves to prayer." It is an image of unity and devotion… unity of purpose and devotion to prayer in order to gain wisdom and knowledge from God.

Application

The success of the early church and the success of any church rests on these two foundational stones. First, there must be a sense of unity among the believers. Ever been in a church filled with disunity? Nothing gets accomplished. There is no spirit of growth, no zeal for evangelism, no compassion among members, no contagious spirit to draw others. The truth is that as a church, we move forward when we move together, being of like mind and purpose. Doing the mission of the Kingdom must always be the unifying and driving force of the church. The second foundational stone is that of fervent prayer. If prayer is the way in which we connect to our Heavenly Father, then doesn't it make sense that to accomplish God's plan and purpose, we must pray for wisdom? There is an interesting corollary between these two concepts. Unity of purpose will always lead us to pray. Praying together will always lead us to unity. If you are a part of some local body of Christ, let me challenge you to be faithful in gathering consistently with those people of faith, and then let me challenge you to become an advocate for deep and meaningful prayer among the fellow believers in your church. The Kingdom will grow through your efforts.

Prayer

Father, may we learn the fundamental lessons of building your Kingdom. Teach us to always preserve a spirit of unity and to wrap ourselves in the warm embrace of prayerful dialogue with you. Amen.

"They were continually devoting themselves to the apostles' teaching and to fellowship, to the breaking of bread and to prayer." Acts 2:42 NASB

Observation

The second chapter of Acts is one of the most dramatic and powerful passages in all of scripture. As promised, the Holy Spirit descends on the apostles and they are given the ability to speak in the various languages of the world. Men from many nations were able to hear the apostles speak in their own tongue. As the Spirit empowered the early disciples, the church experienced phenomenal growth. After Peter offered a brief sermon on the day of Pentecost, more than 3000 people were added to the church that very day. Our focus verse describes what the disciples did to continue the growth of the church. They devoted themselves to the teaching about Christ that the apostles offered. They were devoted to being together, to sharing meals, and to praying together.

Application

While there are many directions to go with this focus verse, let's focus on the idea of being "devoted to fellowship." The early disciples knew the importance of sharing life together with other believers. In fact, they knew that their existence depended on having one another to empower and sustain them. Fellowship for them was more than having coffee and cookies after the evening service... it was a vital sharing of life. They found strength in each other. They found hope in each other. They found the presence of God in each other. No one attempted to live the faith in solitude. Each lived their faith in the context of community. They knew how desperately they needed each other.

It is my prayerful hope that believers of our age can gain the same insight. There are so many who attempt to live the faith on the fringes. They attend church every once in a while. They gather with other believers maybe at Christmas and Easter. If they study the word, they do so at home in the comfort of a leather chair. I call them "lone ranger" believers. They have missed the vital importance of surrounding themselves in the company of fellow Christians. They desperately need the church. They just don't know it. I pray that you will be devoted to fellowshipping with other believers. Be intentional about being in the presence of committed Christians. It will change your life.

Prayer

Father, teach us the importance of connecting to a community of faith. Amen.

Acts 3: Use What You Have

"But Peter said, 'I do not possess silver and gold, but what I do have I give to you: In the name of Jesus Christ the Nazarene—walk!'"
Acts 3:6 NASB

Observation

Empowered by the indwelling Spirit of God, Peter and John are able to do miraculous things. As they approached the Temple at the hour of prayer (3 p.m.), they encountered a man who had been lame from birth. Daily, he had been placed at the Temple Gate to beg alms. This day would be different. Peter and John demand his attention. Instead of giving him alms, Peter declares him to be made well. Peter seized him by the right hand and raised him to his feet. Suddenly his feet and ankles were strengthened and he began to walk. Notice again Peter's words to him. He doesn't offer the beggar that which he expected, a few coins... he offers him the ability to walk by the power of Jesus Christ.

Application

What is it that you possess that will bring glory to God? In this passage, Peter clearly declares that he does not possess silver and gold. Instead, he offers what God has placed in his life... the ability to heal through the work of the Spirit. So again... what do you possess? What is your gift? What is your talent? What is your thing? And are you using your gift to the glory of God? To be sure, there are some who do possess silver and gold and they should be using that gift to further the Kingdom, not simply to "build bigger barns." Others possess the gift of singing, or management, or compassion, or intellect, or teaching, or writing, or cooking, or one of a thousand different things. God has uniquely blessed each of us with those things that we do well. The key is not to hoard the gift as though God gave it to us for "self-blessing." The key is to use the empowerment of God to change lives and build the Kingdom. It is my hope and prayer that each of us will become willing to use that which God has given to us in order to make a difference. The lame of the world, those crippled by fear, by loneliness, by guilt, by brokenness, and by low-esteem, need the people of God to once again call them to a better life. So take whatever it is that you do possess, and in the name of Jesus Christ the Nazarene, join their need to the healing power of God.

Prayer

Father, thank you for gifting all of us in unique and special ways. May we be willing, daily, to use our gifts to your glory and for the Kingdom's work. Amen.

"Now Joseph, a Levite of Cyprian birth, who was also called Barnabas by the apostles (which translated means Son of Encouragement), and who owned a tract of land, sold it and brought the money and laid it at the apostles' feet." Acts 4:36-37 NASB

Observation

The fourth chapter of Acts continues the story of the phenomenal growth of the early church and the way in which the Spirit of God continued to be poured out on the early believers, giving them boldness of witness and strength of heart. These early believers worked for the common good. They recognized that the work of the Church was more important than even their own possessions. In our focus passage, one believer named Joseph, sold a valuable tract of land and brought the money to the Apostles to be used solely for the Kingdom's work. Apparently, such an action was true to his nature. He was such a supporter of the early church that he was given a nickname... Barnabas... "the one who encourages."

Application

If the leaders of your church were to give you a nickname based on your involvement in the life and ministry of the church, what would it be? Don't we wish that someone would call us Barnabas? Don't we wish that our reputation for encouraging the believers and giving to the church would earn us a nickname of such respect? Unfortunately, our nicknames might sound more like this... "He who comes when it's convenient," "She who comes because it is good for business," "He who scans the audience for a potential date," or "She who thinks church is a huge fashion show." You get the point. All of us continue to earn a reputation, if not a nickname, for the way we regard the work of the church. How glorious it would be if our motives became pure, our hearts became passionate, and our gifts became generous. The truth is that the church needs the encouragers of the world to fill its pews. The church needs for us to bring what is "best within us" as an offering to the Lord. As you prepare to head to church this week, ask yourself, "What do I bring to the table? Am I offering encouragement? Do I spread joy? Do I welcome people gladly and receive them warmly? Do I bring grace?" Let's work on that nickname. Let's develop the kind of reputation that honors the Lord.

Prayer

Father, today, may we become the encouragers of the church. May we understand that the work of the church is worthy of our best offering of self. Amen.

> "So they went on their way from the presence of the Council, rejoicing that they had been considered worthy to suffer shame for His name. And every day, in the temple and from house to house, they kept right on teaching and preaching Jesus as the Christ." Acts 5:41-42 NASB

Observation

As the story of the early church unfolds in the pages of Acts 5, the Apostles are arrested by Jewish officials for their preaching and teaching of the gospel. After a miraculous escape from prison they return to the Temple to preach some more. Again, the Jewish leaders bring them before a council and warn them to discontinue their preaching. The apostles are then flogged and sent on their way. But as our focus passage indicates, they rejoiced that they were worthy of suffering shame for the name of Christ and they kept right on preaching Jesus as the Christ.

Application

Quite a stubborn lot, were they not? Though they had been arrested, beaten, and sternly warned, nothing about their priorities changed. They "kept right on teaching and preaching Jesus." For them, the message of salvation in Christ was more important than any threat or personal inconvenience. It begs a question for us. "Where is our breaking point? What factors are strong enough to keep us from making our faith sharing a priority? Could we ever become silenced from sharing the message of Christ with others?" It's a question of boldness. It's a question of how important the sharing of our faith really is. Most of us are quickly deterred at the first hint of an uncomfortable conversation. We don't like confrontation and so we avoid it at all cost. It's as though we would rather look the other way than engage a person about their need for Christ. Christ left the church with one great commission... that of sharing the gospel. What does our unwillingness to do that single task reveal about the level of our commitment to Jesus? Let's be better. Let's be bold. Let's risk a conversation in which we talk of spiritual things to someone we know who is struggling with spiritual matters. It's what we are called to do.

Prayer

Father, give us a boldness of faith and a conviction of spirit that will prod us into the sharing of our Christian experience with others. Amen.

> "So the twelve summoned the congregation of the disciples and said, 'It is not desirable for us to neglect the word of God in order to serve tables.'" Acts 6:2 NASB

Observation

Acts 6 contains what most Bible scholars believe to be the first description of the role of deacons, or church "servants," in the New Testament church. Apparently, the early church took very seriously the ministry of caring for widows within the church. There was a daily distribution of food for widows needing assistance. Conflict arose when some in the church felt that the native Jewish widows were receiving more than those from a Greek background. In order to solve the conflict, seven men were appointed by the church to head-up the ministry so that the Apostles could continue to focus on teaching and preaching the word of God.

Application

The word "deacon" is translated from the Greek word *diakonos*. It is a combination of two smaller words. The word *dia* is a preposition meaning "through." The word *konos* means "dirt or ground." The literal meaning, "through the dirt," gives an image of those willing to take on whatever task is necessary in order to do the work of the church. In the case of our focus verse, the task was that of serving tables. Deaconship was not a position of power, nor that of an overlord, but rather that of a servant. In effect, all of us have been called as deacons in the life of the church. Are we not called to do whatever is needed in order for the work of the church to move forward? Ministers, who are called to specific functions in the life of the church, can easily be pulled away from a primary task in order to solve a ministry need within the congregation. In a perfect world, church servants use their gifts and find a place to help in the Kingdom's work. It is never a question of some functions being more important than others. All the work, from preaching, to teaching, to cleaning, to visiting, is all needed and important. My challenge for you this morning is to wrestle with the question of what do you need to be doing in the life of your church? What place of ministry needs your involvement? Where can your gifts and talents best be used? We are all called as servants. Let's find our place so that the Kingdom marches onward.

Prayer

Father, thank you for envisioning the church as a group of people with varying abilities and talents whom you draw together to do ministry. May we find our place and gratefully serve. Amen.

Day 96 Acts 7: Check Your Attitude

"Then falling on his knees, he cried out with a loud voice, 'Lord, do not hold this sin against them!' Having said this, he fell asleep."
Acts 7:60 NASB

Observation

This chapter records the death of Stephen, the first Christian to be martyred as a result of his faith. After giving a defense of his faith, using a very accurate history of the Israelites, the religious leaders became enraged and in their anger they took Stephen to the outskirts of the city and stoned him to death. Notice Stephen's attitude toward them as they kill him. He speaks of word of redemption. He offers a word of forgiveness. He pleads that God would not hold this crime against them. Such an attitude can only come from one whose heart is fully possessed by the love of Jesus Christ.

Application

Whenever Jesus Christ is truly Lord of someone's life, attitudes are altered forever. The way a person once thought, acted, and responded towards others, is forever changed by a sense of overwhelming grace. In other words, if each of us is fully possessed of Christ, it should become more and more impossible for us to hold attitudes towards others that fail to honor our Lord. For example, how can we claim to hold an attitude of prejudice towards any person, race, or nationality and still claim the Lordship of Christ? How can we hold an attitude of anger and revenge and think we are somehow following in the footsteps of Jesus? How can we gaze lustfully on members of the opposite sex and think that such thoughts bring honor to Christ? The simple answer to these questions is that we can't. Somehow the true measure of our faith can be taken by a look at the attitudes we hold. It is not just that Christians hold the right attitudes about death, it is that we are to hold the right attitudes about living each day. The reason most of us fail to get it right is due to the fact we have not allowed ourselves to be fully possessed by the Spirit of the Living Lord. Jesus Christ has come to transform our lives, not to give sanction to our misguided beliefs. So check your attitudes. If they fail to honor Christ, then let the first order of the day to be that of asking Jesus to cleanse and forgive in order that his Spirit can find a place to dwell.

Prayer

Father, remind us that all of life should reflect your Lordship. May our attitudes be pure, our motives honest, and our lifestyles Godly. Amen.

"Then they began laying their hands on them, and they were receiving the Holy Spirit." Acts 8:17 NASB

Observation

Because of rising persecution against the Christians in Jerusalem, Philip was led by God's Spirit to Samaria to preach to the people there. The Samaritans received his message gladly and many were baptized in the name of the Lord Jesus. Soon, Peter and John were sent from Jerusalem to celebrate with these new believers. They prayed for the new converts to receive the Holy Spirit. And as our focus verse indicates, they "laid their hands on them" in order that they might receive the Spirit. Notice the importance of touch. When those who had the Spirit touched those believers who had yet to receive the Spirit, suddenly their lives were transformed. It is significant that it took personal contact between two ethnicities, who formally hated each other, to finally claim their unity in Christ.

Application

Let's be honest... there are a lot of things that divide people. We are separated by race, gender, economics, political opinion, language, denomination, loyalties, nationality, and belief. Until someone or something begins to press the point, many of us stay segregated from those different from ourselves. But every once in a while, a moment unfolds that allows us to mix and mingle with those who are different. When that happens, walls begin to fall and barriers are weakened. In the time of the early church, there was no hatred or divide any worse than that of the Jew-Samaritan conflict. But suddenly, the transforming power of Christ began bringing the two sides together and it happened with the ministry of touch.

It is amazing what Christ can do whenever we begin to "touch" people in his name. Our touch may begin with a conversation, a prayer, a shared event, a dialogue, or even a shared crisis. It may begin when we offer aid in a time of destruction. The point is this... the love of Christ is often conveyed best when we dare to "touch" different cultures, races, and ideologies, not with harsh words of rebuke or judgment, but with the grace and civility of Christ. How open we are to "touching" others who are different from ourselves is indicative of how serious we are of spreading the gospel.

Prayer

Father, we pray that you might touch the world through the simple touches that we offer those different from ourselves... touches filled with grace, respect, and love. Amen.

> "Now in Joppa there was a disciple named Tabitha (which translated in Greek is called Dorcas); this woman was abounding with deeds of kindness and charity which she continually did." Acts 9:36 NASB

Observation

As writer Luke continues to tell the story of the early church, he describes the early ministry of Peter. Peter, who was filled with the Spirit, was able to do extraordinary things. While traveling near Joppa, he is summoned to the home of a woman named Tabitha who had suddenly died. Tabitha was a proven disciple of the Lord. She had filled her life by doing deeds of kindness and charity. When arriving on the scene, Peter was taken to the upper room where her body had been laid. He knelt down, prayed, and commanded her to arise. Peter was able to present her alive to all of her family and friends.

Application

Certainly the raising of the dead in the name of Jesus is the extraordinary miracle contained in this passage. And certainly, because of the miracle event, others also came to faith in Christ. But I want to focus briefly this morning on this woman named Tabitha. Notice what is said of her in our focus verse... "She was abounding with deeds of kindness and charity which she continually did." Something about her faith in Christ caused her to develop a reputation of kindness and charity. Her faith governed and shaped everything that she did. Notice that she did not just "occasionally" do such things, but that acts of grace were "continually" a part of her life. There was a consistency of lifestyle. There was a pattern of kindness and charity because her faith was authentic.

I wonder if those of us who have claimed faith in the Lord Jesus have such a proven reputation? Do we live a consistent lifestyle that honors Christ because we too have been claimed by Christ? In other words, are our actions, thoughts, and words governed by the faith we claim? Is our faith genuine enough to change our demeanor, alter our attitudes, and control our actions? Is there consistency? Do we occasionally act like Christ or do we consistently pattern our lives after his example? Let us resolve to prove our faith each day, not only by what we claim with our lips, but with how consistently we live out our lives.

Prayer

Father, may we live "all-out" for Christ. May his Spirit control our actions and may his words fill our minds. Amen.

> "The believing Jews who had come with Peter couldn't believe it, couldn't believe that the gift of the Holy Spirit was poured out on 'outsider' Gentiles, but there it was—they heard them speaking in tongues, heard them praising God." Acts 10:45-46 THE MESSAGE

Observation

The tenth chapter of Acts represents a huge leap forward for the early church. Until this point, the efforts of the apostles had been directed towards making Jewish converts. In other words, as the apostles spoke in various cities and towns they did so in local synagogues attempting to convert fellow Jews to belief in Jesus Christ. Suddenly in chapter 10, God reveals to both a Gentile man named Cornelius and to Simon Peter that the gospel message is to have no boundaries. The hope of eternal life in Christ is inclusive of all nations. The "pouring out" of the Spirit on those Gentiles who heard the message of Peter was evidence that God had intended a broader audience for the gospel.

Application

The only limits placed on the sharing of the gospel are those that we place upon it. A "limited audience" has never been the intention of God. God wills that all would come to salvation through Christ. The problem has always been that sometimes believers have tended to draw circles around those who are deemed worthy to receive it, while excluding those deemed unworthy. What could be farther from the truth? Who among us is even worthy of salvation and forgiveness in Christ? If the story of Jesus is to be good news for us, then it must also be good news for everyone living on the planet. The dangerous trend among many modern-day Christians, is that we have lost a sense of our missionary zeal. We have bought into a "live-and-let-live" mentality that offers little compassion for the lost world. We have somehow deflected the force of the Great Commission, which tells "us" to go and preach to all nations. We have seemingly lost interest in trying to reach any and all with the message of hope that the gospel brings. We need to once again broaden our circle. We need to gain a sense of the worldwide embrace of the Kingdom. May God forgive our lethargy and give us new vision and burden so that we consider every tribe and nation as lost brothers we are striving to claim.

Prayer

Father, remind us again that not only is it your desire for all nations to know the gospel, but that you also desire for each of us to help tell the story. Amen.

"The followers all decided to help the believers who lived in Judea, as much as each one could." Acts 11:29 NCV

Observation

In the 11th chapter of Acts, believers, who had been scattered to various places because of persecution, made their way to Antioch where a number of Greeks heard the gospel message through their preaching. Barnabas was sent from Jerusalem to encourage these new believers. Barnabas then traveled to Tarsus to find Paul and bring him to Antioch so that the two of them could preach and teach the way of the Lord. For over a year they taught these early Christians. When it came to their attention that a famine was going to cause a need in Jerusalem, the believers in Antioch chose to collect an offering and send it to help their brothers in Christ.

Application

One of the distinguishing characteristics of the early church was the generosity with which they offered their lives. When a need was recognized, both spiritually and physically, the early believers were quick to respond. They gave "as much as each one could." They gained a sense of community. They pulled together so that the needs of one another could be met. Their faith in Christ led them to live with a generous attitude.

Has not Christ invested in each of us a spirit of generosity? Something about the heart of Christ in us, gives to us a sense of compassion to help others. We take whatever it is that we possess, and we share it as much as we can. For some, Christian generosity is expressed best through financial support to the church. For others, support for the church comes through fervent prayer. Still, for others, generosity is expressed through acts of service and compassion. Others give through their teaching abilities. Some contribute through various talents and skills as they volunteer to meet needs. Here's the point... all of us have something to contribute to the work of the Kingdom. It is as we offer all that we have to the Lord and to his Church that needs are erased, spirits are lifted, and the Kingdom marches forward. As you make your way to worship this week, consider what you can bring to the table and offer that gift as an act of worship.

Prayer

Father, teach us to be generous with that which you have provided for each of us. Open our eyes to need and our hearts to generosity. Amen.

Day 101 — Acts 12: Knowing Your Place

"And immediately an angel of the Lord struck him because he did not give God the glory, and he was eaten by worms and died."
Acts 12:23 NASB

Observation

Weird verse, right? This verse is part of the story of the death of King Herod. Herod had begun a ruthless campaign of persecution against the early church because of the political advantages he gained among the Jews. He had already killed James by the sword and had attempted to do the same to Peter, until an angel of the Lord rescued Peter from prison. Our focus verse centers on an incident when King Herod was attempting to give a speech before the people of Tyre and Sidon. They were hoping to gain his generosity and so when he began to speak, they kept shouting, "The voice of a god and not a man!" Herod apparently enjoyed the praise and refused to make the people stop. As a result, he was struck dead by an angel of the Lord because he attempted to claim some of God's glory for himself.

Application

It is never a good idea to think too highly of ourselves. What's the old saying? "Pride goeth before a fall." I seriously doubt that anyone is going to accuse us of being a god, and I seriously doubt that any of us would make such a claim about ourselves. And yet, at times, there can be a little question as to Lordship. If we are not careful, any of us can actually claim a higher position in our minds than we should. We sometimes make ourselves out to be the Lord of Life. Whenever we put our priorities, our wishes, our desires, and our attitudes above those of Christ, have we not usurped his place? Do we not, at times, enjoy our "self-praise" making us think a little too highly of ourselves? Somewhere along the line we need to figure out that it is not about us. We have not been created by God to bring glory to ourselves. We have been placed on the planet to bring glory to God. So as you start a new day, take a moment to reflect on whose agenda will fill your calendar this week. Yours or God's? And just to help you from being eaten by worms... I'd advise you to put yourself second.

Prayer

Father, make us humble enough to act as your servants and graceful enough to live as your children. Amen.

Day 102 — Acts 13: How Hungry Are You?

"Then, when they had fasted and prayed and laid their hands on them, they sent them away." Acts 13:3 NASB

Observation

Chapter 13 of Acts begins with a look at what was happening in the life of the church in Antioch. In that one local church were prophets and teachers. The Holy Spirit commanded the church to set apart Barnabas and Paul for the work appointed for them. This marked the beginning of Paul's missionary efforts. Notice how the church prepared them for their work. They fasted, prayed, and laid hands on them. The "laying on of hands" is a fairly common practice, even in most churches today. It is a way of commissioning and blessing someone to a specific task. Prayer is also a common practice. Fasting, however, is not as widely discussed, nor practiced.

Application

So what's the deal with fasting? Is it important? Is it necessary? For me, it's all about focus. Sometimes we need to give up the normal routines of daily life in order to seek and discern the movement of God in new and different ways. Included in the normal "things of daily life" can be our obsession with eating. Most of us get caught up in an almost automatic ritual each day. We eat, not because we are necessarily hungry, but simply because it is the time when we always eat. We are programed to head to the table when the clock strikes a certain hour. But what if we took the time and energy to alter our day in order to draw a more deliberate focus on seeking the voice of God. What if instead of rushing to the table, we consciously set aside our meal as a spiritual discipline? Rather than fill our bodies with calories, what if we filled our minds with the careful reflections of God's leadership in our lives? What if our physical hunger reminded us of our need for spiritual hunger? What if we gave up physical desires in order to focus on spiritual needs? Sometimes, it takes a different angle and perspective to see things more clearly. May I suggest that personally and privately you at least fast for most of a day as a way of clearing your mind and routine so that you may hear from God more clearly? Who knows, fewer calories may mean greater blessings.

Prayer

Father, may we be willing to do whatever it takes to connect with you. Give us a hunger for your purpose that equals the hunger within our stomachs. Amen.

"But Jews came from Antioch and Iconium, and having won over the crowds, they stoned Paul and dragged him out of the city, supposing him to be dead." Acts 14:19 NASB

Observation

In the city of Lystra, Paul and Barnabas, through the empowerment of the Spirit, were able to heal a man who had been lame from birth. The people of the town were so astounded that they attempted to worship them as though they were gods. In fact, the two were even compared to Zeus and Hermes. Paul and Barnabas immediately repudiated such a notion and begged the people not to view them as anything but mere men. But the attention caused by the event forced the Jews from Antioch and Iconium to travel to Lystra. (Previously, Paul and Barnabas had suffered persecution in those places.) These Jews were able to stir up the crowds against Paul to the extent that they were able to stone him and leave him for dead.

Application

Sometimes there is a downside to ministry. Sometimes, in our attempt to help others in their times of great need, we become in some ways victimized. Sometimes people associate us with their difficulty and even though we may have been instrumental in offering help, still we become connected with a difficult moment in their lives. Even the attempt at helping others is not always met with open arms. It is those types of moments that tend to jade our perception and keep us from offering the compassion that we know we should offer. Regardless, we must carry on with the love of Christ in spite of the risks. Better to lose a friendship than lose a soul from heaven's bliss. Better to risk a conversation than be silent in a time of need. Better to be rejected than to ignore opportunities for helping others. All that to say, that sometimes, there is a risk to ministry. We may pour our hearts and souls into offering help and never see anything come to fruition on this side of glory, nor ever hear a word of gratitude, nor receive any credit for a difficult job well done. So what? We minister, not for the self-glorification it brings, but for the joy of knowing we sometimes serve greater causes. Please know that your "labor in the Lord is not in vain." The God who sees in secret, may be the only One to ever reward your effort. But isn't that enough?

Prayer

Father, teach us that in our risk of ministry, that we gain the greatest rewards. Make us faithful, compassionate, and humble. Amen.

"For it seemed good to the Holy Spirit and to us to lay upon you no greater burden than these essentials: that you abstain from things sacrificed to idols and from blood and from things strangled and from fornication; if you keep yourselves free from such things, you will do well. Farewell." Acts 15:28-29 NASB

Observation

As the influence of the early church continued to spread to regions well beyond Jerusalem, some issues developed in regard to requirements to be met for non-Jews to find their way into the life of the church. Some devout Jewish converts insisted that new Christians should begin practicing a very dedicated allegiance to all the traditions of the Jewish faith, including circumcision. A council was held in Jerusalem to wrestle with the issue. Our focus verse is the result of that council. In their wisdom, the early church leaders felt that it was important to make it simpler to gain access to God through Christianity, rather than harder. And so they only asked for new Gentile converts to adhere to a few items.

Application

I wonder if we sometimes make it rather difficult for new believers to make their way into the life of the church. Rather than celebrate with great joy the excitement of finding faith in Christ, we sometimes get distracted by insisting on a lot of requirements in order to be a "good" member. We insist on doctrinal adherence long before such issues are even understood by the new believers. Surely the church can do better. Surely the Spirit of Grace and inclusion should trump any rigid requirement. We should make it easier to join the church, not harder. Now don't get me wrong... doctrine IS important. Understanding what we believe and why we believe it is critical. It is important that we maintain the essentials of our faith and the core values of our church. New believers need to be patiently taught and consistently affirmed. Let's insist that people mature in belief and understanding. But let's educate new believers with grace and patience. Let's allow faith in Christ to be the first step. Let's affirm with joy THAT decision and then do our part to help the new believers come to a better understanding what it means to practice daily Christianity.

Prayer

Father, give us wisdom enough to create a welcoming community of faith that will draw the lost, inspire the Christian, and build the Kingdom. Amen.

"But about midnight Paul and Silas were praying and singing hymns of praise to God, and the prisoners were listening to them;"
Acts 16:25 NASB

Observation

Paul and Silas had been teaching and preaching in the city of Thyatira and were having success. Lydia, who was a citizen in that place, became the first convert in Europe. As they continued to teach in that place, they encountered a demon-possessed woman who was being quite a distraction. They healed her of her demons, which made her "owners" quite angry because they had been making a nice profit by exploiting her odd behavior. The angry owners stirred up the crowds and actually had Paul and Silas arrested, beaten, and thrown in prison. Notice the reaction of these two when faced with great uncertainty and still nursing the wounds that had been inflicted. They were praying and singing hymns of praise to God. Even in the prison, they were offering praise and affecting the lives of those imprisoned with them.

Application

Their story begs some great questions, "What is your natural reaction whenever you face difficulties in your life? Whenever you walk through difficult moments when fear and uncertainty long to defeat your spirit, what then? Is your faith strong enough and your inner joy great enough that you could sing praises to God?" It certainly takes a depth of faith and a heart of courage to rejoice when everything about your life says to cower in fear. What makes the difference? Trust. Clearly Paul and Silas trusted in the provision and protection of God. They knew that no matter what circumstances came their way, that God's presence would be with them to walk them through the present peril. I doubt that any of us could claim the faith of these early disciples, but the power and strength available to them, is the same still afforded us in Christ. We are "more than conquers," right? I don't know what pressures you face today. I can't know all of your fears. But I do know that we are called to cast our cares on God, who cares for us. So maybe today, instead of fretting your life away, you ought to try singing a hymn of praise to God, Master and Lord who longs to hear your voice.

Prayer

Father, remind us that in the dark nights of our lives, that your presence is ever with us and that your power will always sustain us. Give us the faith to praise, even when the moments are difficult. Amen.

"Being then the children of God, we ought not to think that the Divine Nature is like gold or silver or stone, an image formed by the art and thought of man." Acts 17:29 NASB

Observation

During one of his missionary journeys Paul found himself in the city of Athens. While there, he argued theology and philosophy with the leading men and women of the city. He told them that he had seen an inscription on one of their statues to "an unknown god." He then said to them, "What you worship in ignorance, I will proclaim to you." He then began explaining the scriptures to each of them, teaching them that God cannot be bound in gold, silver, or stone. God is not a mere object to be worshiped.

Application

As modern-day, enlightened believers surely we know more than the ancient Greeks. Surely we know that God is not bound up in golden statues or formed by chiseled stone. Surely we know the boundless, unlimited sovereignty of God... or do we? Though we would never cast a golden image of God, my fear is that we sometimes attempt to form an image of God in our thoughts. You see, rather than allow God to shape and mold us, we often attempt to shape and mold God into our expectations. Rather than conform to God's image, we often attempt to manipulate God to conform to our agendas. We use God-talk and carelessly throw around a few out-of-context verses in an attempt to make it seem that God is somehow siding with our narrow-minded opinion or driving our selfish agenda. In other words, we attempt to manipulate God into some small box of thought that conforms to our thinking. Rather than let the unlimited grace and power of God change us each day, we attempt to narrowly define God and God's teachings. Like the ancient Greeks, we often create a God that fits the way we want to think or worship. Shame on us. Certainly the God of the Universe deserves more from us. Rather than limit God by human manipulation, let us learn to worship the One whom we cannot ever fully define, but in whose presence we stand amazed.

Prayer

Father, remind us that you are all-powerful and all-knowing and that it is a sinful gesture on our part to think that we can draw limits around your heart of compassion and your teaching of grace. Amen.

Day 107 — Acts 18: Faith Coaching

> "And he began to speak out boldly in the synagogue. But when Priscilla and Aquila heard him, they took him aside and explained to him the way of God more accurately." Acts 18:26 NASB

Observation

While in the city of Ephesus, Priscilla and Aquila, who had been co-laborers with Paul, met a man named Apollos. Apollos was a strong believer in Christ and had an extensive knowledge of the scriptures. His knowledge of Christ, however, was not as complete as it needed to be. There were some teachings and insights that he had yet to understand. And so Priscilla and Aquila took on the role of mentoring Apollos so that he would be even better equipped for his role of preaching and teaching. With the encouragement of the brethren, he later departed from Ephesus and made his way to Achaia where he was warmly greeted. There he was able to speak powerfully the message of Christ.

Application

It's called mentoring. Sometimes, those who are mature in the faith and have experienced a little more of life, are able to take a newer convert and help them to understand the intricacies of faith a little more clearly. Sometimes a parent takes on the role of mentoring a child. At other moments, a friend takes on the role of mentoring another friend who is still growing in the faith. At other moments, it could even be a teacher mentoring a student. A Christian mentor is one who is willing to invest time, energy, and prayer in the life of a young Christian in order to help that person grow in the faith. Most of us were mentored at some point by someone a little older and a bit wiser... maybe a Sunday School teacher, a pastor, a deacon, or a friend. We have grown in our faith because of their investment or "coaching" in our lives. Maybe it's time for you to return the favor. Maybe it's time for you to make the commitment to mentor someone with the wisdom and knowledge you have gained from Christ. I want to challenge you to consider making a spiritual investment in the life of a student, a friend, or a coworker by dedicating yourself to the task of teaching and training that person in the faith. Pour your heart into the life of a younger Christian and watch as God uses you to help them grow in their faith. Isn't it time that you started making a difference?

Prayer

Father, thank you for investing gifts of time, teaching, and faith in all of us. May we use our talents well for the growing of your Kingdom. Amen.

"God was performing extraordinary miracles by the hands of Paul, so that handkerchiefs or aprons were even carried from his body to the sick, and the diseases left them and the evil spirits went out."
Acts 19:11-12 NASB

Observation

The miraculous events mentioned in our focus passage occurred while Paul was teaching and preaching in the city of Ephesus. It is apparent that the Spirit of God was great in the life of Paul. When handkerchiefs that had touched the body of Paul were taken to the sick they were healed of their diseases. The power went from God to Paul, and then from Paul to those who were ill. God chose to heal many by using Paul as an instrument through which God's grace and healing power would flow.

Application

God uses all kinds of people to do all kinds of things. In this story, God used Paul, and even cloth touched by Paul, to bring healing to many. There is no way to explain such an occurrence other than to say that God's Spirit was at work in a very powerful way. Let's be honest. Most of us are not going to be used of God in quite the same way. Touch my old t-shirt and you probably won't get much of a blessing! But touch my life and you might. God chooses to work through people. We become God's hands and feet on the earth. Whenever we make ourselves available, God can do extraordinary things through us. God might use a talent, our words, our compassion, or our strength. God might even use our wealth. There are many ways that God can and will work through us, because there are many people who need to be touched by the healing power of God's grace. My question this morning is, "Are you willing to be used?" It's that simple. God will use your life if you make it available. Think about it... your willing spirit can convey grace, lift the brokenhearted, soothe wounds, and offer hope. All you have to do is to ask God to make you an instrument. Who knows what lives you may touch even this day?

Prayer

Father, thank you for calling each of us into the Kingdom's work. Remind us that you long to do extraordinary things through us, if we will but offer a willing heart. Amen.

"And there was a young man named Eutychus sitting on the window sill, sinking into a deep sleep; and as Paul kept on talking, he was overcome by sleep and fell down from the third floor and was picked up dead. But Paul went down and fell upon him, and after embracing him, he said, 'Do not be troubled, for his life is in him.'" Acts 20:9-10 NASB

Observation

While in Troas, Paul offers a very lengthy teaching session. A group of believers were gathered in a room on the third floor. It's late at night. The room is stuffy with many lamps. Paul's teaching goes on and on. You get the picture. One poor young man, trying to get a little fresh air by sitting in the windowsill, falls asleep and then falls out of the window. Tragedy is averted when Paul rushes down and restores him to life. Paul then returns to the third floor and teaches some more.

Application

Let's talk for a moment about sleeping in church, but not in the same sense as the young man who fell out the window. I know a lot of people who come to church fully awake physically, but are asleep spiritually. It's called lethargy or apathy. So many seem to get into a spiritual rut of doing the same thing, the same way, over and over again. They lose the joy of their faith and the excitement of worship. They simply go through the motions of a spiritual life devoid of any real meaning or growth. Many of us simply need to wake up. We need a celestial alarm clock to ring, awakening us to new life in Christ. Let's be honest... any of us can grow weary in our pursuit of Christ. So how do we maintain a sense of vibrancy? How can we reawaken our faith? Let me offer you one of the best solutions I know... service. Find a way to serve a greater world. Volunteer to be a part of a "hands-on" ministry. Take the time to discover a place where you can give expression to your faith. It may be through a local non-profit. It may be through a church-sponsored missions experience. It may be through sharing the love of Christ by volunteering at a local school or helping to build a Habitat House. You choose. So if your faith seems a little sleepy these days, try serving a greater world. You may be amazed at how vibrant your faith can become.

Prayer

Father, forgive us when we care little for our faith and become complacent about our worship. Show us this day a place to "plug-in." May our sense of service restore the excitement of our faith. Amen.

"Then Paul answered, 'What are you doing, weeping and breaking my heart? For I am ready not only to be bound, but even to die at Jerusalem for the name of the Lord Jesus.'" Acts 21:13 NASB

Observation

In the scene described in our focus verse, Paul is slowly and steadily making his way to Jerusalem. While in the city of Caesarea a prophet of God named Agabus tries to warn Paul about the dangers awaiting him there. Jewish opposition will be great and the prophet warns that Paul will be bound and tied and led away by Gentiles. (All of which will indeed happen as Paul is arrested and sent to Rome to stand trial.) Because of the report from the prophet, many of the believers try to persuade Paul not to travel to Jerusalem. Notice his resolve and courage... "I am ready not only to be bound, but even to die at Jerusalem for the name of the Lord Jesus." He faces the uncertainty of the journey with the assurance that each moment will be lived out under the watch care of God.

Application

Let's talk about our resolve for a moment. In terms of faith, how willing are we to march boldly into the future, ready to do the will the God no matter the cost? How courageous will we live? How strongly will we defend our faith? Truthfully, there is always a sense of uncertainty surrounding the days we live. There is always peril and danger around every corner. But if our resolve is to walk in faith, with our lives placed securely in the hands of God, then God's presence goes before us. We will discover that we gain courage and assurance for the living of each day. As the old hymn reminds us, "Because He lives, I can face tomorrow, because He lives, all fear is gone. Because I know He holds the future, and life is worth the living just because He lives." So back to this question of resolve. You have choices to make. Do you live your life, bouncing from one fear to another, from one anxious moment to the next, or do you place your life in God's hands knowing that God will direct your path and defend your life? Go with God. Set your resolve to trust fully and to live the life you are called to live.

Prayer

Father, grant us courage for the living of each day. May our resolve be that of trusting you fully and walking joyfully into the moments ordained for us. Amen.

"But when they stretched him out with thongs, Paul said to the centurion who was standing by, "Is it lawful for you to scourge a man who is a Roman and uncondemned?"" Acts 22:25 NASB

Observation

In this scene, Paul is about to be scourged for the accusations made by the Jews. A scourging was a horrific beating with a leather whip, usually 39 lashes. Just as the Roman centurion is about to carry out the scourging, Paul raises the issue of Roman citizenship. Under Roman law, no citizen could be beaten without a proper trial. In fact, anyone scourging someone without proper procedure, could himself be scourged. So in this scene, when the centurion discovers Paul's citizenship, he immediately releases him until proper procedures can be followed.

Application

Sometimes, it's all about your citizenship. Because we are Americans, we know that there are certain rights afforded us under the Constitution. There are rights and privileges granted us, some of which even extend beyond the borders of our nation. It is not because of anything that we have earned, but simply because we were born in the right place. As Christians, we also lay claim to an even greater citizenship. We are the children of God and residents of the eternal Kingdom. Because we belong to God, there are certain rights and privileges afforded us. We have grace that covers our sins. We have power that protects our lives. We have joy that lengthens our days. We have God's Spirit to nurture us and teach us how to live. Because of our Heavenly citizenship, we have worth, value, and status... none of which we have earned, nor deserved. We have simply been claimed as God's child, and in that relationship, we live.

As with any privilege, comes responsibility. Because we have found inclusion, protection, and privilege as a part of God's Kingdom, it becomes our role to welcome new "immigrants" to that same soil. Let us seek to "save the lost." Let us work untiringly to share with others the gospel story so that they too will know the love of Christ and the joy of being a citizen of Heaven.

Prayer

Father, thank you for claiming each of us as your child and for welcoming us into your Kingdom. May we strive to be good citizens of that realm. Amen.

"When it was day, the Jews formed a conspiracy and bound themselves under an oath, saying that they would neither eat nor drink until they had killed Paul." Acts 23:12 NASB

Observation

In this scene, Paul is once again under attack by the Jewish leaders in Jerusalem. After hearing him speak, they become so angered by his words that they vow to kill him over his beliefs and preaching. In fact, more than 40 of them take a vow not to eat or drink until they have killed him. They make plans to ambush Paul when he is being led before the Council of the Jews. Paul's nephew hears of the plot and reports both to Paul and to the Roman centurion what he has heard. As a result of his warning, Paul is safely moved to a different city.

Application

It is one thing to disagree with someone's beliefs and religion, it is quite another to long for his/her death. Here's where religion sometimes gets it wrong. If the love of God is truly in us, then our hope for those who think differently from us, is not for their deaths and elimination, but for their salvation. If we truly possess the love of God, then suddenly we are bound, not to hate, but to love our religious enemies. Let's be honest... there is a lot of rhetoric these days, even among "Christian" people about members of the Islamic faith and the terror and violence many think they espouse. It is easy to get caught up in such fervor and stereotype every Muslim as being a radical terrorist. Instead of looking for ways to reach them with the gospel, we look for ways to push them out of our communities and schools. Many have bought into a hatred for people they don't even know.

When will we learn that the gospel often walks across the bridges of relationship we build with others? Is it not the way of our Lord to "love our enemies and pray for those who persecute us?" Rather than respond as the Pharisees of the 1st Century, let us learn how to first offer the love of Christ with an open-mind and a peaceful dialogue. We will never build life-changing and soul-saving relationships out of hatred. We change the world when our religion is authentic and when our attitudes reflect those of the Savior whom we claim to follow.

Prayer

Father, we acknowledge that there are many who believe very differently from ourselves. It is our prayer that they would one day know Jesus Christ as Savior and Lord. Remind us that it is our role to love them until that day comes. Amen.

Day 113 Acts 24: Waiting for the Right Moment

"But after two years had passed, Felix was succeeded by Porcius Festus, and wishing to do the Jews a favor, Felix left Paul imprisoned."
Acts 24:27 NASB

Observation

At this point in the Biblical narrative, Paul had been taken to Caesarea where he was to be quickly tried by his Jewish accusers. The Roman Governor, Felix, was intrigued by Paul and often called upon him for discussions of faith. More than anything else, however, Felix wanted Paul to offer him a bribe, which he never did. Being in no real hurry to resolve the issue, Felix left Paul imprisoned for over two years.

Application

Sometimes there is mystery to God's unfolding plan. It seems odd that the same God who rescued Paul from prison before, the same God who protected his life numerous times, the same God who used Paul to start countless churches and win thousands of converts, would now allow Paul to sit in a dark and dank prison cell for over two years. Why the delay in his trial? Why the long period of imprisonment? Was it in order for Paul to have an audience with the Governor? Was it in order to have Paul strengthen the believers in Caesarea? Who's to say? Sometimes there is mystery to God's unfolding plan, right? So what about your life? Ever feel like you are stuck in a "life rut" when opportunities just don't seem to click and relationships seem to grow stale? Ever feel like your life is in neutral when the rest of the world is racing by at break-neck speed? Sometimes it is frustrating and difficult for us to "wait on the Lord." We get stressed out over the seemingly uninterested action of God. But let us remember a few things. 1. God has a plan for our lives. 2. God's plan will unfold on God's timetable and not ours. 3. Time is under God's control. What are a few days or even months to a God who is transcendent of time? Our task is to truly "wait on the Lord." Not to worry... as we remain faithful to God's call, the events and moments of our lives will be arranged for God's glory. Don't fret because your life occasionally seems to be "on hold." Rejoice that God is arranging the pieces of your life to do great and mighty things. The moments will come. Your life will count.

Prayer

Father, thank you for using each of us to build your Kingdom. Teach us patience and faithfulness while we wait for your purposes to be accomplished in our lives. Amen.

"Then Agrippa said to Festus, 'I also would like to hear the man myself.' 'Tomorrow,' he said, 'you shall hear him.'" Acts 25:22 NASB

Observation

Paul's imprisonment led to yet another chapter in his life story. When Fetus desired to bring Paul back to Jerusalem where the Jews were plotting to kill him, Paul appealed to Caesar which was a right granted to him as a Roman citizen. While being held, King Agrippa visited the region and was told by Festus all of the history behind his arrest and about the accusations made by the Jews. Intrigued by Paul's story, reputation, and teaching, Agrippa wanted to personally hear Paul speak. And so Paul gained yet another opportunity to share the gospel with powerful and influential men.

Application

Read the passage carefully and you will notice how Paul's life, his testimony, and his boldness in the face of persecution led to a certain curiosity about his life. Not only did Festus long to hear more, but in our focus passage, even the King wanted to hear his story. Something about the mystery of faith was captivating by those who had never heard.

When our faith is lived authentically, shared boldly, and expressed lovingly, we too have the ability to create a sense of curiosity. The world will long to know why we think like we do and act in the ways we act. Genuine faith always draws a crowd. True Christianity is always a contagious force. It is our distinctiveness, our humility, our compassion, and our grace that draws the non-believing world to examine our lives more closely. The challenge for us then, is to live a "thoroughly-Christian" life. When we are ready to stand counter to our culture, ready to forgive our enemies, and ready to offer our lives in service for the needs of humanity, the world will notice. We will create a curiosity that draws others to hear our story. So let me challenge you to live a curious life. Live a life so radically different from the culture of the world that people will notice. And if they notice... perhaps they too will explore the reasons behind such a faith.

Prayer

Father, create in each of us a genuine heart, a pure spirit, and grace-filled lifestyle so that the world might see something different in us. May their curiosity lead them to explore the realities of faith in Christ. Amen.

"And Paul said, "I would wish to God, that whether in a short or long time, not only you, but also all who hear me this day, might become such as I am, except for these chains."" Acts 26:29 NASB

Observation

Chapter 26 of the book of Acts shares the story of Paul's defense before King Agrippa. He gives a brief overview of his life, including his former persecution of the Jews, his conversion on the Damascus Road, and his call to minister in the name of Jesus Christ. The King listens carefully to Paul's testimony and even declares that if he, the King, listened long enough, that he too might be persuaded to become a Christian. Paul then declares in our focus verse, that he would wish all people would come to faith in Christ.

Application

Paul had a single vision… a focused passion that drove his life. That vision was telling others about salvation through Jesus Christ. So Paul poured out his life in pursuit of that one passion. He gave up popularity, position, power, safety, and even health. Spreading the gospel became the sole purpose of his life. He found contentment and joy in no other pursuit.

Perhaps none of us will ever have the passion and sacrificial spirit of Paul. God called and empowered him to do incredible things. Paul's obedient heart allowed him to be used by God in extraordinary ways. So here's the thing... we too have the same Spirit that empowered Paul, giving strength to our lives. We serve the same God. We proclaim the same Savior. So why are we not changing the world the way Paul did? Could it be a matter of the heart? Are our hearts completely devoted to God's purpose? Do we have a true passion to live each day in pursuit of God's will? Changing our world is never a problem of opportunity; it is a problem of obedience. Today, this very day, you will encounter people in whose lives you can make a difference, if you choose to live a bold faith. Maybe it starts with a simple conversation. Maybe it starts with an inquiry about how they spent their Sunday. I challenge you to risk a conversation in which you talk about spiritual things. Be open to what the Spirit might say through your life. Remember that the world will not be changed by your private devotion. It will be transformed when your faith is courageous and your witness becomes bold. Look for opportunity. Pray for obedience.

Prayer

Father, today, make us bold, obedient, and faithful. Amen.

"Yet now I urge you to keep up your courage, for there will be no loss of life among you, but only of the ship." Acts 27:22 NASB

Observation

Chapter 27 of Acts contains a very detailed description of Paul's perilous journey to Rome. As a prisoner, Paul was being transported by ship all the way across the Mediterranean Sea. Ignoring the fact that they were traveling late in the year and being warned by Paul not to press on further, the ship's captain chose to keep going. As a result, the ship encountered a vicious storm that lasted for more than two weeks. Eventually, the ship ran aground near a small island and began to break apart. All 286 people on board were forced to plunge into the sea, but by God's grace they all survived as they made their way to shore. Paul had told them in the midst of the storm that they would survive. His word for them was, "courage."

Application

Most of us have never been caught at sea in the midst of a life-threatening storm, but all of us have experienced the storms that life hurls at us—poor health, broken relationships, financial pressure, job loss, transition and change. None of us are immune. The pressures are real, the winds are intense, and the journey uncertain. Like the ancient sailors with Paul, we too look for a word of hope in the midst of the darkest night, and once again, the Spirit of God provides such a word. It's the word "courage." It's the word that helps us to survive. By definition courage is... "moral strength to persevere, to withstand danger, fear, or difficulty." The question becomes, "Where is the source of such courage and strength? How do we find the power to endure and survive?" Remember the rhetorical question of the Psalmist? "From where shall my help come? It comes from God, the maker of heaven and earth" (Ps. 121). Our hope, our help, and yes, our courage are all bound up in the same source. They come from God. We have courage because God's presence is always with us, our prayers are always heard, and God's power is always greater than our fears. So in the midst of whatever storm you currently face, let me offer to you a word of courage. God has not abandoned you and has not forgotten your plight for even a moment. Hold fast to God in the darkest storm and stand amazed by God's miraculous deeds.

Prayer

Father, remind us today of your abiding presence in our lives. May we have the courage needed to face even the darkest storms. Amen.

"And the brethren, when they heard about us, came from there as far as the Market of Appius and Three Inns to meet us; and when Paul saw them, he thanked God and took courage." Acts 28:15 NASB

Observation

In this final chapter from the Book of Acts, Paul is making his way toward Rome and a very uncertain future. What would be his fate? Would he be treated harshly? Would the Romans treat him fairly? Would the Jews in Rome bring more hostility? Would he be imprisoned for long? Having escaped the shipwreck and having wintered in Malta, he makes his way to the outskirts of Rome where he is greeted by fellow Christians. When he sees them, notice that he thanks God for their presence and that he takes courage in their company.

Application

It has been said from some sage of an earlier time that, "the longest journey is made shorter in the company of close friends." You have probably found that to be true. We tend to weather the rough seas, escape the dark nights, and survive the perils of daily living while in the company of friends. Most of us have lived life long enough to know how desperately we need each other... especially those who believe strongly in the Christian faith. Fellow Christians offer much. They gladly pray when the needs are great. They offer encouragement when the struggles are real. They speak of hope when the days seem long and tedious. They give strength when our own energy is insufficient. How desperately we need one another.

So how do we find the kind of relationships that offer such joy and encouragement? Where do we go to build the kind of connections that last for a lifetime? Simple. We go to church. We go to church and we invest our lives with the people of God. It is the church that will help us to raise our kids, fortify our convictions, give strength to our lives, and build our faith. Like Paul, each week when we walk in the doors we should thank God for our fellow believers and discover the courage that comes through those relationships. It is my hope and prayer for you this day that you will know the power of the gospel as it becomes "fleshed out" in the lives of fellow Christians. Take courage. You are not alone.

Prayer

Father, thank you for offering us the gift of the Christian Church. May we have enough sense to surround ourselves in the protection, grace, and joy that the Church longs to offer to each of us. Amen.

"For ever since the world was created, people have seen the earth and sky. Through everything God made, they can clearly see His invisible qualities—His eternal power and divine nature. So they have no excuse for not knowing God." Romans 1:20 NLT

Observation

The book of Romans is clearly a letter written by the Apostle Paul to Gentile Christians living in Rome. In the opening verses, he describes himself as a slave of Christ, chosen by God to share the gospel message to the Gentile world. He praises the faithful at Rome for their reputation, which was being discussed around the world. Apparently, there were many strong believers in the midst of that very cosmopolitan city. Paul prayed constantly for the church, knowing of its strategic place of influence in the Mediterranean world.

Application

Paul speaks against all who practice ungodliness and unrighteousness... those who, in his words, "suppress the truth." He suggests that no one has a valid excuse for not knowing about God or acknowledging God's authority. In our focus verse Paul points to the world of nature as a testimony to the greatness of God. God's power and nature can be clearly seen in the splendor of the natural world. Anyone with eyes to see, must know of a Purposeful and Powerful Creator God who is worthy of all praise. In Paul's mind, there is no excuse for acting as though there is no God, nor for acting as though God is not important. My fear is that many of us sometimes lapse into a casual attitude about God. We pray when it is convenient to do so. We praise God when the notion strikes. We obey God when doing so fits our situational ethic. We act as though God deserves part-time allegiance at best. Who are we kidding? We live without excuse if we think that God doesn't matter. As you begin another day, don't try to see God in everything... try NOT seeing God. It can't be done. Everything around us declares God's power and presence: the heavens declare glory, the birds of the air fly, the seas roar in glad adoration. The only thing that seems inconsistent in offering praise is "us." What a dangerous notion. You have no excuse today for not praising God, who is worthy and powerful. He is God.

Prayer

Father, forgive any excuse we would offer at being silent with our praise. Teach us to declare your glory… openly, consistently, fervently. Amen.

"And this is the message I proclaim—that the day is coming when God, through Christ Jesus, will judge everyone's secret life."
Romans 2:16 NLT

Observation

In this passage, Paul offers a very strict warning about the judgment of God. In verse 11, he speaks of the impartiality of God's judgment. God will judge the Jews who have the law but fail to obey it, and God will judge Gentiles who live with a sense of right and wrong but who choose to do the wrong thing. He warns that there is no "get-out-of-jail-free" card based on heritage or bloodlines. All will be judged according to their actions, thoughts, and words.

Application

Here's a scary thought... God will judge our secret life. Uh-oh. Most of us are pretty good at living out our faith publicly. As a general rule, we can control our tongues, associate with the right people, do the right things, avoid the wrong places, and faithfully attend church. On the outside, we tend to measure up fairly well. Most of us rarely stumble while in public view. But it's not our outside, "pretend life" for which we will be judged... it's the secret life, the life we live while no one is looking. Are not most of our sins committed within the confines of our hearts and minds? Don't most of our impure thoughts, desires, and motivations occur within the deep recesses of our beings where we are alone with our thoughts? We all have the secret life, don't we? We hold resentment towards a certain person, but we would never tell anyone. We lust after someone's spouse but can never speak of it publicly. We have thoughts of harming someone whom we dislike, but others will never know. Here's the problem... we can hide our secret life from everyone except God, but then again, God is the only One who matters. God sees the secret life within us. And according to God's word, we will be judged by the secret life. So where is our hope? First, our hope is found in the forgiveness that Jesus Christ alone can offer. Second, our hope is found in confession. It is as we claim our private sins that we are able to place them at the feet of Christ. Third, our hope is in the strength that God's indwelling Spirit can provide. We choose what thoughts, emotions, and desires we will allow to linger within us. God's Spirit can offer us the power to purge the evil away if we will give him full access to every facet of our lives. So be careful today with the secret life. In God's eyes it counts.

Prayer

Father, we pray for authenticity in our Christian lives. May we truly be on the "inside" what we profess to be on the "outside." Amen.

> "For no one can ever be made right with God by doing what the law commands. The law simply shows us how sinful we are."
> Romans 3:20 NLT

Observation

In the 3rd chapter of Romans, Paul announces two things very clearly. The first, we are all sinners. In very plain language Paul declares that none of us are righteous, "for all have sinned and fall short of the glory of God" (v. 23). He also points out, however, that all of us are made acceptable in the eyes of God through faith. "We are made right with God by placing our faith in Jesus Christ. And this is true for everyone who believes, no matter who we are" (v. 22). The key to salvation for any and all is faith in Christ. Unable to justify ourselves by any means, we discover a saving grace that comes through our trust in Jesus and in his sacrifice for our sins.

Application

There are many things in our day-to-day world that can point to how "sinful" we are; yet those things are powerless to fix the problems. For example, slip on a blood-pressure cuff and take a reading. If it reads "high" you know that an overindulgent lifestyle, or lack of exercise, has given you a problem. Or, step onto the bathroom scales. Again, the numbers might tell you what you have done wrong, but in and of themselves, the scales can do nothing to help you lose weight. Or speed excessively down the interstate and you will soon get a ticket. The ticket will tell you what you have done wrong and how much it may cost, yet it does nothing to solve the problem. Paul reminded the first-century world that the Law of Moses did not offer a saving grace. All the law could do was to point to everyone's inability to please God fully. The law could point to mistakes, but fail to ease the punishment. You see the problem... most of us know how badly we disappoint God. We just don't know how to fix the problem and make things right. But God does. As 1 John 4:14 states, "The Father sent the Son to be the Savior of the world." The truth is that we are hopelessly lost in our sins, but endlessly loved by our Savior. In spite of what we have done, or what we have become, Christ offers his life for ours. Take hope this morning. God's grace is greater than your sins. Trust in Christ and claim your pardon.

Prayer

Father thank you for offering us the hope of forgiveness through Christ. Amen.

"He was fully convinced that God is able to do whatever He promises.
And because of Abraham's faith, God counted him as righteous."
Romans 4:21-22 NLT

Observation

Chapter 4 of Romans is all about the faith of Abraham and how his faith brought him peace with God. Abraham knew the joy of entering a relationship with God. It was not that Abraham was a perfect man and sinless in every way. It was that Abraham believed in God, spoke with God, and attempted to be obedient to God. His faith in whom God was and in all that God could do brought him into righteousness. With God, it's always about relationship rather than religion.

Application

Abraham was fully convinced that God was able to do whatever was promised. It was that simple God-can-do-it trust that gave such passion, fulfillment, and reward to his life. Even when he and his wife Sarah were old, Abraham believed that God would keep the promise of creating a great nation from his offspring. How securely do we believe in God's promises? Are we convinced beyond the shadow of a doubt that God keeps promises? Surely such faith on our part would revolutionize our walk with God. God promises to save us as we call on His name (Rom. 10:13). God promises to be present with us always, even to the end of the age (Matt. 28:20). God promises to forgive us of our sins and to cleanse us from all unrighteousness (1 John 1:9). God promises to supply all our needs according to His riches in glory (Phil. 4:19). God promises to offer us peace in the midst of our anxiety (Phil. 4:6). The promises are many. What is revealed in those promises is the heart of God, who longs to be in relationship with each of us. Whenever we become convinced that God is a promise keeper, our faith increases exponentially. The greater our faith, the closer the relationship grows. Learn the lesson of Abraham. Pleasing God and knowing God's blessings is not about keeping all the rules, speaking in King James' English, or wearing stain-glass contacts. It's about living in a trusting relationship with God. How much do you believe about God?

Prayer

Father, I pray that you would count us as righteous. May our faith be strong and may our relationship with you flourish. Amen.

"So just as sin ruled over all people and brought them to death, now God's wonderful grace rules instead, giving us right standing with God and resulting in eternal life through Jesus Christ our Lord."
Romans 5:21 NLT

Observation

Paul spends a lot of time in this 5th chapter contrasting the sin of Adam with the grace of Jesus. He makes the argument that through one man, Adam, sin entered the world. He juxtaposes that thought with the idea that through one man, Jesus, grace conquers the world. It is apparent that without the sacrifice of Christ, we are hopelessly bound to our sins. But with the sacrifice of Christ, we are forever and completely forgiven of our transgressions.

Application

Until the coming of Christ, sin ruled the world and destroyed the hearts of men. But when Christ came, suddenly grace became the victor. To use Paul's words, "grace rules." What does such a word mean to us? What happens when grace wins out over sin? First, it means that our hope will find assurance. "Grace that conquers sin" reminds us that our hope will be realized. Our salvation will be brought to completion. Second, "grace wins" also reminds us that the wrath of God is always tempered by love for us. Though we are often deserving of punishment, God chooses to forgive our sins and restore the brokenness of our relationship. Third, grace also means that a better tool for both human and spiritual relationships has been put into place. Just as God models grace towards us, we must learn to model grace in our dealings with others. Relationships deepen, stress lessens, and burdens ease when we learn to live by grace and not by revenge. Grace calls us to a better life. I would remind you that grace is a choice. God chose to offer it to us and we must choose to now offer it to others. As you embark upon the beginning of a new day, let me ask, "Will others characterize your interaction with them as being 'grace-filled,' or will you insist on retribution and judgment?" I hope that you will let grace rule in your life so that others can see at least a glimpse of the reaction they can expect to receive from the God you claim to follow. Hatred, selfishness, and judgment have ruled long enough. It's time to let grace rule.

Prayer

Father, teach us to model the grace that you have shared with each of us. May we know the joy that comes when we learn to live like our Father. Amen.

Romans 6: Taking Back Control

"We know that our old sinful selves were crucified with Christ so that sin might lose its power in our lives. We are no longer slaves to sin."
Romans 6:6 NLT

Observation

Sin can only have power over our lives until we claim faith in Christ. From that time forward, sin can only have the power that we allow it to have. We are no longer slaves to its control. Does that mean that we will no longer sin? Of course not... but it does mean sin becomes a choice. Where once we were powerless to do anything about the influence of sin in our lives, we now have the ability, through Christ, to gain control over it. We are no longer slaves to sin, but obedient servants of Christ.

Application

To what are you a slave? If you take a moment to think about it, you may discover that you are a slave to many things. Some are enslaved by health issues. Others are enslaved by financial obligations. Still, others are enslaved by job pressures. I know others who are enslaved to their electronic taskmasters... cell phones, laptops, and web browsers. Such things dominate their lives. Here's what's crazy... most of us have the ability to choose our masters. We don't have to live unhealthy lifestyles, we don't have to spend more than we earn, and we don't have to let our possessions possess us. But we do. We surrender the control of our lives to foolish things. We can do better. Paul reminds us that in Christ, we are no longer slaves to sin. Faith teaches us that Christ has defeated such an enemy. But did you know that Christ also stands ready to help you defeat the other taskmasters in your life? The Bible promises that we can be more than conquerors (Rom. 8:37). It also promises that "greater is He that is in me, than he who is in the world" (1 John 4:4). It also teaches, that "God will supply all our needs according to His riches in glory" (Phil. 4:19). So maybe we do have a choice. Here's the secret. If we give our total allegiance to Christ, then nothing else can enslave us. Only one thing can truly be our Master. Living for Christ will re-prioritize our living. Do this. Name one of your taskmasters this morning. Pray specifically that Christ will give you the strength to put it to rest.

Prayer

Father, may we, in the powerful name of Jesus Christ, stand up and defeat one of the earthly things that tries to make us its slave. Amen.

> "I want to do what is good, but I don't. I don't want to do what is wrong, but I do it anyway." Romans 7:19 NLT

Observation

Our focus verse is among the "better known" verses of the book of Romans. In this passage, Paul describes our sin nature and how sin, which lives within us, seeks to control and manipulate us, causing us to do the very things that we know are wrong. It's a battle, right? We want to do what is good, but we somehow end up doing wrong. It's a reminder that the potential to be drawn into sin is still very great within us. Apart from the presence and power of Christ inside of us, surely we would fail.

Application

In the Garden of Eden, God gave Adam and Eve a single rule... "Do not eat from the tree that is in the middle of the garden." It wasn't long until the serpent appeared and made the suggestion to do otherwise. "Surely, you won't die... you will be like God, knowing good and evil." Eve ate of the fruit and encouraged Adam to do the same. Both Adam and Eve had the choice of obedience or disobedience. Both chose poorly.

Paul explains at length the limited power of the Law. The Law only speaks of Godly expectation. It outlines the boundaries. But in our twisted human nature we very quickly play with the possibilities of disobedience. It's as if the rules suggest an enticement. For example, when God commands, "You shall not commit adultery," we begin to wonder more deeply about why adultery is so forbidden. We play with the possibilities. We think about how such a sin would feel. And suddenly we are lured into disobedience. It's like the "Do not touch" sign on a freshly painted bench. Something drives us to disobedience. That something is our sin nature. It's the powerful voice within us that seeks to draw us away from God. So today, we have choices to make... listen to the voice of God's Spirit, or listen to the voice of temptation within us. Warning: temptation has an insatiable appetite. It will pursue us until it controls us. So where is our hope? It is in the power of Christ at work within us. We choose to yield to that power, or we choose to hear the destructive voice of sin and its possibilities. Which will you choose this day?

Prayer

Father, remind us that the potential to do evil is always powerfully embedded within us. Make us dead to our sin nature and call us to life through Godly obedience. Amen.

Day 125 Romans 8: A Better Prayer

"And the Holy Spirit helps us in our weakness. For example, we don't know what God wants us to pray for. But the Holy Spirit prays for us with groanings that cannot be expressed in words." Romans 8:26 NLT

Observation

This verse contains one of the greatest promises of the Bible. Paul reminds us that God has sent the Holy Spirit to help us in times of need and weakness. As an example, Paul talks about this matter of prayer. He reminds us that even when we don't know what to pray or how to pray, that the Spirit prays on our behalf, speaking the deep longings of our hearts that we cannot even express with words.

Application

Have you ever not known what to pray or even how to pray about a certain need? Most of us have experienced such a moment in our spiritual journey. Sometimes needs are so complex, problems so great, and solutions so vague, that it is beyond our wisdom to even know how to lift our petition before God. Sometimes we work through the solution that we desire from God before we even begin to pray. It's as though we don't really need God to help us find answers as much as we want God to do what we want. Maybe there is a better way. Maybe the soul-searching, no-idea-what-to-do kind of prayer is more honest, more humble, and more effective. Sometimes not knowing what to pray forces us to be totally God-dependent. It takes our wisdom, our thoughts, and our opinions totally out of the mix when we pray, "I have no idea what to do. I just need you to take control and demonstrate your miraculous power." Let me give you an example... Not long ago I was praying for a friend whose bad decisions have ruined his marriage, his career, and his reputation. Though I have prayed for him on many occasions, I find myself at a loss currently, to know what else to pray or how to even go about it. What I find myself doing is simply praying a prayer in which I place my total trust in God by saying, "Thy will be done." The truth is I don't have the answer to my friend's needs. But God does. So I have chosen to get out of the way and let God work. The Spirit groans the inexpressible words of my heart and I am comforted, knowing that a better prayer than I can pray has been offered. So take a little comfort this morning... the Spirit works mightily when your simple life falters.

Prayer

Father, thank you for filling our lives with your indwelling Spirit. May we find grace, hope, and comfort this day, knowing he intercedes for us. Amen.

Romans 9: "Working" on Faith

"But the people of Israel, who tried so hard to get right with God by keeping the law, never succeeded. Why not? Because they were trying to get right with God by keeping the law instead of by trusting in him. They stumbled over the great rock in their path." Romans 9:31-32 NLT

Observation

Boil down Paul's discussion in Romans 9 and you will discover that he offers a simple truth about God's acceptance and rejection of Israel. Many Jews believed that keeping the Law would justify them in the eyes of God. It was a salvation-by-works kind of mentality. "Do the right things and God will have to accept us." Paul tells us that it is not a rigid keeping of the Law that makes one right in the eyes of God, but simple faith instead. When we are joined to God through simple faith we find ourselves in the right relationship with Him.

Application

Perhaps we tend to think that the more "good things" that we do, the more that God will like us. We act as though we will earn our salvation by the things that we can do. If we go to church, give to the poor, use the right language, and treat people fairly, how can God resist loving us? Don't get me wrong... all those things are good practices, but they should be the result of our faith and not the catalyst for it. We simply don't "do" enough good things until the day comes that God is pleased with us. Instead, we discover that God already loves us and in response to that love, we do good things. That's a different way of thinking about God. Paul's message still needs to be heard. Getting right with God is still all about having a trusting relationship. God loves us, promises to save us, and offers the gift of Jesus. It is as we begin to trust in those promises that our salvation comes to life. Remember that God already loves us. We are already the objects of God's grace. Those who try to "earn" their salvation labor in vain. The gift is already offered. All we do is accept it and let God's grace begin to transform us. As you start your day, instead of trying to do enough good things to be loved by God, why not accept the fact that you already are and then concentrate on ways to draw closer?

Prayer

Father, teach us that it is more important to spend time in your presence than it is to spend our days trying to do good deeds. Give us a simple trust and a better faith. Amen.

"If you confess with your mouth that Jesus is Lord and believe in your heart that God raised him from the dead, you will be saved." Romans 10:9 NLT

Observation

In this chapter, Paul outlines the simplicity of the Christian faith. He reminds both the Jewish and Gentile audience that being made right with God comes through faith and nothing else. Notice the assurance of this verse... if you confess your faith and if you believe with your heart, you WILL be saved. Pretty straight forward, right? Following this word of promise, Paul then writes about the important role of sharing the Good News. "How shall they (non-believers) believe in Him whom they have not heard?" (v. 14). The gospel is a word of great hope and promise as long as it is shared.

Application

Many of us grew up with the "Roman Road" as a simple way of sharing our faith. Walking through several passages provided an easy way to at least begin the conversation of how to become a Christian. The presentation consisted of Romans 3:23—"All have sinned...," Romans 6:23—"The wages of sin...," Romans 5:8—"While we were yet sinners...," and Romans 10:9—"If you confess..." It was simple then and it is simple now. For whatever reasons, we tend to complicate the Christian message. We get hung up on discussions of ethics, the role of women, political ideology, church membership requirements, baptism, communion, and about a hundred other things. In fact, we are so fearful that someone will engage us in a discussion that we can't handle that we are hesitant to even begin faith-sharing conversations. Maybe it's time to strip away all that baggage and just present the simple promise of God's word. Read the focus verse again... "If you confess with your mouth that Jesus is Lord and believe in your heart that God raised him from the dead, you will be saved." It's a simple promise about salvation. Confess the Lordship of Christ and believe in the resurrection. In so doing you will gain salvation. Not too complicated, right? More than 90% of Christians have never led a non-believer to faith in Christ. I hope you can become one of the 10% that does. Take a moment and memorize our focus verse. Let it bolster any attempt you might make to share Christ with a non-believer. Simplicity can be a beautiful thing.

Prayer

Father, give us a simple passion for the lost and a simple message to share. Amen.

"For everything comes from Him and exists by His power and is intended for His glory. All glory to Him forever! Amen."
Romans 11:36 NLT

Observation

In Chapter 11, Paul discusses at length the ways in which God's grace is extended to the Gentiles. Using the metaphor of a tree, he speaks of how the disobedient branches of Israel have been stripped away and how other branches have now been grafted in. He reminds his audience that all people have the potential to share in Abraham's inheritance. Our inheritance comes through our faith in Christ.

Application

Our focus verse speaks clearly to the omnipotence of God. "For everything comes from Him and exists by His power." We are reminded that nothing has been created by accident. Creation is more than a random "bumping together" of cells and molecules. We have been purposefully created by God who spoke us into being. With both intentionality and power, God authored our existence. We are the result of God's willful and purposeful creative energy. Go back to Genesis 1:1... "In the beginning, God created..." as Paul asserts that we come from God and exist by God's power. Now check out the second part of this verse... "And is intended for His glory." Did you catch that detail? God has created everything in order to bring Himself glory. Put it together... we were created by God, we exist by God's power, and our purpose for being on the planet is to bring God glory. So the important questions of the day become, "Are we doing that? Do we glorify God through our actions, our words, our attitudes, our thoughts, and our relationships? Is all that we do, done to the glory of God?" Let's be honest and admit that not all days are lived that way. Often we stumble and fail to represent God well. So how can we glorify God by our existence? It takes intentionality. We have to awaken each day with the realization that glorifying God is the purpose of our lives. That realization will force us to make specific, deliberate, God-honoring choices. We don't accidentally bring God glory. We glorify God as we love Him with all our heart, soul, and strength. So today, be conscious of your calling. Remind yourself that every thought, every word, and every deed should bring God honor.

Prayer

Father, thank you for creating us uniquely, among all the people of earth. Remind us today that we are to glorify you with the totality of our being. Amen.

"Dear friends, never take revenge. Leave that to the righteous anger of God. For the Scriptures say, 'I will take revenge; I will pay them back,' says the LORD." Romans 12:19 NLT

Observation

Chapter 12 of Romans has a seemingly endless supply of wisdom. Paul talks of being a living sacrifice and of being transformed by the renewing of our minds. He speaks of Christian piety and humility. He speaks of the many parts of Christ's body and how each of us should play our role well. He also reminds us to be devoted to each other in brotherly love.

Application

"Never take revenge." Easier said than done, right? We humans seem wired for revenge. "Hurt me and I will hurt you," is how many of us think. The problem with revenge is that it eats away life's joy like cancer. In fact, revenge tends to escalate anger and injury. Remember the Law of Moses we sometimes quote? "An eye for an eye and a tooth for a tooth." We throw out this rule as though it gives us the right to enact revenge, when in reality this rule was offered in an attempt to keep revenge from getting out of hand. Moses was limiting the extent of retribution. A person could only injure someone else to the extent they had been injured, and never more. The demands of the Christian faith limit our right to revenge even further. Christ tells us to love our enemies and pray for those who persecute us. As Paul further explains in this passage, revenge is not a right that is ours to claim. It is God alone who will wield justice. In fact, Paul writes, "Never take revenge." How much of your life is consumed by the thought of "getting even?" How many days have you squandered by wallowing in anger and hatred? You are only cheating yourself of joy and limiting the life God intends for you to live. Theologian Fredrick Buechner reminds us that revenge is "like sawing off the very limb we are sitting on." We only destroy ourselves when thoughts of revenge overtake our hearts. Even while being nailed to a cross, Jesus said, "Father, forgive..." As you think of your enemies, what words are on your lips and what thoughts reside in your heart?

Prayer

Father, may we know the joy of offering forgiveness and extending grace. Amen.

"Give to everyone what you owe them: Pay your taxes and government fees to those who collect them, and give respect and honor to those who are in authority." Romans 13:7 NLT

Observation

Chapter 13 is a very powerfully written chapter in which Paul describes the respect we are to have for those who are in authority over us. Paul recognizes that good government provides a peaceful environment. A peaceful environment provides the best soil in which the gospel can spread and grow. Paul's insistence on paying taxes and fees may seem rather political to some, but understand his instruction is offered in the context of allowing government to aid in the protection of its citizens and in providing for the common good. Those who are respectful of the law will, in turn, be more respected by those who govern.

Application

"Give respect and honor to those who are in authority." Often, we give respect and honor when those in office happen to belong to OUR political party and espouse OUR political agenda. Republicans tend to honor fellow Republicans and Democrats tend to honor fellow Democrats. Respect is given only to those whom we like. We've lost a basic sense of respect and civility. Even as Christians who are called to offer respect and honor, we have exchanged our Christian duty (according to Paul) for a loyalty to political ideology and party. With an "ends-justify-the-means" mentality, we have talked ourselves into believing that it's okay for Christians to act very non-Christlike when we are talking politics. We use slurs, tell off-color jokes, resort to name-calling, and speak with disrespect. Sadly, it is often groups of Christians who offer the worst name-calling and venom spewing. Truth is, something greater than a political agenda is at stake—our Christian witness and our right to raise a respected voice. You and I can make a difference. It's okay to disagree with government or oppose a political leader. It is not okay to hate or to treat those with whom we disagree with disrespect. What if the Christians in our land lived this political year differently than we have the past few years? What if we listened patiently, differed respectfully, and prayed fervently? Could we not bring a sense of peace and reason to the stormy politics of our day?

Prayer

Father, may we become Christian citizens in every respect of that word. May our love for Christ be evident even in the ways we respond politically. Amen.

"For we don't live for ourselves or die for ourselves. If we live, it's to honor the Lord. And if we die, it's to honor the Lord. So whether we live or die, we belong to the Lord." Romans 14:7-8 NLT

Observation

In Chapter 14, Paul speaks about the dangers of criticizing others. He pleads for tolerance, especially among believers. Who are we to condemn or judge another's faith? His words really seem aimed at those who claim a moral superiority for how they practice their faith in comparison to others. Paul's advice is to live-out our faith in ways that we feel led, but don't condemn those who choose different expressions of faith. In particular, he writes about the eating of certain foods insisting that we live our faith in ways that don't provide a stumbling block to others.

Application

Our focus verse offers a very important word of teaching and challenge. All that we do should be done in a way that honors the Lord. In other words, we must live with a greater sense of accountability. We do not live to simply please our own desires or selfish whims. We live to honor the Lord. Such a calling forces us to be accountable to Christ and to others. We have to be conscious of the fact that our actions and words reflect on Christ and have the potential of influencing others. We cannot ignore our calling as Christians to live disciplined lives that are governed by the Lordship of Christ. We must understand the rippling effects of our example. We live to please Christ and to encourage others to do the same. It is not about us. To borrow from the great reformer, Martin Luther, "Our thoughts must be captive unto the word of God." We must govern ourselves to live within restraints so that our witness is a positive one. We must think in terms of what others might find offensive in our lifestyles in order to keep them from "stumbling." We must be willing to give up "self" in order to help others discover faith in Christ. We are called to encourage, lead, and invite with our actions, not repel and offend. So be conscious of the Savior you represent. We live to honor him and not simply to please ourselves.

Prayer

Father, teach us to develop the life-goal of honoring Christ in all that we do. Remind us that we must sometimes sacrifice selfish wants in order to help others grow in their faith. Amen.

"My ambition has always been to preach the Good News where the name of Christ has never been heard, rather than where a church has already been started by someone else." Romans 15:20 NLT

Observation

As Paul winds down his letter to the Christians in Rome, he offers them some final words of instruction. Specifically, he challenges them to encourage those who are weak in their faith. He reminds them that those who are strong must bear the "weaknesses" of those without strength. Knowing it is easy to become overwhelmed by the demands of the gospel, coupled with the pressures from one's culture, Paul calls those who are strong in their faith to give support to the weak.

Application

Paul felt a strong desire to reach out to those who had never heard the gospel. His mission was not to simply strengthen believers, but to introduce Christ to those who were unfamiliar with the story. That missionary zeal must find its way into the heart and life of the modern church. Though a portion of our work should be dedicated to helping believers to mature, a much larger portion should be devoted to giving hope to those who have yet to hear the gospel message. Sadly, most mainline churches have a better record of baptizing sons and daughters of their own members than they do of baptizing formerly unreached people. In other words, most churches tend to do more evangelism within the church walls than they do on the outside. Such a mentality only fosters a more limited gospel and a much larger unsaved world. There is something to be said for plowing new ground. The reason that many mature Christians fail to lead others to faith, is because they tend to surround themselves exclusively with believers. We tend to cling to those who think and respond the way that we do. So what happens to the lost soul in our midst? Nothing. No witness. No invitation. No significant conversation. So here's today's challenge. Begin a relationship with a non-believer. Initiate a dialogue with someone whose world-view and faith position does not match that of your own. Build the bridge of relationship and let the gospel find a way to walk across the divide. It will take time and effort, but how else will you impact the world? Claim a friend in the name of Christ. Pray that doors will open and hearts will warm.

Prayer

Father, give us a heart for people who have never heard the gospel of Jesus Christ and then give us an opportunity to start the conversation. Amen.

Day 133 Romans 16: Who's Avoiding You?

"And now I make one more appeal, my dear brothers and sisters. Watch out for people who cause divisions and upset people's faith by teaching things contrary to what you have been taught. Stay away from them."
Romans 16:17 NLT

Observation

This final chapter of Romans serves two important functions. First, Paul takes a moment to pass along his greetings to faithful friends who have aided him in his ministry. He mentions 29 different individuals by name, including the first Christian convert in the Province of Asia. Second, Paul offers final words of instruction, which are to strive for unity within the church by avoiding those who cause divisions. Clearly, there were some who were causing dissension by teaching false doctrine.

Application

It is interesting that Paul's final appeal to the Christians in Rome was a warning to avoid those within the church who cause divisions by their false teaching. Sadly, in the life of every church, there are always those who seek to cause division, and typically, it has nothing to do with doctrine. There are always those individuals who find some point of discontent and they long to have others join them in their frustration. They seek to infect others with the same unpleasantness that has settled into their own lives. These folks are easily recognizable as they keep the "corridor talk" stirred up, they gossip and spread their negativity by any means they can. Because they are angry or upset, they assume that others will be, too. Paul simply warns us to watch out for such people and "stay away from them." Such people do nothing to build unity in the life of the church. They tend to draw attention away from the greater goals of the church like encouragement of the saints and spreading the love of Christ to non-believers. I read recently that in that past 2000 years of human history, there have only been 4-5 years of total worldwide peace. I wonder if statistics are any better in the life of any church? Let me challenge you to think carefully about how you act in the life of your church. Do you heal or hurt? Compliment or complain? Soothe or stir? Commit to being a grace-filled person whose love for the Lord finds practical expression even at church.

Prayer

Father, forgive us when we substitute our personal agendas in place of your agenda for the church. May we be people of great faith and gentle passion. Amen.

"God is faithful, who has called you into fellowship with his Son, Jesus Christ our Lord." 1 Corinthians 1:9 NIV

Observation

In this first chapter of the book of 1 Corinthians, Paul makes a very clear call to unity among all Christian believers. He has heard that divisions are arising in the Corinthian Church as various factions are forming around those baptized by various individuals. Some claim to follow Paul. Others claim to follow Apollos. Still others claim to follow Cephas. He pleads for unity. There is to be no division in mind or thought. They have all been claimed by God for salvation. He reminds them that Christ is not divided and neither should they be as well.

Application

Our focus verse reminds us of God's faithfulness. It is God alone who has called us into fellowship. God didn't create division when creating the church, but called us into fellowship and that bond forces us to discover fellowship with each other. Think for a moment about all the various things that have tended to divide the people of God. Division has come along the lines of communion practice, worship style, clothing worn, doctrinal issues, pastoral leadership, Bible version used, the role of women, the color of carpet in the sanctuary, and a thousand other things. I even heard of a church that once divided along the lines of whether or not to put up a hat rack in the back of the church! Here's what happens... we begin to interject personal opinion and preference into the church. We assume ownership of an institution that was never created to be owned by anyone. We quickly lose sight of core values in exchange for personal preference. And so division arises among the faithful. And when division begins to separate hearts, the Kingdom loses both effectiveness and witness. The things that unite us must remain stronger than the arguments that seek to divide us. We find our unity in Christ. It's always our allegiance to him that creates harmony in the midst of personal-opinion-caused disruption. As you consider the role you play in the life of your church, always ask, "Is it about me, or is it about serving Christ?" May God help us to keep our focus on him.

Prayer

Father, we thank you for the Church, the body of believers in which you have placed us to grow and live. May our passions always be on serving Christ and not on pleasing self. Amen.

Day 135 — 1 Corinthians 2: Peeking at God

"No one can know a person's thoughts except that person's own spirit, and no one can know God's thoughts except God's own Spirit. And we have received God's Spirit (not the world's spirit), so we can know the wonderful things God has freely given us." 1 Corinthians 2:11-12 NLT

Observation

These two verses offer us a little dose of Pauline theology. Paul reminds us that we receive the Spirit of God at that point in which we become believers in Christ. Because we have the "indwelling" Spirit, we are able to understand God's heart, thoughts, and passion. In our focus verse, we are reminded that we can know much about God because the Spirit, who knows all things, reveals God to us.

Application

Sometimes when someone does an unexplainable thing we think, "You just never know what's going on inside of a person." By that, we mean that is impossible to ever fully know and appreciate the deep thoughts, emotions, and passions that are swirling inside of another human being. Even those closest to us sometimes do things we can't quite understand. Have you ever said, "I don't know what's gotten into you today," or, "I obviously don't know you as well as I thought I did." Our thoughts, emotions, and feelings are hidden deeply within us and it is rare for anyone to fully understand us. But God does. God knows the thoughts, the emotions, the fears, and the secret desires that rattle around in each of us. God formed us and watches over us. God is intimately acquainted with all our ways. Paul teaches us that such knowledge can go both ways. He reminds us that we can know, or at least begin to understand the mysteries of God. God is revealed to us through the Holy Spirit. It is the Spirit that prompts, teaches, and convicts. The Spirit also gives us the ability to pull back some of the curtains that hide the mystery of God. There are things that we can know about God, only through the Spirit's work. We will never know all there is to know about God but we are allowed a chance to peek at the wonderful inner mysteries of God's heart. God is revealed to us through the Spirit, placed in each of us. This day, you can know God's love, watch care, and patience because the Spirit reveals that to you.

Prayer

Father, thank you for revealing yourself to us through the work of your Spirit. Amen.

Day 136 1 Corinthians 3: Firm Foundation

"For no one can lay any foundation other than the one we already have—Jesus Christ." 1 Corinthians 3:11 NLT

Observation

Paul continues to work on a problem deeply rooted in the early church at Corinth. There was division in the church caused by a false pride over who had led which believers to faith in Christ. Some boasted of being in Apollos' group, others boasted about being in Paul's, still other boasted about being in Peter's group. Paul reminded them that they were acting like "people of the world." He told them that he needed to speak to them as "infants" in the faith. They were not yet ready to take on the solid food of his teaching. He was careful to remind them that the foundation of their lives was not resting on any man, but on Jesus Christ.

Application

We all know how important a strong and solid foundation can be for any structure. If the foundation is not well designed and well placed the entire structure will one day collapse. A neighbor of mind recently discovered a crack in a wall. He had to pay thousands of dollars for a company to come and jack up his house and repair a faulty foundation. To have ignored the problem would have resulted in further damage to his home. In a recent sermon, I made a reference to the foundation under the Empire State Building. That 90+ year-old building has remained sturdy, due in large measure, to the foundation that extends over 60 feet into the ground below. You get the point. Build a strong foundation and the structure tends to remain strong. Pay little attention to what you build upon and you are asking for trouble. Just ask the guys who built the Leaning Tower of Pisa! So what is your life built upon? What is the foundation that grounds your existence? People often attempt to build on any number of things... wealth, intellect, personality, pop culture, and maybe human wisdom... There is a long list of faulty and weak foundational stones. Notice Paul's counsel. Build your life on the foundation of Jesus Christ. Remember the words of the great hymn? "My hope is built on nothing less than Jesus' blood and righteousness. I dare not trust the sweetest frame but wholly lean on Jesus' name. On Christ the solid rock I stand all other ground is sinking sand... all other ground is sinking sand." So what or upon whom is your life being built?

Prayer

Father, grant us enough wisdom to build our lives on that which matters most. Thank you for the solid foundation of Jesus Christ. Amen.

Day 137 — 1 Corinthians 4: Mentor Worthy?

"So I urge you to imitate me." 1 Corinthians 4:16 NLT

Observation

Paul had a concern for the Christians in Corinth. His concern was whether or not they viewed themselves as servants or celebrities in Christ. There was a sense of spiritual arrogance and moral superiority on the part of some. Rather than take on the role of a servant, many held themselves in very high regard. Paul reminded them that true praise comes from God and not from men. He challenged them to imitate his life... one of dedicated work performed with a servant's heart.

Application

I wonder how many of us would dare to say to someone younger in the faith, "Imitate my life." Would our faith-example bear-up under such scrutiny? Would our words, lifestyle, and dedication be Christ-like enough to welcome someone's imitation? Probably not. In fact, most of us would be petrified with the notion of welcoming someone's close watch of our conduct and faith. And yet, such role modeling is vitally needed. In fact, I would suggest that it is our inability to mentor those younger in the faith that continues to weaken the witness of Christ to our culture. In other words, many of us are not "mentor worthy" because we don't want to be "mentor worthy." We don't want to be held to such a high standard because such faith would require so much of us. We would have to be disciplined in our words, our conduct, and our relationships. Authenticity and consistency would be required of us and most of us simply are unwilling to pay such a price. We shirk our responsibilities in exchange for an easier, less-demanding lifestyle. May God forbid. And may God forgive our casual Christianity. The world needs mentors. Your children need mentors. Your co-workers need mentors. There is great competition for the very souls of your friends and family. Are you willing to simply concede the battle to the enemies of faith? Or will you take on the challenge of being a worthy mentor? Whether you want them to do so or not, people have already begun to imitate your faith. Be worthy.

Prayer

Father, may we feel the weight of responsibility that rests on our shoulders as believers in Christ. Prepare our hearts for mentorship. Give us distinctive lifestyles and a dedicated passion for serving Christ. Amen.

"Your boasting about this is terrible. Don't you realize that this sin is like a little yeast that spreads through the whole batch of dough?"
1 Corinthians 5:6 NLT

Observation

This chapter stands at the heart of the Corinthian controversy. According to what is written in the text, one of the members was practicing sexual immorality by having a sexual relationship with his stepmother. Not only did the church tolerate such behavior, they even boasted about it happening within their midst. Paul blasted the church for allowing such behavior to go on. In no uncertain terms, he called for this member to be removed from the fellowship. Paul insisted on the right to judge those within the body who were not living up to Christian standards.

Application

Paul was concerned that any form of evil or immorality in the life of the church had the potential of spreading throughout the church and soiling the reputation of God's people. His thoughts are a careful warning to every church, reminding us of the important line to draw between acceptance and tolerance. Although the invitation to the gospel of Christ is certainly inclusive of all people, certainly all sins cannot be tolerated once that person is joined to the body of Christ. When we become believers, we accept the call to transformation. Christ loves us for who we are, but he calls us to a new and better life. Old ways of thinking, acting, and living have to be redefined by the light of the gospel. Christ has not saved us in order to give sanction to our sins but to redeem us from our sins and call us to new life. We must understand that any and all types of behavior are not to be accepted by the church. Those who refuse to allow the Spirit of Christ to transform their lives, calling them out of their former ways, must bear the discipline of the church. Paul goes so far as to say that they should be removed from the fellowship! Let's make it personal. Ask yourself, "Am I living a life that honors both the Lord and His church?" If the answer is no, then attack the problem areas of your life. Pray for strength. Seek counsel. Develop an accountability partner. Don't be the evil yeast that harms the dough. Be the redeemed sinner whose testimony will challenge others.

Prayer

Father, remind us that our reputation as individuals reflects on the reputation of Christ's church. Teach us to remove the sin from our lives so that we may bolster the witness of our church and lead others to a stronger faith. Amen.

"Even to have such lawsuits with one another is a defeat for you. Why not just accept the injustice and leave it at that? Why not let yourselves be cheated?" 1 Corinthians 6:7 NLT

Observation

In the first half of the 6th chapter of 1 Corinthians, Paul takes up the subject of lawsuits. Apparently, there were fellow members who were taking each other to court for various reasons. Rather than solve their differences through understanding and compromise, they took matters to the secular courts. Paul was disturbed that such a practice could harm the reputation of the church. What message would it send to the outside world if people within the church couldn't resolve their differences without using a judge?

Application

Winning is not always winning. (That's not a misprint!) Sometimes, we may win an argument or get our much-insisted way. But winning is not always the most important victory to claim. Paul insists that there are things that we do for the sake of the gospel and one of them is compromise. Such compromise is not the erosion of values, or the watering-down of belief, nor the giving-in to peer pressure. The compromise that Paul describes is our willful setting aside of our agendas, opinions, and egos in order to maintain a sense of unity and harmony within the Body of Christ. Paul says that sometimes it is better to accept injustice if it means a lack of conflict within the church. Paul was so concerned about the reputation of the church in the context of culture that he urged a willful keeping of the peace, even at the cost of compromise. Sometimes, in our stubbornness, we insist on getting our way. We insist on being right and belittling those who think differently from ourselves. We insist on winning even at the cost of disrupting the fellowship of the church. Many a church has split over firmly entrenched hotheads insisting on their way. Don't do it. The damage of winning can be much more destructive than the humility of defeat. Being a part of the body means striving for unity more than striving for personal victory. You may need to accept an injustice for the sake of keeping the peace. What matters most... a personal win or a protected witness? Winning is not always winning, especially if it hurts the church.

Prayer

Father, may we be willing to swallow our pride if it serves the greater good of the church. Amen.

Day 140 1 Corinthians 7: Will of God or Personal Opinion?

"Now regarding your question about the young women who are not yet married. I do not have a command from the Lord for them. But the Lord in His mercy has given me wisdom that can be trusted, and I will share it with you." 1 Corinthians 7:25 NLT

Observation

Chapter 7 is a rather lengthy chapter that touches on several subjects including advice on marriage, sexual relations within marriage, and the advantages of remaining single. Paul also writes with a sense of urgency as though it is his expectation that the Coming of the Lord would be very soon. In fact, he challenges his listeners to avoid distractions of any kind, including the taking of a wife, because each person's priority needs to be focused on their devotion to Christ.

Application

I am intrigued by our focus verse. I find it to be refreshingly honest. Paul is writing about the topic of single women and whether or not it is best for them to marry in light of the soon-approaching Day of the Lord. Put that discussion aside for a moment and notice Paul's approach on this topic. He honestly admits that he "does not have a command from the Lord for them." In other words, he is very careful to distinguish specific instructions revealed to him by Christ from those about which he only has an opinion. He is hesitant to use "It's God's will" kind of language when he has only Godly wisdom to share and not a direct word from the Lord. Refreshing, isn't it? Imagine finding a preacher who doesn't state his opinions as though they are the divine will of God. I'm a pastor, right? I spend a great deal of time pouring through the scriptures, asking for guidance, and seeking the intentions of God. I'd like to think that what I offer to folks week in and week out is insightful, accurate, and in keeping with God's purposes. But to claim a spiritual superiority is quite another thing entirely. I'd be a little leery of someone who always claims to know God's perfect will for your life. It's a journey we all walk and none of us have all the answers. So as we journey together, let's share what we know honestly and compassionately. You help me to understand God's will more fully and I will promise to help you to do the same.

Prayer

Father, we thank you for revealing yourself to each of us. Give us humility and honesty as we strive to teach each other in the faith. Amen.

Day 141 — 1 Corinthians 8: Be Careful How You Walk

"But you must be careful so that your freedom does not cause others with a weaker conscience to stumble." 1 Corinthians 8:9 NLT

Observation

This verse is at the heart of Paul's topic in this 8th chapter. The entire chapter discusses the subject of eating meat sacrificed to idols. The question was whether or not it was okay to do so. (Food used in pagan worship practices was often sold by local vendors after it had been offered in worship.) Because idols are not real, Paul insists that eating such food is not wrong. However, because all believers had not yet reached the same level of spiritual maturity, Paul reminds his hearers to be very careful as to the way they live out their faith. Something of no consequence to one believer may be offensive to another. Paul reminds his hearers to practice their faith conscious of the fact that they live in community with other believers.

Application

As we live out our faith, we must do so always remembering that we are part of a greater body of believers. There is a sense of accountability under which we live. Part of our charge is to encourage and "build each other up." We must be cognizant of the fact that our actions can have rippling effects on others. We may have come to terms with a certain topic when others have not, and we should not ignore how others percieve our actions. Paul determined that if eating "meat sacrificed to idols" caused another believer to stumble, then he would refrain from doing so. Most of us don't struggle each day with the issue of eating meat sacrificed to idols. But we may struggle with issues like social drinking, how we spend our Sundays, watching certain movies, or wearing certain fashions. Families will ultimately decide what is right in terms of Christian conduct. And though we are not placed in the position to judge others, we must, in fact, judge ourselves. We must always ask ourselves if our actions are offensive to the point that they may lead others astray. Again, we have to live knowing that part of the call of being a Christian is a calling to guard reputation, witness, and sphere of influence. It's a tough question to ask… "Are their aspects of our lives that need to be governed by a sense of faithfulness to younger, weaker Christians?" Let us remember that it is never about our selfish wants and desires, it is always about accountability to Christ.

Prayer

Father, remind us that we live in community with each other. May our lives build up and encourage, not offend and weaken others. Amen.

Day 142 1 Corinthians 9: Finding the Common Ground

"When I am with those who are weak, I share their weakness, for I want to bring the weak to Christ. Yes, I try to find common ground with everyone, doing everything I can to save some."
1 Corinthians 9:22 NLT

Observation

In this chapter, Paul describes his calling to preach the gospel. He outlines the "rights" he has to ask for food and drink as payment for his work, but doggedly refuses to accept anything from them so that he will in no way hinder the gospel by becoming a burden. Not in it for personal gain, Paul describes why he is compelled to preach the gospel—because of Christ's calling. In our focus verse, he describes his strategy for sharing Christ. Paul tries to find common ground with everyone in order to identify with them and lead them to faith.

Application

We connect with each other on the common ground of experience, occupation, hobby, and interest. That's how relationships form—something that we share in common helps to initiate a conversation and a potential friendship. There are a million ways of connecting to each other. For example, recently I was preaching a funeral and after the service, I met the grandson of the deceased. He told me that he was attending the University of Alabama and we quickly entered into a conversation about Alabama football. Those kinds of conversations happen all the time. We discover a connection, an interest, or a topic that becomes the bridge to a conversation and maybe to a friendship. That was Paul's evangelistic strategy. He sought to discover "common ground" with others so that potential faith-sharing relationships could be built. There was a great intentionality about his strategy that we should model. We ought to be in the constant process of building intentional relationships in order to share the story of Christ with others. Let's look for the common ground. Let's find a place where our interests intersect those of another in order to begin a relationship. And then with intentionality, let's use the relationship to initiate faith-sharing conversations. God can do much as we stand on the common ground.

Prayer

Father, teach us how to connect with others in ways that will allow us to share our faith in simple but deliberate conversations. Amen.

Day 143 1 Corinthians 10: The Way of Temptation

"The temptations in your life are no different from what others experience. And God is faithful. He will not allow the temptation to be more than you can stand. When you are tempted, He will show you a way out so that you can endure." 1 Corinthians 10:13 NLT

Observation

In this passage, Paul is using the story of the ancient Israelites' experience in the desert as an illustration of sin and consequence. They were tempted to do evil and therefore they had to bear the results of their action. Paul points to their idol worship, sexual immorality, and constant grumbling as ways in which they were tempted. He reminds his audience, and modern day believers as well, that we too must deal with the same pressures and problems of being tempted.

Application

We often use "tempted" or "tested" to describe the various pressures and urges in our lives that lure us away from God. But these words represent divergent concepts. Temptation is always evil. It is authored by Satan and the purpose of temptation is to disrupt our relationship with God and our adherence to God's will and purposes for our lives. Take for example, the tempting of Christ in the wilderness as Satan attempted to divert the ministry of Jesus. Testing, on the other hand, has the purpose of building in us a stronger faith. Testing originates with God and has as its result a stronger, more obedient faith. Consider Abraham, whose faith was tested on Mount Moriah when he was told to sacrifice his son. New Testament writer James gives further clarity. "Consider it all joy, my brethren, when you encounter various trials, knowing that the testing of your faith produces endurance" (James 1:2-3). "Let no one say when he is being tempted, 'I am being tempted by God'; for God cannot be tempted by evil, and He Himself does not tempt anyone" (James 1:13). So let's be clear about the promise that Paul is making. He reminds us that none of us are immune to temptation, but that God will give us the power to overcome that which tries to lead us down the wrong paths to journeys away from God's intention for our lives. So if you are feeling the draw to do the wrong thing, before things get worse, ask God specifically for the power and presence of mind to just say "no."

Prayer

Father, we thank you that you promise to give us strength as we face temptation. Give us discernment to see clearly and courage to act bravely. Amen.

Day 1441 Corinthians 11: Put on Your Faith, Not Just Your Hat

"A man dishonors his head if he covers his head while praying or prophesying." 1 Corinthians 11:4 NLT

Observation

In this chapter, Paul discusses two specific issues in the life of the church in Corinth. The first is a discussion of how to behave in public worship, specifically about whether or not it is appropriate to cover one's head while praying. The other topic is that of a proper observance of the Lord's Supper. Paul reminds them that they are to treat the Lord's Supper, not as a normal meal to be greedily consumed, but as a celebration of the Lord's death.

Application

Ever wonder why it's considered proper for all the men to take off their caps during a prayer? It all comes back to this word of instruction that Paul offers to the Corinthians, and serves as an example of how scripture affects modern church. This verse and discussion raises an interesting question in terms of Biblical interpretation and the veracity of scripture. A lively discussion can always be found among those who contextualize Paul's words and those who treat every teaching as binding on all churches in all places in all ages. Did Paul mean to dictate that men can never pray in worship with a hat, or that women can only pray while wearing one? Or, did Paul intend for this instruction to be a special word of counsel specific to Corinth? For example, when women pray in our churches, if they do so without a hat, is that a sin? Is this teaching considered as timeless instruction or a specific word to a specific church? It's a matter of interpretation that will go on as long as the church exists. However, let me pick up my earlier thought... should Bible verses affect modern culture and dictate behavior? Absolutely. But maybe not in a coercive way. God's word will touch and affect culture only if it has touched and affected the lives of God's people first. Here's my point... Scripture certainly has the potential to shape culture, but it can only do so as the people of God are willing to be shaped by it. We can certainly bemoan our God-less culture all day long, or we can shape our culture by actively living out our faith. We will impact the world to a much greater extent when we practice what we preach more than when we belittle those who don't share our theological perspectives.

Prayer

Father, make us careful students of the word who are not merely hearers only, but doers. Amen.

> "It is the one and only Spirit who distributes all these gifts. He alone decides which gift each person should have." 1 Corinthians 12:11 NLT

Observation

Chapter 12 is devoted to a discussion of spiritual gifts. In this chapter, Paul describes the various ways in which the Spirit of God equips each member of the body of Christ. A spiritual gift as defined in verse 1, as a "special ability" that the Spirit gives to each believer. Paul goes on to describe a number of various diverse gifts given to the body of Christ, in order that the body will have the ability to function and minister in the ways that God intends.

Application

Paul teaches us some very important things about spiritual giftedness. First, he reminds us that all of us who are a part of the body of Christ have been gifted by God's Spirit to perform an important function in the life of the church. Paul lists abilities like offering wise counsel, or possessing great faith, or declaring great truth. He reminds us that we all have a part to play—that each of us has been uniquely equipped and placed in a body of believers so that Kingdom work gets done. Second, he reminds us that it is the Spirit alone who decides which gift each person should have. In other words, you are who you are because God's Spirit has made you that way. And because we are all crafted by God and gifted by God, who among us should boast in possessing one gift over another? The real question in terms of the church is this, "Are you investing your gift in the life and ministry of the church?" Remember that God has not equipped us for individual work, but for contributing to the work of the Body of Christ. Whenever even just one of us chooses to be uninvolved we hurt the effectiveness of the church. God needs all of us, serving out of a sense of our giftedness, to effectively accomplish all that God wants done. So do this... pray for discernment about your spiritual gift. Try to discover what "spiritual ability" God has placed in your life. And then, as you begin to understand your gift, work on finding your place. Your gift is vital and your involvement is needed. The Body will be lessened by your absence, but strengthened by your presence. Go share your gift.

Prayer

Father, thank you for equipping us for the work of ministry by placing spiritual gifts within each of us. Make us good stewards of the gift. Amen.

"If I had the gift of prophecy, and if I understood all of God's secret plans and possessed all knowledge, and if I had such faith that I could move mountains, but didn't love others, I would be nothing."
1 Corinthians 13:2 NLT

Observation

Most of us are very familiar with the 13th Chapter of 1st Corinthians. We know it to be the "love" chapter because in it Paul describes the importance of love over and above all spiritual gifts. He reminds his audience that love becomes the passion and grace that tempers all our efforts. To those who might long for one spiritual gift or another, Paul emphasizes that a greater gift to possess is always the gift of love. We can possess many wonderful abilities that have the potential to help and heal, but undergirding any success that we might enjoy, is the spirit of love.

Application

Our focus verse offers a very real image of the importance of love. Look at the comparison that Paul makes. To have the gift of prophecy (or fervent preaching), to have the wisdom to understand all of God's secret plans, to have faith that literally could move mountains... wouldn't you think that in the eyes of the Kingdom, that you would be well-equipped to do amazing work? Who wouldn't want such gifts? But Paul insists that to love others, is still a greater gift. And what fascinates me about this verse is that the gift of love is one that we all already possess. Remember the Fruit of the Spirit... "Love, joy, peace, patience, kindness, goodness, gentleness, faithfulness, and self-control." It's listed first among the nine qualities that Paul lists in Galatians 5. But just because we possess this gift, doesn't mean we use the gift. Love is a choice. We choose to offer it, to share it, to be controlled by it. To share the gift is the greatest of all Kingdom work. It is what should motivate us, captivate us, and inspire us. People really don't care if you are a great orator, or an amazing Bible teacher, or if you can pray up a storm and cast the mountains into the sea. You will catch their notice when you catch their heart. Love will become the bridge over which the Spirit of Christ will walk. So choose to love... extend grace, offer forgiveness, speak kindly, listen carefully, and share sacrificially. Loving others will become the greatest legacy of your life.

Prayer

Father, we love because you first loved us. Teach us to share the love you have entrusted to us. Amen.

Day 147 — 1 Corinthians 14: Tell the Truth

"Let love be your highest goal! But you should also desire the special abilities the Spirit gives—especially the ability to prophesy."
1 Corinthians 14:1 NLT

Observation

In this chapter, Paul continues to discuss a variety of spiritual gifts and specifically discusses the importance of prophecy. Prophecy, in the context of Paul's instruction, did not refer simply to "foretelling" the future. It also referred to a "forth-telling" of God's truth. Paul suggests that the gift of prophecy strengthens, encourages, and comforts the entire church. Paul insisted that boldly proclaiming God's truth, to both believers and nonbelievers, offers valuable instruction.

Application

When God reveals a special word of insight or wisdom to any of us as believers, we must be careful with what we do with that word. According to Paul, we are to strengthen, encourage, and comfort the entire church. We are NOT to become arrogant, nor assume a sense of spiritual superiority over others. For example, one of the spiritual gifts that I believe I possess is this gift of prophesying. Week after week, I am blessed by God to offer a word of teaching to the congregation. My motivation for doing so is not to pretend that I'm better than any others, or that I am smarter or more spiritually qualified than the rest. I'm not. It's just one of the ways God has gifted me to function within the context of the church. Some in the church possess the same gift, others teach, some practice hospitality, while others display discernment. We all have gifts. God has gifted each of us for the common good and not personal gain. When we learn to share our gifts, the church is blessed and the Kingdom moves forward. In fact, I rather suspect that most Christians have a hint of the gift of prophecy within them. As God reveals truth to each of us, we should look for ways to encourage the church. It may not be through a 22-minute sermon, but in a simple conversation, or a gently offered word of advice. The point is not to hoard the wisdom we gain from God, but to share it. We need each other, and we need the spiritual insight that others offer. What has God revealed to you this week? Look for opportunities and conversations in which you can share that insight with others.

Prayer

Father, remind us yet again, that we are gifted for the common good. May we use our abilities and gifts to build the church and to encourage others. Amen.

"Don't be fooled by those who say such things, for 'bad company corrupts good character.'" 1 Corinthians 15:33 NLT

Observation

In this chapter, Paul offers a very careful reminder of Christ's resurrection appearances and then moves into a discussion of how our "earthly bodies" will one day give way to our "spiritual bodies." He writes with great hope and assurance as he describes the way in which we will be raised to life through Christ. Much of his writing is to counter false teaching that had surfaced in the life of the church. There were some who suggested that there was no resurrection from the dead. He warns his listeners not to "be fooled by those who say such things."

Application

Verse 33 is an important verse, not only in terms of false teaching within the church, but also in terms of life management. The company we keep will shape our character. If we surround ourselves with good, noble, and moral people, our lives could soon reflect such character. Surround ourselves with those who are just the opposite and soon our lives could move in a completely different direction. We live in community with each other. Our lives are affected positively or negatively by those around us. Joyful people can make us joyful... negative people can spread their negativity into our lives. So be careful of the company you keep. Weigh out the "character qualities" that begin to surface in your life as a result of the time spent in their presence. In Paul's words, "bad company can corrupt good character." I think the opposite is also true... "good company can build better character." Ever travel to a different region of the country where people speak with a different accent and dialect? After just a few days ever notice yourself using a new expression or saying some words in just a slightly different way? (I have a friend who is Swiss and every once in a while she slips and says the word, "Y'all," and I just have to laugh. We've corrupted her!) People affect us. So take on this question... "How are you influencing the lives of those around you?" Do you corrupt or correct? Do you encourage good behavior or bad? Do you teach Christian ethics or worldly compromise by your actions? Be mindful of your influence and pray that you might be as "salt and light."

Prayer

Father, give each of us a situational awareness. Make us conscious of the influence that others are having on us and that which we are having on them. Amen.

Day 149 — 1 Corinthians 16: What's Your Hurry?

"Perhaps I will stay awhile with you, possibly all winter, and then you can send me on my way to my next destination."
1 Corinthians 16:6 NLT

Observation

Paul ties up a few loose ends in this final chapter of 1 Corinthians. He writes about the offering that he is collecting for the believers in Jerusalem who are suffering such great persecution. He also offers a few words of final instruction about how they are to treat various leaders in the faith who will come through Corinth. He then wraps up the letter with a few final greetings. It is written with an attitude of great affection for a church he dearly loves.

Application

As I read through this final chapter I tried to understand Paul's timetable in terms of his travel schedule. In our focus verse, he speaks of his plans to possibly spend all winter with the believers in Corinth. Yet, a few verses later, he writes that he will stay in Ephesus at least until after the Feast of Pentecost before coming their way. Pentecost always falls in the late spring. It is 50 days after Passover. So at some point Paul will travel, maybe during the summer months, through Macedonia and then to Corinth, where he will enjoy an extended stay. These were not quick trips and short stays. Why does any of this matter? Relationships take time. Paul knew that it was impossible to invest in people without spending time with them. And so he would plant his life in various cities, sometimes for years. We likewise should invest carefully and deliberately in the lives of others, and take time to nurture relationships. I truly believe that one of the shortfalls of 21st Century Christianity is our lack of attention to relationships. Most of us have more on-line "friends" than we do the flesh and blood type. We "chat" but seldom talk. We offer quick words of greeting and maybe a casual conversation, neglecting the hard work of deeper relationship. Transformative relationships are never the shallow type. They take time, effort, and intentionality. I encourage you to go deep into some relationships for the purpose of sharing your faith. You can only impact those lives where the relationship is not rushed and where the conversations are anything but casual. Invest the time for the sake of the Kingdom and watch how God will work.

Prayer

Father, give us depth in our relationships. Allow us to build bridges of friendship over which the gospel may one day travel. Amen.

Day 150 2 Corinthians 1: The Give and Take of Comfort

"He comforts us in all our troubles so that we can comfort others. When they are troubled, we will be able to give them the same comfort God has given us." 2 Corinthians 1:4 NLT

Observation

The book of 2 Corinthians opens with a typical Pauline greeting in which he identifies both himself and the intended recipients of his writings. He tells his readers of the terrible persecution that he has endured in Asia Minor. It was all but unbearable, but it taught him to rely on God for both comfort and deliverance.

Application

Paul describes the give and take of comfort. He reminds us that God comforts us in the midst of all our troubles. And then, as recipients of comfort, we are expected to offer comfort to others in God's name. That's the give and take of comfort. We receive it, and we are expected to give it. I see this Kingdom demand lived out weekly in the life of a woman in my church. A couple of years ago, she lost her husband of many years to death. The loss was devastating. It placed her in a deep emotional hole that only now has she begun to escape. It's been a long journey, but here is what I have started to notice. Somewhere deeply within her heart, she has found the capacity to offer compassionate care to others in the midst of their grief. She understands it. She gets it. And so she reaches out to help others cope in quiet and profound ways. The comfort of God's Spirit in her life has led her to be on the giving end of grief. That's how it works. We receive the grace of God and we role model it before others. We find a comfort to share from our own experience of grief. We find grace to offer from our own acceptance of God's kindness. We find hope to proclaim from the hope offered to us in Christ. Use the experiences of life that have come your way. Learn to become a contagious Christian. In whatever ways God has touched your life, touch others in God's name. It's a give and take kind of thing. It's how the gospel becomes flesh and blood, over and over again.

Prayer

Father, thank you for being the God of all comfort. Thank you for rescuing us from all alarms. Turn our gratitude into gifts of grace that we can offer to others. Amen.

"But thank God! He has made us His captives and continues to lead us along in Christ's triumphal procession. Now He uses us to spread the knowledge of Christ everywhere, like a sweet perfume."
2 Corinthians 2:14 NLT

Observation

In our focus verse, Paul uses two very distinct images. The first is of a triumphant procession. In the Roman world, conquered armies were often taken captive and paraded in a victory procession. Paul uses the image to describe the way in which we are rescued from sin and made glorious captives by Christ. We are led by him in a triumphant procession. The second image is one of sweet perfume that spreads throughout the air. Often, again in a triumphant parade, incense was burned. People not only saw the parade, but its sweet smell filled their nostrils. Paul mentions that our witness spreads the knowledge of Christ like a sweet perfume.

Application

Scents can be rather distinctive, and scent is often attached to memories. For example, when I was a young boy, my grandmother used to take my brother and me to a local park. A bakery was located across the street and so as we played, we could always smell that bread. To this day, the smell of baking bread chases me back to that memory. Here's another example... Years ago, I participated in several mission trips to Brasilia, Brazil. I noticed that the city seemed to have a certain smell. I didn't notice it at first, but on a second trip the scent immediately caught my attention. On a third trip I experienced the same reaction. It was not a good smell, nor a particularly bad smell, just a distinctive one. Almost 20 years later I can still conjure it up in my mind. Paul reminds us that as believers, we are to be like a sweet perfume. Our witness, our testimony, and our faith should be so distinctive that people notice. In fact, every time people are around us, they should be reminded of Christ. We should be like an unforgettable scent that fills the air. So how distinctive is your faith? Is it memorable? Does something about your life cause others to think of Christ? It's not about your smell, but your distinctiveness. Live in such a way at others are caused to remember Jesus.

Prayer

Father, may our Christian influence be like a sweet perfume that spreads its aroma to all those with whom we have contact. Amen.

"But the people's minds were hardened, and to this day whenever the old covenant is being read, the same veil covers their minds so they cannot understand the truth. And this veil can be removed only by believing in Christ." 2 Corinthians 3:14 NLT

Observation

Paul contrasts the old covenant with the new. He speaks of the ways in which God once related to people and how they found justification through the law. In contrast, he offers words about the "glorious" new covenant found in Christ. In Christ there is freedom from the law of do's and don'ts. Faith is bound up in relationship and not religion.

Application

Paul borrows an image from the day of Moses. When Moses descended from the mountain after being in the presence of God, his face shown so brightly with the glory of God that he had to cover it with a veil in order for the people to look at him. God's glory, in a very real sense, was veiled from their eyes. In like fashion, because of disobedience, their lives were veiled from God's truth. They failed to fully see and appreciate the glory of God. Paul writes that until each of us finds faith in Christ the glory of God will be veiled in our lives and we will not fully understand God in the ways He longs to be revealed. In other words, we live a "veiled life" until our faith is placed in Christ. Some people simply go through the motions of living. Sure, their hearts beat, their lungs fill with air, they walk, and they work. But for these people life is an endless succession of empty days and meaningless moments. It is as though a veil shrouds their lives blocking joy, purpose, and zest. They have never discovered the joy of a relationship with Christ. Remember that Jesus has come to give us life and give it in abundance (John 10:10). Real life doesn't come about through the chasing after a new job, the next car, the next house, or the next spouse. Real life comes through a relentless pursuit of Christ, for when we find our place in him we discover peace, joy, and purpose. Do you need to remove the veil? Seek the things of Christ... serve, forgive, heal, love. Give yourself away in God's name and watch how the clouds of despondency soon part and the real joy of living floods your life.

Prayer

Father, forgive us for living a veiled life... one that doesn't honor you nor use your invested gifts in our lives. Teach us to find real life through our pursuit of Christ. Amen.

Day 153 2 Corinthians 4: Gazing on Things We Can't See

"So we don't look at the troubles we can see now; rather, we fix our gaze on things that cannot be seen. For the things we see now will soon be gone, but the things we cannot see will last forever."
2 Corinthians 4:18 NLT

Observation

Paul spends a lot of time in this passage speaking about the transcendent power of the gospel, which is embodied in each of us. Though we are weak, fragile, and woefully inadequate as vessels that would hold any treasure, God has chosen to place the gospel story in each of us. We become the keepers of the treasure and the guardians of the gospel. What joy to know that even in our fragile state, we hold the eternal truth of God.

Application

It is important to remember to look beyond what we can see, to hope in that which we cannot yet experience. Faith is always that way. It challenges us to fix our gaze on things we cannot yet see. It invites us to travel to destinations not yet imagined. In fact, the very essence of faith is the "assurance of things hoped for and the conviction of things not seen" (Hebrews 11:1). A few years ago, while on a youth beach trip, one of our students had the experience of seeing the ocean for the very first time. He had heard others talk about the ocean and had seen pictures and watched movies—he knew what he should expect to see. But he had never felt the warm sand between his toes and the power of the waves. He had never watched small crabs rush back to their holes or seen the sea oats blow in the breeze. When the day came for him to walk down to the ocean for the first time, he was at a loss for words. His eyes danced up and down the shore. He played at the edge of the surf like a timid young child. He built castles in the sand. He had dreamed of the day when he would stand in such a place. To actually be there, brought him immense joy. Something of God's unfolding Kingdom is like that teenager's first trip to the beach. We long for it. We pray about it. We dream of what we will experience. And when that day finally dawns we will revel in it. But for now we can only gaze on the unseen, knowing that even our wildest imaginations can't begin to conjure up its glory. How exciting to know that at the end of our pursuit of faith, we will experience that of which we can only now dream.

Prayer

Father, give us the hope of heaven. Keep us steadfast as we move toward that day. Amen.

Day 154 2 Corinthians 5: "Tell Me I'm Forgiven and Loved..."

"For God was in Christ, reconciling the world to Himself, no longer counting people's sins against them. And He gave us this wonderful message of reconciliation." 2 Corinthians 5:19 NLT

Observation

This is one of those chapters that needs to be read repeatedly in order for Paul's words to really sink in. It begins with a passage about death and how we are raised in Christ with "heavenly bodies." In fact, going against the popular Greek thought of the day that separated body from spirit, Paul writes, "For we will put on heavenly bodies; we will not be spirits without bodies" (2 Corinthians 5:3 NLT). Paul also speaks about our role as believers in being ambassadors for Christ through whom God makes appeal. Finally, Paul closes the chapter by speaking of the ministry of reconciliation that we are challenged to share.

Application

I want you to notice the amazing promise made to each of us in our focus verse. Through the work of Christ, God is continually in the process of reconciling the world to Himself. And in order to do that, God no longer counts our sins against us. Yes, you read that correctly. In Christ, God no longer counts our sins against us but removes them so that we might enjoy a life with Him. Sin separates. It places a huge barrier between God and us. Our sins are many and so our separation from God is vast. But because of Christ's death on the cross as payment for our sins, God reconciles, or "reconnects" us with Himself. As the popular song suggests, "Our chains are gone, we've been set free." Understand that sin is a real problem... always will be. We will struggle with our transgressions for as long as we are on the planet, and yes it is important to know the cleansing that comes each day through confession. But also understand that what we will NOT struggle with is having a method by which we find our cleansing. The method of grace was established long ago. The price has been paid; the debt has been erased. In Christ, we are reconciled with God, our sins no longer counted against us. So go and live a good life today... one filled with joy and grace and peace, knowing that as bad as your past has been, you awoke this day forgiven, loved, and in the presence of God.

Prayer

Father, this morning, we praise you and thank you for the gift of grace that continually calls us to a new and better life. Amen.

"Therefore, come out from among unbelievers,
and separate yourselves from them, says the LORD.
Don't touch their filthy things,
and I will welcome you." 2 Corinthians 6:17 NLT

Observation

In our focus verse, Paul is challenging these early Christians to maintain their purity as they learn to be the Temple of the Living God. His point is not to be separated and aloof from the unbelieving world, but rather to be unstained by it. He warns them about "touching their filthy things..." He is speaking about idol worship and things dedicated to such a practice. Paul does not want them to corrupt themselves by embracing any part of such practices.

Application

Influence can be a two-way street if we are not careful. We always influence the people around us and they have a tendency to influence us in return. That give-and-take can be a very positive thing, especially in terms of being among other Christian believers. My faith can rub off on you; your faith can rub off on me. That exchange of ideas, truth, and insight can be a very needed and positive thing. But Paul's warning concerns how we deal with non-believers. By all means, we are to embody the Christian faith in their presence with the hope that something of the gospel will touch their lives and lead to further dialogue. We are certainly called to change the world and that happens through each relationship and conversation we have with those yet to know Christ. But we must be careful to control the flow. In other words, in our contact with nonbelievers, let us guard our hearts and minds, lest we be drawn into doing things that mar our witness and corrupt our faith. We must seek to influence others while carefully guarding the treasure within us, lest we corrupt the image of Christ in us. Please understand... our place is not to judge others, nor trick ourselves into some hubris that gives us a moral superiority. Our place is to live authentically with hearts that are impassioned to love others with the love of Christ, in the hope that we might offer them a greater way of living. So be careful of the flow... be mindful of which direction the influence travels.

Prayer

Father, give us courage to live bold lives and grace with which to temper our contact with others. May we never offer a rude nor offensive Christianity, but one that leaves others longing to know more of the mystery of our faith. Amen.

"Because we have these promises, dear friends, let us cleanse ourselves from everything that can defile our body or spirit. And let us work toward complete holiness because we fear God." 2 Corinthians 7:1 NLT

Observation

Our focus verse is a carry-over from the previous chapter in which Paul describes the ways in which we are sons and daughters of God. Paul reminded the Corinthians that God had promised to be a Father to them and also to us. In light of those promises, Paul challenges us to cleanse ourselves from that which can defile body or spirit. We are to work at being completely holy, distinct, and set apart, because of our reverent respect for God.

Application

Cleansing is a constant challenge. Whether we speak of our homes, our cars, or our bodies, it seems that there is never an end to the process of washing away the dirt and setting things right again. I like to drive a clean car and so I probably wash my car more than most. Cars get dirty because we drive them around in this world. Our bodies get dirty. We take daily showers and baths because we want to keep the dirt and grime away from our bodies. Keeping a house clean is also a constant struggle. No matter how much you dust, vacuum, and wipe clean, it doesn't take long before the process needs to be repeated. So Paul's challenge makes great sense. We have to cleanse ourselves from everything that defiles body or spirit. He is speaking about cleaning our minds and purifying our hearts. And like everything else, spiritual cleansing is a constant process that demands constant attention. It's not like we can pray a "one time" prayer of forgiveness and never have a need for grace again. It's not like we can read the Bible every once in a great while and consider ourselves "well-fed." Maintaining our lives before God takes daily attention, effort, and yes, cleansing. We need to confess our sins and seek the grace of God with each new day. The longer we neglect our spiritual lives, the darker they become. Start the day with a little cleansing. Confess your sins as honestly as you can before God and vow to do better. Ask God to purify, forgive, and cleanse. And remember, as long as you travel around this world you are going to get dirty again. So repeat the cleansing process often, even daily.

Prayer

Father, remind us that our sins separate us from you. Teach us the value of cleansing ourselves spiritually so that we can enjoy moments in your presence. Amen.

Day 157 — 2 Corinthians 8: A Little Give and Take

"Right now you have plenty and can help those who are in need. Later, they will have plenty and can share with you when you need it. In this way, things will be equal." 2 Corinthians 8:14 NLT

Observation

One of the on-going tasks that Paul continued to write about in his letters was the offering that he was collecting to take to the church in Jerusalem. The church in Jerusalem was suffering great hardship and persecution. Paul had asked many of the churches to which he wrote to aid the Jerusalem church by collecting an offering that would help to alleviate their suffering.

Application

In our focus verse, Paul describes a little "give and take" scenario. Out of their current prosperity, he asks the Corinthians to give to those in need. He reminds them that the day will come when they themselves will have need and those once impoverished, will remember their generosity and will gladly share with them of their own resources. There is a fine line between prosperity and poverty and most of us have known how easily the pendulum swings between the two. Certainly Paul writes about monetary things, but his words can also be applied to a "poverty of spirit" as well. There are moments when life will rob us all of joy and gladness. Moments will come that will force us to be in need of encouragement, grace, and prayer. And in those moments, we will certainly look to the Christian community that surrounds us to renew our strength and give us hope. We will also live on the other side of hardship, meaning that we will also know abundant joy and contentment. In those moments, Paul asks us to consider how to help those in need. We live in community with one another. Part of our Christian faith demands that we learn to give and take. In times of emotional, spiritual, and yes, financial abundance, we are to share with those in need, knowing that the days may well come when we will have to rely on the strength of others to help us in our times of crisis. There is a sharing of life that enriches us no matter what life throws in our direction. The Greek word of the New Testament that describes this sharing of life is "koinonia," translated "fellowship." We will live well when we live in the community of God's people. Share what you have and take what you need. Together, we will survive.

Prayer

Father, thank you for surrounding us with communities of faith. May we learn the value of careful investment in those communities. Amen.

"Remember this—a farmer who plants only a few seeds will get a small crop. But the one who plants generously will get a generous crop."
2 Corinthians 9:6 NLT

Observation

Paul is talking about way more than agriculture. Although it is true that a farmer can grow more crops if he plants more seeds, Paul is actually teaching the Corinthians about being more generous in their giving towards the needs of the church in Jerusalem. It is as they give generously towards those needs that God will in turn, continue to bless those who have given. Those who have learned the joy of giving will find both abundance and assurance.

Application

Do you have a "rainy" day fund? Do you keep a little cash stashed away somewhere in case of an emergency? Some people have a special savings account they never touch unless the need is very, very critical. Others use a safety deposit box. Some place their savings under a mattress while others fill up mason jars and bury them in the back yard! Many think that the tighter the grip on their wealth, the more protected their lives (and wealth) will be. But Paul offers a little different strategy. Rather than hoard it all, Paul suggests making a careful investment in others. The real security for life is not the investment you make in the bank, but rather the investment you make in people. So the challenge is to plant your life generously in the lives of others. Our real savings is not measured in dollars and cents but in the depth of friendships built with others. Friendships take time. They take attention. They take nurturing, commitment, and energy. But the dividends are priceless. Who better to walk you through a crisis than your closest friend? Who better to hold your hand in the midst of grief, or speak a word of hope in the midst of trial, or pull you up when life has thrown you down? The poor of the world are not those without money... the poor are those without friends. So plant a lot of seeds. Give yourself away in relationships. Nurture lifelong friends by connecting often. Develop new friends as often as you can. Let your life-saving investment become the people in your life who love you, support you, and carry you. Sow generously and you will live well.

Prayer

Father, we thank you for the key relationships in our lives that really matter. Teach us how to invest well in the lives of people. Amen.

"When people commend themselves, it doesn't count for much.
The important thing is for the Lord to commend them."
2 Corinthians 10:18 NLT

Observation

Paul spends a few verses defending his work and ministry. He reminds his readers that anyone can boast about themselves and the glorious things they think they have done. Such boasting is worthless. It is what God thinks about our work that is important. We live not to please ourselves or even others, but to please God. It is God's praise that we seek.

Application

We like a word of praise every now and then. We like to be told that we have done a good job. As children, we craved a word of affirmation from our parents or teachers. We wanted our coaches to tell us that we had played well. As adults, we still crave affirmation. We want to be told that we are good parents, or that we have been a good spouse. We want the boss at work to pat us on the back every once in a while and tell us, "Good job!" Words of affirmation and praise keep us going. They soothe the psyche and feed the ego. They help motivate us to keep moving toward important goals. I hope that you have those people in your life who offer you that kind of support and encouragement. I hope you receive a little praise every once in a while from the people in your life who matter most. And, I hope you are that kind of person for someone else. It doesn't take a lot to offer a positive word of encouragement but it can mean a great deal. It's needed in every life and maybe you have someone you need to praise before the end of the day. Back to Paul's words... As important as it is to receive the praise of others, there can be no higher praise than that of our Lord. The goal for which we should all strive is for Christ to say on that final day, "Well done, good and faithful servant." Could there be any higher affirmation than for Christ to recognize our faithful witness and dedicated service? We will earn that praise through daily discipline and dedication. It is when we live authentically, forgive abundantly, and share sacrificially that we will know the joy of his affirmation. Sure, it's nice to be told every once in a while that we are doing well by our co-workers, friends, and families. But how much greater joy will be ours as we complete a faithfully lived life in the eyes of Christ?

Prayer

Father, find us faithful, consistent, loving, and thoroughly Christian. Amen.

Day 160 2 Corinthians 11: Living in Community

"Who is weak without my feeling that weakness? Who is led astray, and I do not burn with anger?" 2 Corinthians 11:29 NLT

Observation

Paul takes a few moments to defend his ministry to the Corinthians. He reminds them of all the extensive beatings and abuse he has suffered for the sake of the gospel. He also speaks about his intense love for all the believers. In a statement that declares his empathy and sensitivity for them, he writes, "Who is weak without my feeling that weakness? Who is led astray, and I do not burn with anger?"

Application

There is something about the Christian faith that forces us to feel the hurts, joys, and emotions of others. Christ calls us into community with each other as a "body of believers" and as such, we must understand, know and even feel the hearts of our fellow Christians. We should not see someone's hurt, or learn of his or her pain, and not be affected by it. How can we claim to love our brothers and sisters in Christ and be insensitive to some moment of turmoil in their lives? The truth of the matter is this... we long for others to feel our pain. We want someone to appreciate all that we are going through. We long for someone to help us carry our burden in a time of crisis. So why would we fail to offer it to someone else? There are always those moments when faith gets messy. There are those moments when we would rather look the other way or distance ourselves from someone's needs, but true faith doesn't give us those options. We hurt when others hurt. We bear their burdens. We share their joy. We listen to their doubts. None of us can live this life of faith as "lone rangers." We need each other. So take a moment and consider your place in the community of faith. Are you fully invested? Have you made the needs of others as YOUR needs? Will you carry another's pain? Share another's hope? Rejoice in another's triumph? May each of us learn the value of community and may we give ourselves fully to being connected to one another.

Prayer

Father, thank you for placing us in a community of faith. Thank you for the support, encouragement, joy, and strength it provides. May we be as eager to contribute to the body as we are to take from it. Amen.

Day 161 — 2 Corinthians 12: Finding Strength

> "Each time He said, 'My grace is all you need. My power works best in weakness.' So now I am glad to boast about my weaknesses, so that the power of Christ can work through me." 2 Corinthians 12:9 NLT

Observation

In this passage, Paul is still trying to defend his apostleship by describing both a vision he had of paradise and further persecution he suffered as a proclaimer of the faith. He says that, in order to keep from becoming proud, God had "given him a thorn in the flesh." What Paul means by that phrase has been discussed for generations. Was it a physical ailment? Was it a persistent adversary? We are not told. But we are told that Paul discovered great peace and power in his life when pride was replaced with humility, and when arrogance was replaced with dependency. He discovered that "more of Christ and less of self" made for a better life.

Application

Most of us tend to be rather self-sufficient. We want to control every aspect of our lives. We want to do things the way WE want to do things. But every once in awhile, life hands us one of those crippling moments when we soon discover that life is not ours to control and that sometimes we can only hang on and see where the storms take us. It may be a physical illness that removes us from the captain's chair. It may be a financial collapse that wrestles control away from us. It may be a relationship snag that leads to upheaval. Sooner or later we will discover that we are not as self-sufficient as we once thought. What happens then? Hopefully, we rediscover the peace of God-dependency. We learn the lesson of once again placing our trust, our hopes, and our lives in the powerful hands of our Father. Like Paul, we may well discover that when we are at our weakest point, that God can work most powerfully in our lives. As we surrender control to God's guidance and will, we discover a peace and contentment that reminds us that, in God's grace, all is well. Sure, we don't want to go through times of stress and illness that bring us to our knees, but aren't we glad that when such storms come, that we can discover again where our hope and dependency should always rest. In that discovery, we will find God's amazing power and plan. Feeling a little weak these days? Life overwhelming you? Maybe you are just in the exact place God wants you to be.

Prayer

Father, teach us to lean more on you and less on ourselves. We thank you for those moments that draw us closer to you. Amen.

"Examine yourselves to see if your faith is genuine. Test yourselves. Surely you know that Jesus Christ is among you; if not, you have failed the test of genuine faith." 2 Corinthians 13:5 NLT

Observation

In this final chapter to the Corinthians, Paul tells of his up-coming visit to Corinth and how he hopes to find them faithful once he arrives. His words carry a little sting as he warns that he will "not spare anyone," meaning that he will not hesitate to preach very powerfully to them about their lack of repentance. He calls them to self-examination to determine if their faith is genuine.

Application

Notice that twice in our focus verse that Paul uses words like "examine," and "test." He wants them to do a little self-assessment to see if their faith is real and if their lives reflect the Lordship of Christ. He asks them to do a little spiritual check-up to see how well they measure up. Self-examination can be a difficult discipline, especially if we are honest with ourselves. Most of us do a little self-assessment each day. We check ourselves physically by taking our blood pressure or recording our weight. We check ourselves financially by looking at the various balances in our accounts. We even check the status of the gas in our tanks as we drive to work. We know that to neglect various aspects of our lives can lead to ruin. So what about spiritual assessment? Are we as vigilant to monitor what's going on with us spiritually? Paul asks us to see if our faith is genuine. Let me probe a bit further. Is your faith growing? Are you keeping up with the disciplines needed to mature in your faith, like those of prayer and Bible Study? Is your faith stronger, your resolve greater, and your Christian influence broader than it was in the past or have you begun to atrophy a bit? Do the check-up thing and be honest. Have you plateaued? Is your faith less active than it needs to be? Is there some measure of growth? To neglect spiritual assessment can lead to ruin. If you are not in the place you want to be, then take some deliberate and intentional steps. Commit to weekly worship. Join a small group Bible study. Keep a prayer list. Talk to a friend about your spiritual walk so that they can pray for you. Don't let your faith grow dim out of neglect. Be strong. Be bold. Be intentional. Be courageous.

Prayer

Father, allow us to make a very careful and honest spiritual assessment. Challenge us to strengthen the areas where we are weak. Amen.

Day 163 Galatians 1: Good Planning

"Jesus gave His life for our sins, just as God our Father planned, in order to rescue us from this evil world in which we live." Galatians 1:4 NLT

Observation

Writing to several regional churches, Paul can only "marvel" (1:6) that the Galatian Christians have turned from their freedom in Jesus back to the rules of Old Testament Judaism. Some even tried to compel Christians "to live as do the Jews" (2:14). Paul emphasizes in this letter that men are not justified in the sight of God by the law, but rather by faith. In our focus verse, Paul is reminding his readers of God's plan for the redemption of the world.

Application

Don't you like it when a plan comes together? Whether planning a family dinner, or going to see a movie, or working on a new strategy at the office, all of us enjoy seeing the formation of a good plan and watching it come to fruition. We enjoy seeing ideas work together in order to accomplish a goal. Recently our church participated in a "Day of Mission" to partner with local non-profits in our city. The day went well, the participants were excited, and work was done efficiently, all because good plans had been put into place. There was a method to the madness. It's like the old adage suggests, "Poor prior planning prevents proper performance." But good plans result in good action. Notice the details in what Paul writes. The redemption of the world was God's plan from the beginning. God always knew that our sins would create a barrier. And so God planned the coming of Christ before any of us had committed our first sin. God's desire has always been to rescue us from this evil world. So a plan was put into place... Christ would come, die on a cross to pay our "sin debt," and would be raised to life again. As we trust in him, we discover eternal life. Our hope of salvation and our promise of forgiveness are all bound up in that plan. From the start, the plan was implemented for our benefit. Motivated by love, God put the mechanism in place by which we could be saved. It's a good plan and it still works today. Plug into the plan and discover the life that God longs for you to live.

Prayer

Father, we thank you that in your wisdom and providence, you have provided a plan by which we can be forgiven and rescued. Thank you for the gift of Christ and for the plan of salvation. Amen.

"My old self has been crucified with Christ. It is no longer I who live, but Christ lives in me. So I live in this earthly body by trusting in the Son of God, Who loved me and gave Himself for me."
Galatians 2:20 NLT

Observation

In this passage, Paul is writing to the Galatians about a conversation that he once had with Peter in which he'd confronted Peter about an inconsistency that he had seen in Peter's life. Though free in Christ, Peter seemed to have felt the pressure to give in to those who still required a very rigid keeping of Old Testament law. Paul reminded him of his own journey and of the freedom found in Christ. Our focus verse arises out of that conversation.

Application

Years ago I was challenged to find a "life verse," a verse that for me caught the essence of living the Christian faith. Our focus verse has become the one to which I cling. It reminds me that I have been crucified with Christ. In other words, I have been forever joined to him through the power of his death and resurrection. My life, once controlled by my will, my desires, and my self-motivations has been cast aside. Christ has taken control and now lives in me. So the life I now live "in the flesh" I live by faith in the Son of God, who loves me and who gave himself up for me. This verse reminds me that I am not my own. I now live under the guidance and grace of Christ. I belong to him. When I sin, I choose to take this body that now belongs to him and use it for purposes that are not in keeping with his will. This verse calls me to accountability and reveals to me daily what my purpose and motivation should be. It calls me to a higher ethic and greater responsibility. It's a verse that has had great meaning for my life, and which continues to govern my ways. So my challenge for you this day is to reflect on your life and seek out a verse to claim as your own. Is there a verse that continues to call you, correct you, or motivate you? Is there a verse that holds profound meaning in your life? You certainly don't have to answer those questions this morning, but you should at least consider searching for a life verse that becomes a guiding entity for your journey. Sometimes, a single verse can become the continual reminder that calls you to consistent faith. So what's yours? Name it and claim it.

Prayer

Father, may your word live in us fully, calling us to a greater walk of faith. Amen.

"But the Scriptures declare that we are all prisoners of sin, so we receive God's promise of freedom only by believing in Jesus Christ."
Galatians 3:22 NLT

Observation

In this third chapter, Paul goes to great lengths to illustrate why freedom in Christ is better than the oppression of the Law. The Law can only point to our sinfulness. It can only tell us what we have done wrong. It can do nothing to correct the problem and provide forgiveness. Only in Christ can our sins be erased and our lives find grace and forgiveness.

Application

For years, Alcatraz was said to be the most "escape proof" prison in the country. Because it was constructed on an island, there was only one way of escape. Too far to swim, prisoners could only escape by boat. Many, of course, tried to escape through the years but very few ever had success. In fact, during the 29 years the prison was operated, 36 attempted to escape, but none were known to survive. (Five are stilled listed as missing and are presumed to have drowned.) By all accounts, it was a very secure prison that offered no real hope of escape. Paul writes about a different kind of prison in our focus verse. He reminds us that God's word declares that we are all prisoners of sin and have no way, in our own strength and intellect, of having any hope for escape. Our sins, our past mistakes, and our failures enslave us and keep us from experiencing the life that God longs for us to know. But, there is hope. The promise of freedom comes through only one source, Jesus Christ. Apart from his grace extended to us through the cross, we have no hope of freedom and no hope of eternal life. John 8:36 reminds us, "that if the Son sets us free, we shall be free indeed." A lot of us struggle in prisons of doubt, despair, loneliness, anxiety, fear, and grief. But Christ has come to offer us new life, joy, hope, and freedom. Through our faith in him, all the barriers and chains that keep us separated from God are removed. We escape the past to live expectantly in the present. How long have you been in your private prison? How long will you choose to stay there? Christ offers you a better life... a life of freedom. Put your trust in him and ask him to break the chains. A better life awaits you.

Prayer

Father, give us enough hope and courage to dare a prison escape. Unshackle us from fear, from guilt, and from death. Set us free in Christ to live with joy and grace. Amen.

Day 166 Galatians 4: We Are Family

"Now you are no longer a slave but God's own child. And since you are His child, God has made you His heir." Galatians 4:7 NLT

Observation

In this passage, Paul attempts to explain how we are children of God through faith. He explains the way in which we once were enslaved by our sins, but now have been adopted as God's children. No longer to live as a slave, we are heirs to God's Kingdom.

Application

We all have family. No matter how well or how poorly we are treated, we will always be someone's son or daughter. Biologically, we are the product of those who created us. The DNA has been cast and we are forever linked to our parents. We share their tendencies, looks, mannerisms, and even likes and dislikes. In situations where relationships are positive and healthy, family means much. Part of being in a family is a sense of belonging. We feel safe, protected, nurtured, and encouraged. But for some, life's journey is not so well scripted. Some are cast aside at birth to be adopted by other families. Others are seemingly cast aside later when the pressures of growing up become too painful for parent or child and the family breaks apart. I know people who have come from all those various worlds. Some know the enduring love of faithful parents and some have had to discover most of their life skills all by themselves. But notice what Paul says about being in God's family. We are adopted in. No longer slaves to sin who are separated from God, we are now welcomed in God's presence and invited to share in the inheritance of the Kingdom. Once adopted in, we do not live under the threat of one day being "kicked out." We belong to God. We are His. We are loved, encouraged, and nurtured. We are gifted with grace and protected by God's strong arm. I may or may not know your life story. I know that for some of you, it's been a struggle because family did not mean all that it should have meant. But I want all of you to know that in Christ, you are now a very important member of a greater family. You are God's child. Always will be. You are loved unconditionally. Accepted readily. Gifted lavishly. Protected carefully. Welcome to the family. He's glad your here.

Prayer

Father, thank you for loving each of us and making us your children. May we know the joy of being in your family and of being welcomed in your presence. Amen.

"But the Holy Spirit produces this kind of fruit in our lives: love, joy, peace, patience, kindness, goodness, faithfulness, gentleness, and self-control. There is no law against these things!"
Galatians 5:22-23 NLT

Observation

Paul is writing about the effect that the Holy Spirit has in our lives. Because the Spirit dwells within us, He begins to change us from the inside out. Our motivations are different. Our demeanor is different. Our actions are different. Our worldview is different. No longer controlled by human nature, we begin to exhibit the kind of life that reflects the Spirit of Christ. Our sinful tendencies are replaced by the Spirit's greater gifts.

Application

A friend of mine owns a 1931 Model A Ford. Because of a physical problem he is unable to drive the car and so my chauffeur skills are called upon to take the owner and his car on the occasional spin. I have to admit that I really enjoy getting to drive the ancient automobile. It's a bit tricky and takes a little more finesse than cars of today. But off we go, traveling the highways and byways at a blistering pace of nearly 45 miles per hour! My friend acquired the car last fall and within a few days we took the car on its maiden voyage around the town of Franklin, Tennessee. Despite my best efforts, it sputtered, backfired, and all but quit, making the trip home a real challenge. On the next trip, we drove to a local Pure station where will filled the tank with fresh gas. Suddenly, it ran like a top... the old engine purring like a kitten. It began to dawn on us that the earlier problem was one of "old gas." When the fresh gas filled the tank, everything changed.

What's on the inside always matters. When our lives are filled completely with God's Spirit, suddenly everything changes. We go from being mean-spirited, angry, jealous, and despondent, to being filled with love, joy, peace, etc. There is only enough space within us for one spirit. Either we are filled with God's Spirit, or the world's spirit. Each has its result. One leads to a positive and joy-filled life... the other leads to the dark side of the human psyche. So what will you choose to put in your tank? What qualities do you long to possess? I invite you to surrender fully to the Spirit of God and see what great things your life can produce.

Prayer

Father, thank you for placing your Spirit within each of us. May we have the wisdom to give the Spirit full control so that our lives produce Kingdom fruit. Amen.

"Dear brothers and sisters, if another believer is overcome by some sin, you who are godly should gently and humbly help that person back onto the right path. And be careful not to fall into the same temptation yourself." Galatians 6:1 NLT

Observation

Paul offers an important word about responsibility within the body of Christ. Whenever we discover that someone has been overtaken by sin, we bear the responsibility of helping that person find the right path again. With a spirit of gentleness and humility, we offer a grace-filled response to their needs. We are not called to condemn, nor to shun, but to display the love of Christ by gently and carefully offering words of encouragement and support. Knowing that we, too, could so easily lose our way, we must be mindful to guard our own hearts.

Application

Ministry can get messy. If we take seriously the responsibility of helping others regain their footing, we will be forced to exert a lot of time and effort, even when inconvenient. In other words, ministry can be hard. To walk a friend through rehab, to help heal a broken relationship, to process some doubt, to overcome an experience of grief, or to mend a heart of guilt, all take investment on the part of those trying to bring healing and wholeness. But that's a part of what it means to be in a community of faith. That's what it means to be a disciple of Christ. We bear the responsibility to help. We do so, remembering that "there but by the grace of God go I," right? None of us are immune from the pull of temptation. We guard our own hearts lest we fall. And if we sense our own vulnerability, shouldn't we look to others with greater patience and empathy as we try to help? It may not be the same sin or temptation with which they struggle, but surely other temptations call to us as well. And so we must learn to be the right kind of Christian friend, knowing that the moment may well come when we will need someone else to be that kind of friend to each of us. So, speaking of ministry, do you know of someone who is really struggling to find his or her way through a difficult time? How have you reached out to offer your support? What kind of investment have you made in their life? It may not be easy or convenient, but it's the right thing to do. Go help.

Prayer

Father, thank you for placing us together in community with one another. May we understand both the joy and responsibility that such a relationship requires. Amen.

Day 169 Ephesians 1: Loved for a Long Time

"Even before He made the world, God loved us and chose us in Christ to be holy and without fault in His eyes." Ephesians 1:4 NLT

Observation

As Paul writes to the church in Ephesus, he reminds them that God has called them to life in Christ and of the spiritual blessings that have been bestowed upon each of them. In our focus verse, Paul is reminding Christian believers that even before God chose to make the world, we were important. God looked beyond the centuries of time to love us and to choose us.

Application

Some of us have known the joy of loving relationships for a long time. I've been loved by my parents for over half a century. I have friends who have loved me for decades. My wife has loved me for nearly 40 years. But according to the book of Ephesians, we have been loved much longer than that. Before the world was even formed, we were loved by God. Before the sun, moon, and stars were set in their courses we were known by the heart of the Father and welcomed as beloved children. Before the Red Sea parted, or Noah built the ark... before the walls of Jericho came crashing down or the Roman Empire came to power... before Solomon built the temple or before Jesus died on the cross, we were loved. I know what you're thinking... "How can that be? How can we be loved before we were even born?" For those of you who are parents, think about how your heart skipped a beat the day you discovered you were having a child. Months before little Johnny or Mary came into the world, you already dreamed dreams, plotted a future, and yes, even loved your expected, but yet-to-be born child. God, who is transcendent of time and space, loved you long before He chose to call you into being. You have been special to God for much longer than you can even imagine. The point is not to try and figure that out, but to simply accept it. And notice that it goes beyond just being loved. We were also chosen to be "without blame." Think of that. In Christ, you are already faultless in the eyes of God. "Holy and without fault," Paul writes. No, I can't explain that either. I can only accept what the Bible says. We still have so much to learn about grace, don't we? Just remember, you've been loved longer than you think.

Prayer

Father, though we cannot even begin to fathom the depth of your love and the offering of your grace, we thank you for calling us into being and for accepting us as your children. Amen.

Day 170 Ephesians 2: Accepting, Not Earning

"Salvation is not a reward for the good things we have done, so none of us can boast about it." Ephesians 2:9 NLT

Observation

Paul is very careful to remind his readers of how each of us is made alive through Christ. Through grace we are welcomed into his Kingdom. It is not as a result of things we have done, but simply because of his love that we are included. Paul attempted to counter the thought of his day that led to boasting. Some believed that because of their heritage or because of their strict adherence to the Law that they had "earned" their salvation. They "boasted" that they were chosen and others were not. Paul reminds them that salvation is a gift, not an earned commodity.

Application

Two thousand years later, there are many of us who still don't get it. In vain, we attempt to earn our salvation. We still think that if we are good enough, giving enough, and loving enough that God will shine on us with favor. And we also believe the opposite side of that coin... if we are bad enough, stingy enough, and angry enough, that surely we are unacceptable in the eyes of God. So we buy into a "salvation by works" mentality. In fact, I was speaking with a college student this week who said to me, "I don't think I will ever be good enough for God to love me." I tried to explain that being good has nothing to do with God's love. We are loved by God simply because we are part of creation. We are God's children and that's where our acceptance begins. Now let's be clear. Being loved by God is not an automatic path to salvation. Not everyone ever created by God will gain salvation. Our sins still have the power to separate us from God's presence. Thus our need for a Savior. Salvation comes through our acceptance of Jesus Christ as Savior and Lord. Because of his willingness to die in order to pay the "sin cost" for our lives, we can be forgiven and ushered into a relationship with Holy God. So step back and see the big picture... God loves us enough to call us into being. God loves us enough to provide a way of grace through Christ. We can't earn that kind of love... we can only accept it. No, you will never be "good" enough to claim salvation. But you will be loved enough.

Prayer

Father, we thank you that we are saved through our faith in Christ alone. Remind us that we long to do good things because we are saved, not in order to earn our salvation. Amen.

Day 171 Ephesians 3: Where Are You Planted?

"Then Christ will make his home in your hearts as you trust in him. Your roots will grow down into God's love and keep you strong."
Ephesians 3:17 NLT

Observation

Paul reminds his hearers that whenever we put our faith and trust in Christ, he will make his home in our hearts. Christ will reside in us. His Spirit will be found within us. We will have inner strength, courage, and lasting joy because he dwells within us. As a part of our faith journey, Christ will allow our roots to grow down deeply into God's love. As we tap into that source of grace, we will be kept strong to live our faith, to share our witness, and to help grow the Kingdom.

Application

Where is your life rooted? Where is the source of your strength? Where do you find wisdom, insight, and courage? Our lives tend to become rooted in the places where we spend the most time. Like a seed that falls to the ground, takes root, and begins to sprout, our lives grow in the soil in which we place them. Placed in fertile soil, our lives will produce much fruit. Placed in shallow or rocky soil, our lives will never fully mature. People choose to plant their lives in all kinds of shallow ground. Some plant their lives in their business life. All they do is centered on being a success in the business community. Others plant their lives in shallow relationships. They claim a lot of friendships, but have very few real relationships. Still others plant their lives in the shallow ground of chasing each new fad or exploring each new Internet experience. Do you get it? The growth and depth of our lives tends to reflect the shallowness of the soil in which we plant them. It is as we invest in things that really matter that our lives find real meaning and purpose. Paul reminds us that as we nurture our faith relationship with Christ that our roots begin to grow very deeply into God's resources. We discover God's love, grace, and plan. The rich soil of grace allows our lives to mature and suddenly our lives begin to matter. Take a moment and consider where your life is grounded. In work? In hobbies? In trivial pursuits? Where do you spend your time? You were meant for so much more. Place your hope, trust, and energy into a pursuit of Christ and discover the depth your life can have.

Prayer

Father, teach us to invest our lives in things that matter. May we learn to plant our lives in the rich soil of your grace where we will find our sense of purpose and produce fruit that matters. Amen.

Day 172 Ephesians 4: Choosing to See Others Differently

"Always be humble and gentle. Be patient with each other, making allowance for each other's faults because of your love."
Ephesians 4:2 NLT

Observation

In this chapter, Paul is stressing the need for unity within the church. He offers some very simple instructions, including those contained in our focus verse. Paul knew that humility and gentleness would go a long way in keeping the peace within a body of Christ. He also knew that unity doesn't happen by accident. It is the result of intentionality. We choose our attitudes and those choices must be made with the Spirit of Christ working in our lives.

Application

"...Making allowance for each other's faults...." Good advice, right? We all have a few little faults... a few imperfections... a few areas that need a little improvement. It's just part of what it means to be human. The joy of relationships is not in finding perfect people to be our friends, but in finding a perfect love for the friends that matter most to us. I've got a few friends that I have had for a long time. In fact, some of my best friendships go all the way back to the days of college. They are not my good friends because they are perfect people, they are my friends because we have learned to look beyond the imperfections and find the common ground of acceptance and support that binds us together. Now think in terms of the church. If you are looking for a perfect church, filled with perfect people, you will live a very frustrated life. No such church exists. We are flawed, at times misguided, overly sensitive, too opinionated, easily offended, and sometimes too closed minded. There are lots of imperfections sitting in every pew. The point is not to find fault in each other, but to look beyond the faults to the glimmer of grace contained within each one of us. Look closely enough and you will see the light of Christ shining in every life. To call our selves a church, is to make allowance for our human weaknesses, while seeing in each other, the grace of God. So be kind. Forgive. Be patient. Try not to be too judgmental. The person you think is unlovable may just be thinking the same about you.

Prayer

Father, remind us that we are in this life together. Teach us to value patience, understanding, and compassion. May we see what is best in each other and not that which occasionally makes us behave poorly. Amen.

"Imitate God, therefore, in everything you do,
because you are His dear children." Ephesians 5:1 NLT

Observation

As a standard to raise by which we can judge our conduct and character, Paul suggests that we imitate God. If our goal becomes that of walking like God walks, thinking like God thinks, extending grace like God extends grace, and showing compassion the way God shows compassion, then our lives will reflect the image of our Father.

Application

Most of us have felt the urge to imitate others at some point in our lives. Maybe there was a time as a child when you imitated some great sports figure. You had to have shoes like he wore and a jersey that had his number. Or remember imitating that rock star? How many young girls have grabbed a hairbrush for a microphone and danced in front of a mirror as they imitated their favorite singer? As adults, we still do the imitation thing. We see the style of clothing that popular people wear and suddenly we are at the mall buying those same fashions. We hear popular phrases and words used by important political leaders and suddenly those words appear in our vocabulary. When someone imitates us, it means they have noted our actions, our mannerisms, and our words and they attempt to replicate them in their own lives. My question is, "Are we worthy of imitation?" Whether we want to be imitated or not, our children will pattern their actions by what they have seen us do. The words we use, the attitudes we hold, and the way we respond in moments of stress will all be imprinted in the hearts and minds of our children. They will learn much by simple observation. That can be a humbling and frightening thought. Need help in being a better role model? Notice what Paul suggests. If we imitate God, surely we will begin to act more like Him. And the more like God we become, the better example we are to those who imitate us. It's a trickle-down effect. If we imitate God closely, then maybe we will provide a better example to those who would imitate us. It's not easy setting the standard of behavior for our children. But as they look to us, let's make sure that we have looked to God.

Prayer

Father, may we imitate you with our actions, our compassion, and our words. As people observe our lives, may they recognize at once, that we are your children. Amen.

"Put on salvation as your helmet, and take the sword of the Spirit, which is the word of God." Ephesians 6:17 NLT

Observation

In this final chapter from the letter to the Ephesians, Paul uses an extended metaphor to describe how we are to dress for spiritual warfare. He reminds his readers that the battles we face are more than flesh and blood contests. It's bigger than that. In order to stand firm, we need the right equipment. Paul reminds believers to put on the full armor of God. Temptations will come. Days of testing will assault. But those whose protection is in place will stand strong amid the struggles.

Application

In our focus verse, Paul mentions two items that are essential for any battle. The first is a helmet. Helmets offer protection, preventing crushing blows that would do us in. I survived a lot of football practices and games because a helmet protected me from a concussion. In my early teenage years, I wore a different kind of helmet to protect my head while riding motorcycles. I've even worn a helmet while doing a little white-water rafting. The purpose is always the same... protect the brain. When Paul advises us to wear a helmet of salvation, he reminds us that protecting the brain is always important. As we are assaulted each day by cultural values, misguided ideology, and the constant pressure to compromise, keeping our minds clear and our thoughts pure becomes increasingly important. It will be our strong faith that will offer the protection needed. Paul also mentions the sword of the Spirit. Though sometimes used offensively, in this passage, I think Paul is referring to the ability to defend one's life. Notice he is careful to teach us that the sword of protection needed to defend our lives, is the word of God. What is there to fortify us more than the promises of God's word echoing through our hearts? What gives better wisdom, guidance, and instruction more than the word of God? Notice that God provides us with all that we need to survive the onslaught of life. Our minds are protected and our hearts are defended by God's power and grace. I don't have to tell you that it's a real struggle out there. Better put on your helmet and grab your sword. You will need both.

Prayer

Father, prepare us for the struggles we will face. May we march boldly into each new day knowing that you offer us protection and power. Amen.

Day 175 Philippians 1: Purpose Driven Life

"Knowing this, I am convinced that I will remain alive so I can continue to help all of you grow and experience the joy of your faith."
Philippians 1:25 NLT

Observation

With sixteen references to "joy" and "rejoicing," Philippians is one of the Apostle Paul's most upbeat and positive letters. Even though he is writing while imprisoned (1:13), he offers encouragement and support to the believers in Philippi. Our focus verse is from a passage in which Paul is musing whether it is better for him to die and be with the Lord or to remain alive and serve the Kingdom. He has a desire to do both. According to verse 25 he has found his answer in knowing that he wants to continue to help the believers to grow in their faith.

Application

We talk from time to time about having a purpose driven life. Pastor Rick Warren certainly "hit the nail on the head" with his book of the same title that challenges Christians to live out their God-given purpose. In the book, Warren raises a key question with which we all struggle... "What am I here for?" Don't we all long for a sense of purpose? Don't we long to know why we have been created and placed on the planet? The Apostle Paul certainly lived out of a sense of purpose. As he writes in our focus verse, his purpose in living was to "help the believers to grow and experience the joy of their faith." He was passionate about helping them grow into maturity. Finding our own passion can be a quest. Warren reminds us that our number one reason for being is to glorify God. We are created to bring God glory in all that we do. I think he's right. The goal for each of us is to live daily in an attempt to flesh out that purpose. How do I glorify God today? How do I glorify God through my work, my relationship with my spouse, in the way I treat my kids, in the way I talk with friends? Glorifying God should become the overarching principle of our lives. It is what governs our actions, thoughts, and words. You may or may not be called to "preach the gospel while living in chains," but you are called to live each day under a sense of purpose that calls you to glorify your Father. So take a look at what you will do with your life this day. Will each action honor God? Will you live out of that sense of purpose?

Prayer

Father, teach us to live out our lives under the governance of your will. Nothing more. Nothing less. Nothing else. Amen.

Day 176 Philippians 2: Sometimes, You Just Gotta Be There

"For he (Epaphroditus) risked his life for the work of Christ, and he was at the point of death while doing for me what you couldn't do from far away." Philippians 2:30 NLT

Observation

Paul refers to a man named Epaphroditus as a brother, co-worker, fellow soldier, messenger, and minister. Other writings record that he will later become the Bishop of Philippi and will be canonized as a saint. He was obviously an important envoy of Paul to the church in Philippi. Additionally, he carefully cared for Paul in the midst of some of the turmoil surrounding Paul's ministry.

Application

Pick up on the last phrase in our focus verse... "doing for me what you couldn't do from far away." Epaphroditus was able to minister to Paul in ways that the believers in Philippi could not because of time and distance. Epaphroditus was able to offer Paul the "ministry of presence." Sometimes, to make a real difference, you just gotta be there. There are moments we can offer ministry from a distance. We can pray for others. We can call. We can send money. But then there are those moments when only our physical presence will make a difference. Sometimes, we need to "show up" and be physically present with someone in a time of need. Friends might not remember all the kind words you say in times of need, but they will certainly remember your being present to support them and to encourage them. Life has those moments, both in crisis and in joy, when there is no substitute for being present and tangible. Sometimes we minister best as we hold a hand, hug a neck, or listen with our ears. The hardest journey is always made easier in the company of a friend, right? Take a moment this morning to think about the people in your life that need your ministry of presence... not a phone call, not a card, but flesh and blood. Is there someone who would be encouraged by your presence, relieved by your presence, helped by your presence, offered joy by your presence? Sometimes you just gotta be there. Sometimes, the love of Christ has to show up dressed in the robe of human flesh. While there is time, go and minister... go and be present... go and be "as Christ" to that friend in need.

Prayer

Father, remind us that there are those moments when there is no substitute for our willingness to be physically present with someone in need. Remind us that we take not just ourselves, but the very presence of Christ as we go. Amen.

Day 177 Philippians 3: A Better Body

"He will take our weak mortal bodies and change them into glorious bodies like His own, using the same power with which He will bring everything under His control." Philippians 3:21 NLT

Observation

Paul writes this 3rd chapter of Philippians with a very forward-looking view. He talks about "reaching forward to what lies ahead," and "pressing on toward the goal for the prize of the upward call of God in Christ Jesus." He reminds all believers that our citizenship is in heaven (v. 20), and that when Christ returns, he will change our weak mortal bodies into the same type of glorious body that he now has. Paul looks to the future with great hope and expectation.

Application

Yesterday, I spent the day doing a lot of Spring yard work. I planted trees and shrubs, weeded some flowerbeds, moved a lot of dirt, and mowed a lot of grass. And this morning, I feel the effects. My body is a little tired. I've got a lot of sore muscles and not a lot of energy. It happens, right? We get those little reminders that we are but human and that our bodies age and sometimes it takes a little longer to "bounce back." There are other ways to realize the effects of time on our bodies. Our hair becomes grayer, our eyes get weaker, and our gait becomes altered. And just as our bodies can grow tired at the end of a long day of work, we also know that our bodies can grow weary after a long life of everyday living. But Paul offers a great word of hope. He reminds us that Christ will take our weak mortal bodies and change them into glorious bodies like his own. What does that mean? What will we one day resemble? Who's to say? Will we look like we did in the prime of our early 20's as the *Heaven Is For Real* book suggests? Will we know and be known? Don't worry about the details... worry about the journey. Our path to that new life and that new body is found in only one source... Jesus Christ. It is Christ who will offer the transformational power needed to make us whole again. It is only through a relationship with him that we will gain everlasting life. Rub a little Ben Gay on your aching muscles, but apply a little faith to your aching life. There is a whole new life waiting for those who have placed their faith and trust in Jesus. Let's reach forward to what lies ahead, confident in the faith that we have in Christ.

Prayer

Father, we thank you for the promise of the glorious life that is to come. As we look to that day, keep us faithful and keep us strong. Amen.

"Don't worry about anything; instead, pray about everything. Tell God what you need, and thank him for all He has done."
Philippians 4:6 NLT

Observation

In his final thoughts to the church at Philippi, Paul reminds those beleivers to substitute prayer in the place of worry. Paul knew of the futility of worry. Many times throughout his ministry, he knew what it was to be in need and have situations that seemed impossible to manage. And yet God "supplied all his needs according to His riches in glory" (v. 19). And so his counsel to believers of all ages is to substitute needless worry for moments in prayer.

Application

Most of us worry... a lot. We worry about the big things and the small. Worry creeps into the deep recesses of our minds and haunts us day and night. We worry about things we can't control. We worry about money, time, problems at work, our kids, our cars, our marriages, our health... the list goes on and on. Right now, if I asked you to give me a list of your three biggest worries, you could spew them out in a millisecond. In fact, you could probably give me a list of 10 or even 12 major worries. What is haunting you today? What worries are creeping into your head this morning? The more time that you spend in worry, the less time that you spend enjoying life. So read our focus verse again... ""Don't worry about anything; instead, pray about everything. Tell God what you need..." Such simple advice, but rarely taken to heart. We need to admit that there are situations in life that are too big for us to control. We can worry endlessly about those things or we can place our trust in the power of The One who has authority and control over everything. Which makes more sense? There is a faith step involved. It's called trusting your Father. Pour out your heart. Talk honestly of your fears and worries. Trust God to do what is best. Read verse 7... "And the peace of God will guard your hearts and minds..." You don't have to spend your days in fear and worry. You have a Father who stands ready to help. Do this... make out a list of your three biggest worries for today. Pray through the list, carefully, specifically, and honestly. Trust God to be at work in your life. Enjoy a little peace rather than anxiety. It's a better way to live.

Prayer

Father, thank you for loving us enough to take on our anxious thoughts and substituting them with your peace. Amen.

"Christ is the visible image of the invisible God. He existed before anything was created and is supreme over all creation,"
Colossians 1:15 NLT

Observation

If you want to read a chapter that contains more wisdom and truth than you can take-in in a brief moment, then read this chapter and then read it again. There is a lot of truth to mine from this passage. The book of Colossians was written by Paul, along with Timothy, to the church at Colosse, to remind them of the superiority of Christ over any Jewish rule or regulation, over angels and anything else. In the book, Paul tries to repudiate some false teaching that had begun to surface in the life of the church.

Application

Reading this chapter puts me in the mind and message of Christmas… what a better way to tell the essence of the incarnation... "Christ is the visible image of the invisible God." Isn't that the point of Christmas? Did not God desire to be revealed in a tangible, physical, visible way? And so God embodied human form in the person of Jesus Christ. The invisible God became very visible in the tender flesh and innocent cooing of a newborn baby. He continued to become visible in the teachings of a 30 year-old rabbi... in the miracles... in the healing events... in the stilling of the seas... in the preaching from the mountainside. God became visible as he rode into Jerusalem on a donkey, broke the bread with his disciples, and as he was nailed to a wooden cross. God became visible when he appeared for 40 days after his resurrection. As John tells it, "The Word became flesh and dwelt among us." The invisible became tangible and it needs to happen yet again. Somehow the love, grace, and redemption of the invisible God needs to be fleshed out even now. How will that happen? It happens in us. As believers we are called to be the visible image of the invisible God. Scary, isn't it... that if the world is to see the love of the Father, it will be revealed through us. That changes everything... how we live, the words we choose, the places we go, the grace we extend. The incarnation is a reminder of great joy. It is also a reminder of great responsibility. Let the word become flesh in you this day.

Prayer

Father, may our lives this very day, reflect your grace, your love, and your priorities. May people catch a glimpse of the Invisible God when they see us this day. Amen.

"And now, just as you accepted Christ Jesus as your Lord, you must continue to follow Him." Colossians 2:6 NLT

Observation

Paul and Timothy are challenging the believers at Colosse to finish what they have started. Now that they have begun a life of faith by following Jesus, the counsel is to continue to follow him in all things. At work in the life of the church were some false teachers who insisted on certain strict disciplines and strange practices. Paul was reminding the Colossians that faith in Christ demands relationship and not ritual.

Application

I'm bad about not finishing some things. For example, I started two books about a month ago that I have failed to finish reading. It's not that they are boring or uninteresting... I've just not given them the priority needed to finish reading them. Sometimes I do the same with medicines prescribed. More than once I have not finished an antibiotic for some infection because I got tired of dealing with the side effects of the med. I figured that I was well enough and so I quit taking the pills. (I know all of my doctor and nurse friends who read this devotion are shaking their heads!) You have probably done some similar things... started something, but failed to finish. It's okay to have an unfinished project taking up space in the garage, or an unfinished book collecting dust on a shelf. What's NOT okay is living an unfinished faith. The call to be a Christ-follower is a calling to two things... a life of transition in which we change from who we once were to what Christ longs for us to become, and a life of completion in which we continue our pursuit of Christ for as long as we live. The "Lordship" of Christ is just that... it implies that we worship, we follow, and we obey. We allow the heart of Christ to beat strongly within our chests. It's never an "on again, off again" kind of thing. It's a pursuit, a calling, a lifestyle, a journey. I hope that most of you who read this are believers in Christ. If you are, let me challenge you to finish what you started. If you are not a believer, let me challenge you to start the journey.

Prayer

Father, we thank you this day for the faith we have in Jesus Christ. May our discipleship be strong, and our faith-commitments solid. Teach us to pursue Christ with passion and desire. Amen.

"And when Christ, who is your life, is revealed to the whole world, you will share in all His glory." Colossians 3:4 NLT

Observation

Paul and Timothy are speaking about the relationship we all have with Christ through our faith in him. We are joined to him... connected. So when the day comes when he is fully revealed to the whole world, we will share in the glory of that moment. It is our association with Christ that lets us share the splendor of the day.

Application

Relationships make or break us. The key relationships that define our lives will determine much about the successes or failures that we will know. When we choose to surround ourselves with those who care about their faith, who love their families, and who care about the needs of others, our lives will be pulled in those directions. People of solid character tend to influence those around them to do the right things. If, on the other hand, we surround ourselves with those who think selfishly, live immorally, and conduct themselves foolishly, their influence will be great in our lives. We are shaped, defined, and molded by the people we choose as our closest associates. Sometimes, it is important to examine the key relationships of our lives and ask, "Is this relationship helping me to become a better person, or is it pulling me in a wrong direction?"

So where can we find the kinds of relationships that encourage, heal, and help? What should we look for in the lives of those with whom we will cast our lot? First and foremost ask, "Is this person, a person of faith? Have they joined their heart to the heart of Christ?" Please understand, I am not suggesting that every friend you have needs to be a Christian. How will your life influence someone for the Kingdom if you have no connection to those who are lost? But I am suggesting that the key relationships that you allow to shape and influence your life do need to be people of solid faith. It's hard enough to live a Godly life in the culture in which we live; we shouldn't even try to attempt it on our own. So look for those who encourage your faith development. Relationships make or break us. What are your relationships doing to you?

Prayer

Father, give us wisdom as we forge the relationships of our lives. May we carefully guard the heart of Christ within us by surrounding ourselves with those who love him passionately. Amen.

Colossians 4: The Right Kind of Prayers

"Devote yourselves to prayer with an alert mind and a thankful heart."
Colossians 4:2 NLT

Observation

Among his final words of instruction, Paul challenges the faithful in Colossae to be devoted to the practice of prayer. He offers two very specific instructions about how they should pray. First, the challenge is to pray with an alert mind. Second, the challenge is to pray with a thankful heart. I wonder how well most of us do with either of these challenges...

Application

What does it mean to pray with "an alert mind?" Part of this instruction surely speaks to our physical selves as we pray. Are we alert? Are we fully awake? Are we focused as we bring our petitions before God? My fear is that many of us pray very distracted prayers. Maybe we feel the pressure of the day that stretches out before us and so we rush through our prayers, not being fully conscious of what we are asking of God as we pray. Maybe our minds are groggy and our bodies are tired when we pray, making it difficult to come into God's presence with our "A" game on. Maybe our lack of "alertness" is not one of physical exhaustion. Sometimes we pray without consideration of the events, opportunities, and moments that swirl around us. God may be at work in some special way and so our prayers should be focused with greater specificity. Is God asking you to pray about a certain need? Is there a problem that needs to be bathed in prayer as you come into God's presence? Is your "spiritual antenna" alert to the movement of God in your life or in the life of another?

The second part of the challenge is to pray with a thankful heart. Admittedly, most of us get right to the "asking" and seldom take the time to do much thanksgiving. I read a little quote the other day... "What if we only have today the things for which we thanked God yesterday?" That's a bit scary, isn't it? Try this... be very intentional today about allowing the first few minutes of your prayer to be moments of giving thanks before you get into asking for the things you need. Express your gratitude for God's blessings with both an alert mind and a grateful heart.

Prayer

Father, how we thank you for the privilege of prayer. May we never treat it lightly or think that it is of little importance. May our prayers be bold, focused, and filled with gratitude. Amen.

"For they themselves report about us what kind of a reception we had with you, and how you turned to God from idols to serve a living and true God, and to wait for His Son from heaven, whom He raised from the dead, that is Jesus, who rescues us from the wrath to come."
1 Thessalonians 1:9-10 NASB

Observation

Paul's letter to the church at Thessalonica, which he helped to establish (Acts 17), is believed by many to be Paul's earliest writing. In the letter Paul teaches on the Second Coming of Christ, apparently an issue of some concern to the Thessalonians. Although Paul does not say when Christ will return to the earth, he does describe how Christ will return. In our focus passage Paul praises the Thessalonians for their continued faithfulness and reminds them that it is Jesus who rescues from the wrath that is to come.

Application

Let's have a little "last times" talk this morning. The Biblical record clearly teaches that a time of judgment is coming, when Christ will return to the world to reward the righteous and to judge the wicked. Paul describes this Day of Judgment as "the wrath that is to come." It will be a day when the power of God will be poured out on the earth judging the hearts of all men. Paul is very careful in his teaching, however, to remind the believers of all the ages, that Christ will rescue his followers from that day of wrath. As we embrace the hope of that promise we must also feel the burden that his message brings. If we know that such a day is coming, should we not do all that we can to help others escape the destructive wrath? In other words, should not our knowledge of that coming day strengthen and quicken our evangelistic zeal? My fear is that many modern day believers have become somewhat ambivalent to our calling to reach the lost. We have seemingly lost the sense of compassion that should birth in us a sense of urgency. Because the love of Christ constrains us, we must care that people are living each day with the threat of judgment. Knowing that we have the answer, the very Hope of the gospel, we must renew our efforts at reaching them with the message of salvation that comes only through Christ.

Prayer

Father, may we never tire, nor grow weary of our task to bear the gospel message to all who have never heard. Give us both compassion and urgency as we wait the coming of the Lord. Amen.

Day 184 — 1 Thessalonians 2: A Worthy Walk

> "So that you would walk in a manner worthy of the God who calls you into His own kingdom and glory." 1 Thessalonians 2:12 NASB

Observation

Paul reminded the believers at Thessalonica that he encouraged them and taught them with great patience and affection so that they would "walk in a manner worthy of the God who called them." He claimed to exhort them like a father would his own children. His desire was for them to be pure in their faith and consistent in their practice of Christianity.

Application

Quite a challenge, is it not... to walk in a manner worthy of the God who calls us? What does such a challenge mean for us each day? First, it has to mean a purity of heart. Our desires, our longings, and our intentions, all have to be pleasing to Our Father. When people hear the words we speak and sense the attitudes within, God should be glorified. Our hearts must reflect a desire to please God in all things. Second, it has to mean a consistency of lifestyle. We cannot claim the Christian faith and not live as Christians should. In other words, if we profess that Jesus is Lord, then our "everyday-walking-around-life" has to be consistent with the teachings and values of Christ. Every day, we must love unselfishly, forgive abundantly, and share extravagantly. We have to live authentically and honestly as believers. Third, it has to mean a willingness to claim the world with a sense of responsibility. If God so loved the world, then we too must love the world and do all that we can to claim it with the redemptive message of the gospel. We must accept the responsibility to reach, teach, and preach with a sense of urgency. Like the sower of Jesus' parable, we must scatter the seed in as many places and in as many ways as we can.

So how is your walk this morning? Is it worthy of the God who has called you? Be faithful. Be consistent. Be active. Be generous. Be loving.

Prayer

Father, may our words, our deeds, our actions, and our thoughts this day bring you glory as we seek to live a life that is worthy of your Spirit that dwells within us. Amen.

Day 185 1 Thessalonians 3: Love God. Love the Church.

"May the Lord cause you to increase and abound in love for one another, and for all people, just as we also do for you;"
1 Thessalonians 3:12 NASB

Observation

Paul's prayer for the Thessalonian believers was that they would "increase and abound" in love for each other. Paul knew that the greatest testimony they could offer on behalf of the Kingdom would be their love for each other, demonstrated each day. Notice that he desires for their love to increase... grow ever stronger and more complete, and that it would abound... over flow, spill out, and wash over every element of their lives. The love that they possessed for each other would soon carry forth to all people. Paul knew that it would be the love of the church that would change the world.

Application

The strongest force that binds together the heart of any church is that of genuine love. Churches can overcome any crisis, any problem, any hardship, any challenge, and any setback as long as love is present. What the church cannot overcome is a lack of love. Love is the distinguishing mark. It's what bears witness to our faith. It's what holds us together. It's what gives us courage and strength. As we pray for our church, the best prayer we pray is not for more blessings, a greater budget, more Biblical literacy, greater spiritual depth, more members, nor even a deeper commitment to the church.Instead, our best prayer is that we would love each other... really love each other. Real love always extends grace. It always listens. It always forgives. It always cares. It always forces our involvement. It always rejoices. It always sacrifices. It always deepens our commitments and strengthens our relationships. It laughs. It weeps. It shares. It protects. It heals. It lifts the needs of others and diminishes our own agendas.

At the end of the day, the world will not be stirred, nor changed by our buildings, our budget, or our business meetings. It will be impacted by our love... our genuine love for each other and our love for our neighbors. Do you love your church... or do you just love going to church? There is a huge difference.

Prayer

Father, may our love for each other grow strong and abound. Remind us that love is always a verb. Amen.

"Make it your goal to live a quiet life, minding your own business and working with your hands, just as we instructed you before. Then people who are not Christians will respect the way you live, and you will not need to depend on others." 1 Thess. 4:11-12 NLT

Observation

In the midst of various words of counsel and instruction, including thoughts on avoiding lust, impurity, and adultery, Paul offers a word about gaining the respect of non-believers. Paul is concerned that one of the ways that we bear witness is through our actions and daily conduct, not just with the words we might offer to others. In our focus verses, he speaks of living a "quiet life," one in which we "mind our own business."

Application

I live in a nice neighborhood in Franklin, Tennessee. There are about 700 homes in the neighborhood. And as you can probably imagine, there is a Homeowners Association that has guidelines and policies to ensure that all properties and common spaces are properly maintained. Property values are enhanced as each homeowner works to follow the guidelines. Some policies relate to the number of trees in each yard, or the type of backyard playground equipment that can be constructed, or the appearance of the front lawn. In wanting to earn the respect of my neighbors, I work hard at following those guidelines. I want to do my part to make our community a nice place to live.

Paul reminds us that we are called to live the kind of life that will garner the respect of non-believers. Rather than cause dissension, provoke anger, or display intolerance, we are to live a quiet life in which we pay attention to the unspoken testimonies that we offer. When I read Paul's list of the Fruit of the Spirit, recorded in Galatians 5:22-23, I am remined of all those noble and important qualities that Christian people are to display. In that list are two of the most important "life-tools" that we should carry with us each day… love and kindness. What if we stepped out into the world each day with those two tools in our hands? What if we spoke in love and acted in kindness? Would we not earn the respect of non-believers? And more importantly, would we not also draw them into the faith by our actions?

Prayer

Father, may we earn the respect of non-believers by living Christ-centered lives that bear testimony to the Savior we long to share. Amen.

"Rejoice always." 1 Thessalonians 5:16 NASB

Observation

Paul closes his letter to the Thessalonians with a list of imperatives for the church. These imperatives relate to Christian conduct. Subjects include: appreciation for those who are leaders in the church, admonishing those who are unruly, turning away from thoughts of revenge, giving thanks, and letting the Spirit have the freedom to work. Sandwiched in between several other verses, Paul adds the imperative to "Rejoice always." That's a tough rule to follow because life gives us plenty of opportunities not to rejoice.

Application

So how can it be done? How can we live a life of constant rejoicing when everything about our life situations wants to rob us of such joy? Let's admit it... life is not always happy and the day-to-day stuff is not always pleasing to endure. What then? How do we find the grace to rejoice when such moments occur? We need to always examine the source of our joy. Many rejoice over the trivial. When a team wins, or a good grade is received, or when a promotion is granted at work, people tend to get excited. But as soon as a tragedy unfolds, or a schedule disruption occurs, or an appliance goes on the blink, such people are back to the fussin' and cussin' of normal life. Go back to the "source" issue. If our joy is found in only the trivial, then yes, we will ride the roller coaster of ups and downs. But what if the source of our joy is found elsewhere? Surely it should be placed in something more important, more powerful, and more permanent. For the believer, the source of our joy is found in our relationship with Jesus Christ. Here is why that is significant. Christ's love for us never changes. His intercession on our behalf never changes. His grace never changes. His watch care over our lives never changes. In the midst of a topsy-turvy world, the Unchangeable Christ remains a constant. So in reality, the bad days should cause us to rejoice even more than usual. On such days, we should delight in the fact that nothing about our present circumstances can alter the heart of Christ for a moment. We are his and he is ours. Rejoice.

Prayer

Father, thank you for the everlasting, always loving Savior. Teach us to rejoice always as we celebrate his presence in our lives. Amen.

"To this end also we pray for you always, that our God will count you worthy of your calling, and fulfill every desire for goodness and the work of faith with power, so that the name of our Lord Jesus will be glorified in you, and you in Him, according to the grace of our God and the Lord Jesus Christ." 2 Thessalonians 1:11-12 NASB

Observation

Paul prays that the faith of the Thessalonians would prove so genuine that God would count them "worthy of their calling." In other words, he prays that the investment that God has made in their lives would bear fruit... that they would be worthy of the Name they bear. Notice that he also prays that the name of Jesus Christ would be glorified in them. Add it up and it's a prayer filled with great hope and expectation. Paul is praying for people he loves and a church that he established.

Application

"Is the name of our Lord Jesus being glorified in you?" We all struggle to live out our faith and model the heart of Christ. We have our moments when glimpses of Jesus emerge, but often we are rather poor examples of what it means to be Christian. Perhaps we harbor a poor attitude, cling to a grudge, act selfishly, tolerate a little impurity in our hearts and a little hatred in our souls, embrace complacency, live with mediocrity, or speak harshly and act rudely. Is Jesus being glorified in us?

The calling to live a Christian life is very much a journey. We stumble, behave inconsistently, and fail miserably. With a little hope and a lot of grace, we strive to do more. Even after decades of practice, we may still find ourselves missing the mark. In our own strength, we will never measure up. But there is help for the journey! God knew that Christ set the bar high. And rather than leaving us to a life of failure, God chose to place within us a solution. Because the Spirit indwells our lives, our hearts change, our attitudes alter, and our minds find renewal. We don't have to languish in half-hearted discipleship. We can be recreated, transformed, and changed by the work of the Spirit. The secret is to open our lives to the complete filling of God's Spirit. If you really want to, you can glorify Christ in your life today. Let go of self in order to let the Spirit work.

Prayer

Father, we thank you this morning for your indwelling Spirit. By his power in our hearts, may we live better lives and bring greater glory to your Son. Amen.

Day 189 — 2 Thessalonians 2: Correct Interpretation

"But we should always give thanks to God for you, brethren beloved by the Lord, because God has chosen you from the beginning for salvation through sanctification by the Spirit and faith in the truth."
2 Thessalonians 2:13 NASB

Observation

In this verse Paul emphasizes the importance of believing the truth. He begins with a word of thanksgiving. Paul was continually giving thanks to the Lord for the believers. He was thankful to the Lord for their salvation. Their salvation was accomplished by the Spirit as they placed their faith in Christ. Yet note the balance of the Spirit and the truth (the word.) The Spirit without the word is mute; He has nothing to say. The word without the Spirit is lifeless; it has no power to act. The work of the Spirit is always united with the work of the word.

Application

This connection about which Paul writes is important to understand. It is God's Spirit, working within us that motivates, guides, challenges, and encourages us. The Spirit is given voice through God's word. As we read the Bible, the lessons that we need to glean, the instruction we need to hear, and the conviction we need to feel, are revealed as the Spirit illuminates those words in order to give us understanding. The word becomes the mouthpiece of the Spirit. Though the Spirit can guide and direct us in a number of ways, he speaks most consistently through our reading of God's word. Note the other side of this connection. To read the word and to attempt its application apart from the Spirit is a dangerous discipline on our part. Who are we that we would dare to claim enough wisdom and insight acting on our own to correctly apply God's instruction to any situation? We need the help of the Spirit to ensure that our thoughts are correct and that our words are accurate. There is always a danger in taking God's word and misusing it. (I would remind you that even Satan quoted scripture in his attempt to tempt Jesus in the wilderness.) Let's be careful with the word of God. It is not ours to manipulate or use as mere leverage in some argument. It's more sacred than that. Read the word and call on the Spirit as you do. Let's be people who seek wisdom and the ability to use it correctly.

Prayer

Father, we thank you for the written word and for the work of your Spirit. May we never lean on our own understanding, but in all our ways acknowledge you. Amen.

Day 190 2 Thessalonians 3: Making Peace with Your World

"Now may the Lord of peace Himself continually grant you peace in every circumstance. The Lord be with you all!"
2 Thessalonians 3:16 NASB

Observation

In the final sentences of his letter to the Thessalonians, Paul offers a prayer for peace in the lives of those believers. It's an easy thought connection to make. Because we pray to the "Lord of Peace," surely the Lord can grant peace to those who claim it in faith. Paul's prayer is that they would have peace in every circumstance. What an important blessing to claim... that of finding peace, contentment, assurance, and hope in the midst of every circumstance.

Application

I would bet that almost everyone who reads this devotional thought could use a little peace in some area of his/her life. Truthfully, most of us struggle each day with some need, some problem, or some burden that robs us of peace and joy. Some are struggling today with finances. They will awaken this morning with a heavy cloud hanging over their heads fretting about how financial obligations are going to be met. I know of others this morning who are not at peace in terms of personal health. Because of serious concerns, they will awaken this day with great uncertainty and angst. Still, there are others who have no peace in terms of the key relationships in their lives. The marriage is strained, there is tension with the teenager, or there is brokenness with a close friend. Others will claim no peace today because of the stress of over-planned schedules or on-going problems at work.

We all live out those various scenarios, don't we? There is always some gnawing tension that robs our joy and eats away at our vitality. We don't have to live that life. It is not the life that God created us to live. In his writing to the church at Philippi, Paul wrote, "Be anxious for nothing, but in everything by prayer and supplication with thanksgiving, let your requests be known to God. And the PEACE of God, which surpasses all comprehension, shall guard your hearts and your minds in Christ Jesus" (Phil. 4:6-7). Maybe this morning you need to claim the promise of God's word and then pray a prayer like Paul. Name that which is troubling to you this day, and then claim the peace of God as you pray to the Lord of Peace for help.

Prayer

Father, may we see clearly this morning that which robs us of peace. Teach us to pray for your perfect peace in that situation. Grant us both grace and hope. Amen.

Day 191 — 1 Timothy 1: Purpose

"It is a trustworthy statement, deserving full acceptance, that Christ Jesus came into the world to save sinners, among whom I am foremost of all." 1 Timothy 1:15 NASB

Observation

In 1 & 2 Timothy Paul offers instruction to Timothy, a young man to whom he has entrusted the church at Ephesus. Paul offers counsel, advice, and wisdom as an older mentor to young Timothy. As he writes about his own spiritual journey, he reminds Timothy of the grace of Jesus Christ that allowed Jesus to forgive him and completely change his heart. He declares that he was once the worst of sinners but Christ came to offer him new life. Notice the sense of purpose about which Paul writes... "Christ Jesus came into the world to save sinners." Pretty clear and direct, right? Jesus' purpose was to rescue sinners and offer them new life.

Application

Sometimes it helps to know your purpose. The mission of Jesus was well defined. He came to offer forgiveness and salvation to those who have lost their way. I wonder what difference it would make to all of us if our purpose and raison d'être were so clearly defined. Surely our lives would be more productive and filled with more joy if we could just define our purpose and spend our days doing the very things for which we were placed on the planet. The good news is that we can have some clarity around that thought. In his remarkable book, *The Purpose Driven Life*, Pastor Rick Warren states that the number one reason we are on the planet is to bring glory to God. As we order our day and plan our schedule suddenly we do so with a different priority. We live, not to serve self or further our careers; we live to push the agenda of God. You see, like Christ, we too are on the planet to save sinners by telling them of the love of Christ. We exist to show compassion, offer grace, extend forgiveness, and represent Christ in all that we do. Our purpose is to see how many lives we can influence for the Kingdom. How that gets done in the everyday experience of life can be as different as each person. It's the mindset that we must develop. In all that we do, wherever we do it, whenever we do it, we live to bring God honor and glory. Today, why not trying living with a sense of purpose. Willfully and obediently choose to glorify God in all that you do.

Prayer

Father, thank you for calling each of us into your Kingdom's work. My we live to glorify you in all that we do. Amen.

Day 191 — 1 Timothy 2: Religion and Politics

"First of all, then, I urge that entreaties and prayers, petitions and thanksgivings, be made on behalf of all men, for kings and all who are in authority, so that we may lead a tranquil and quiet life in all godliness and dignity." 1 Timothy 2:1-2 NASB

Observation

In this letter to Timothy, Paul first addresses the need for prayers to be offered on behalf of all men, and then specifically, he names kings and all those who are in authority. His reasoning is that a stable nation provides for a stable life in which religion can be practiced and dialogue can remain civil. This word of instruction was a difficult word even in the day of Paul. The entire Christian faith was lived out under the influence of the Roman government. Many had felt the sting of oppression and the weight of tyranny and yet Paul urges prayer for the leaders. Paul knew that stability would create a greater environment for Kingdom work.

Application

Do we take this message to heart? Do we actively pray for our government, our leaders, our President, and our senators? There are plenty who spread criticism and cynicism and who even spew hatred toward those elected to lead at every level. Apparently, some have decided that that it's okay to act non-Christian when it comes to political thought and attitude. In recent years it has become acceptable to allow the ends to justify the means. The political divide has become so great in our land that we now tolerate any type of behavior and even applaud those who go to extremes as long as they are on "our" side. Can't we do better? Can't a Christian nation find better ways to dialogue and discuss?

What if we took Paul's challenge seriously? What if we prayed more than we criticized? What if we acted more Christ-like when it comes to politics? What if we attacked problems and not personalities? What if we returned to civility and respect in our political discourse? Please understand that neither side has an exclusive claim on wisdom or truth. America will be at its best, not when we push political partisanship, but when we promote the common good. Join me this morning in praying for our leaders. Let's pray, not for our own agendas, but for the wisdom of God to be evident in each life.

Prayer

Father, thank you for this land that we love. May we do our part as a Christian citizen today by praying for those who lead. Amen.

"These men must also first be tested; then let them serve as deacons if they are beyond reproach." 1 Timothy 3:10 NASB

Observation

Paul offers Timothy some advice in this chapter about the qualifications of both elders (overseers/pastors) in the church and deacons. In his description of those to serve in the office of deacon, Paul specifically indicates that the office is not to be taken lightly. Those who serve as deacons are to be tested. In other words, their merit for serving in the church should be proven over time. They should have a history of doing and saying the right thing. Additionally, they should serve if they are above reproach. Paul demands a high standard. It is his expectation that leaders in the church should truly act like leaders in the church and in the faith.

Application

Though I would certainly echo Paul's scrutiny and challenge for those who serve in key leadership roles in the church, I would actually extend some of his challenge to all those who make up the body of Christ. For me, every Christian, every church member, should be held to a standard of faith and to a level of accountability. There is responsibility demanded of us when we join ourselves to the Body of Christ. We have to be conscious of the fact that we represent the love of Christ to a lost and fallen world. We have to think consciously and act deliberately as we function each day in the world in which we live. We sometimes need to ask the difficult question, "Is my church growing because of me, or is it growing in spite of me?" Let's be honest, none of us are perfect. None of us will speak without the occasional stumble or act without the occasional mistake. But the admission of our flawed humanity is not an excuse for poor behavior. Our constant challenge is to glorify God in all that we do and bring honor to the church we attend. We need to feel the burden and responsibility of Godly living. We need to acknowledge that every individual life reflects on the greater life of the church. Let our prayer be that of faithful, authentic, and honest living. May we live daily as those under the control of Christ's Spirit.

Prayer

Father, forgive us when we conduct ourselves in ways that bring dishonor to both the church and the Kingdom. Make us accountable to each other. Amen.

"Take pains with these things; be absorbed in them, so that your progress will be evident to all." 1 Timothy 4:15 NASB

Observation

As Paul continues to challenge Timothy to be the leader that God intends for him to become, he reminds him to give careful attention to the public reading of scripture, to exhortation (preaching), and to teaching. In other words, Timothy is to maintain certain spiritual disciplines in order to grow in his faith and in order to emerge as a role model and leader for the church. Notice the key word in our focus verse... be "absorbed" in them. Timothy is challenged to a healthy obsession with the things of faith. It will be as he deliberately and consistently maintains specific spiritual disciplines that he will grow in his faith.

Application

It's easy to get "absorbed" in a lot of things. We get absorbed by our work, our hobbies, special causes, organizations, our families, and our various activities. (How many of you get absorbed in watching countless hours of college football each fall or basketball games each March?) We understand Paul's use of the phrase, right? Immerse yourself. Involve yourself. Invest yourself. Paul's challenge is for all of us to become absorbed by the things of God, specifically, the kind of spiritual disciplines we should maintain each day. It's hard to grow in your faith and in your relationship with Christ, apart from the daily disciplines of prayer, scripture reading, and a few moments of careful reflection. I've discovered that we become absorbed by the things we love to do the most. We gravitate toward those activities. When it comes to the things of faith, there are many who approach such activities as being things they "have to do," rather than things they "love to do." See the difference? Obligation is not the motivation that love is. We should want to spend time with Christ, because we love him, not because we feel obligated to do so.

So how do we develop a love for the things of God? It begins by taking the first step of taking the time to spend a few moments with the word and with a prayer list. Do that again tomorrow... and then the next day, and then the next. Over time, your heart will begin to change. What was once arduous will become a joy. What was once a burden will become blessing. Get absorbed and grow your faith.

Prayer

Father, may each of us learn the lasting value of spending moments with our faith each day. Amen.

Day 195 1 Timothy 5: Positive Power of Peer Pressure

"Those who continue in sin, rebuke in the presence of all, so that the rest also will be fearful of sinning." 1 Timothy 5:20 NASB

Observation

While continuing to offer advice to Timothy, Paul gives a charge about those who are leaders (elders/pastors) in the church. He speaks about the honor that comes with the job and the way in which they are to be compensated fairly. Paul also addresses the issue of misconduct. When an elder sins, and the sin is confirmed by multiple witnesses, the sin is to be exposed and the elder is to be rebuked in the presence of all. Paul's council for such action is so that other elders will be fearful of sinning and thus will hold themselves to a higher standard of behavior. Paul hopes to use peer pressure as a positive way to reinforce good behavior.

Application

We often speak of the negative influence of peer pressure. We warn our kids while young, to be mindful of getting in with the "wrong crowd." We know how quickly a group of friends with negative intentions can steer a newcomer to do the wrong things. And so we worry about peer pressure and its negative results. But on a better note, we also know of the positive influence that the "right crowd" can bring. How many testimonies have you heard in which an adult gives credit to the youth group that once helped him to mature and think better thoughts when he was just a teenager? Or what about the once-wayward athlete that gives credit to coaches and fellow players for keeping him out of trouble? Surely we know the value of positive role models and healthy peer pressure. In fact, don't most of us try to steer our families and friends towards the right involvements where the influences will be positive?

So my challenge for you this morning is to consider what kind of peer have you become. As you consider your words, your actions, and your influence over others, are you helping to build up or to tear down? Do you spread encouragement or do you tend to scatter a lot of negativity? Do you raise others to a higher standard, or do you bring them down to your level of pessimism? There's enough negativity out there... let's commit ourselves into becoming the best role models and encouragers that we can be. Let's be part of the positive peer pressure.

Prayer

Father, make us accountable for the people within our sphere of influence. May we be quick to offer grace, good words, and positive ideas. Amen.

"Instruct those who are rich in this present world not to be conceited or to fix their hope on the uncertainty of riches, but on God, who richly supplies us with all things to enjoy." 1 Timothy 6:17 NASB

Observation

In his words to Timothy at the close of his first letter, Paul discusses the dangers of riches and how some, who chase after wealth, fall prey to temptation and are drawn away from the faith. Paul knows that money can be a hazardous material to handle. With wealth, men can bless and build, or they can hoard and hurt. Paul wants those who have wealth to understand that wealth is fleeting and does nothing to prepare the heart for the life that is to come. His challenge is to fix hope on the things that God supplies that lead to greater contentment.

Application

Do any of us really need another lesson in the volatility of money? Nearly each week, the market plunges up and down and many become distraught with the latest economic forecast. It seems that we constantly ride the roller coaster that takes us from prosperity to poverty in just seconds. Surely we have learned by now not to place ultimate trust in our wealth. The key to successful living is one of priority. Why chase that which will not last beyond the grave? Why set our hope on that which can be so quickly devalued?

I'm at a point in my life when I am beginning to assess this whole success vs. significance question. The older, and hopefully wiser I become, I find myself caring more for significance. Sure, I'd love to be financially secure and have plenty of cash to pay for college tuitions, weddings, and cars, but at the end of the day I'm really more concerned about significance. Am I making a difference in the life of my family and friends? Am I building Kingdom foundations in the lives of others that will last for many years to come? Am I living and leaving a legacy of Godly instruction, grace-filled acts, and role-modeling examples? There is an old expression that states, "You can't take it with you." I'm more concerned about what I am leaving behind than what I am taking with me. You should be too. Let's challenge ourselves to fix our hope on God and worry more about people building than portfolio expansion.

Prayer

Father, may we learn to value that which really counts. Teach us that our hope and trust should be in you alone. Make us significant more than successful. Amen.

"Guard, through the Holy Spirit who dwells in us, the treasure which has been entrusted to you." 2 Timothy 1:14 NASB

Observation

Second Timothy contains Paul's "last words." From a Roman prison, the aged apostle wrote his final instructions to his protégé Timothy. Knowing that this letter might be his final contact with Timothy, he imparts words of encouragement to his son in the faith. Paul challenges Timothy to guard and protect the treasure that has been entrusted to him. By "treasure" Paul could have been referring to the instruction given to Timothy by Paul. He may be referring to Timothy's role in caring for the church at Ephesus. Or, he may be referring to the treasure of the gospel—the message that gives life. The instruction is to guard, protect, defend, and care for that which God has placed in his heart and hands.

Application

God has entrusted all of us with treasures to keep. Like Timothy, we are challenged, with the help of the Holy Spirit, to defend and protect that which God has placed in our charge. There are many implications. First, we are called to protect our families. The gift of a spouse, along with children, deserves our best efforts. God expects us to nurture, love, encourage, protect, and defend our families. Part of that challenge is to pray faithfully, love devotedly, and give sacrificially to our families. It must become our acknowledged responsibility to make sure that they know the love of Christ because they have seen him role-modeled in us. We are also called to guard the treasure of the gospel within us. Unlike other treasures, we guard the treasure of the gospel each time that we give it away. The greater the number of disciples, the more the gospel is defended. Guarding such a hope must become a priority for every believer. And so we must share the gospel story as often as we can. We are also called to guard the treasure of our reputations. Whenever we live honest, authentic, and genuine lives before both God and the world, we defend the reputation of Christ that dwells within us. Christ is glorified when we do and say the right things.

We share a big task... that of guarding the treasure. May God help us to guard well all that has been entrusted to each of us.

Prayer

Father, we thank you this morning for the responsibility that you give to all of us as guardians of your treasures. Make us fit for the task. Amen.

"You therefore, my son, be strong in the grace that is in Christ Jesus."
2 Timothy 2:1 NASB

Observation

Interesting verse, right? What exactly is Paul telling Timothy to do? Here's the same verse from the Amplified Version... "So You, my son, be strong (strengthened inwardly) in the grace (spiritual blessing) that is [to be found only] in Christ Jesus." Paul is reminding Timothy to find strength from the sense of spiritual blessing that comes from Christ. It was Paul's hope that Timothy would find all the peace, all the encouragement, all the wisdom, and all the strength needed from his relationship with Jesus. In fact, notice that Paul writes with the imperative voice... "Be strong." Paul encourages Timothy to find great strength through the power of Christ at work in his life.

Application

So where is the source of your inner strength? Where do you find the energy, the stamina, and the poise to maintain your sense of perseverance? People look for inner strength in a lot of places. Some reach for the latest self-help book in the hope that it will provide some small pearl of wisdom to bolster their resolve. Some look for strength in the key relationships of their lives. Find the right friends and life gets less arduous, right? Others look for strength by attempting to master their physical selves through diet and exercise. Still others play the "positive thinking" card, believing that they can conjure up some source of inner strength through some mental exercise.

Do you see the problem with all of those lines of thought? They all are based on self-sufficiency rather than God dependency. We were all brought to life when the breath of God first entered our bodies and we will be sustained only when we allow God to again breathe power into our limbs. Our strength comes only through a genuine relationship with Jesus Christ. If you want to find an inner strength that will sustain you through all of the ups and downs of your life journey, you need to connect in a significant way to the One in whom all authority has been granted. Be strong today. Find the strength you need through your simple faith in Christ.

Prayer

Father, we thank you that our needs are always met in Christ. Through our faith in him, may we have the strength needed this day to meet the challenges that come our way. Amen.

Day 199 2 Timothy 3: Worse Before It Gets Better

"But realize this, that in the last days difficult times will come."
2 Timothy 3:1 NASB

Observation

Paul offers Timothy an ominous warning about the future, based partially on what he perceives in the hearts of men. Later in the passage Paul outlines the way in which men will become lovers of self rather than lovers of God. Greed, arrogance, selfishness, pride, and conceit are just a few of the qualities that will dominate the hearts of men. Those who pursue God with a clean heart and pure mind will feel oppression from others. Paul even states that all who live Godly lives will be persecuted. Such an ominous warning could drive some to despair and despondency. It is not Paul's desire to weaken our resolve, but rather to bolster it. Knowing that the rise of godlessness will become very apparent, we must remain steadfast in our faith, committed more than ever to sharing the love of Christ.

Application

Notice that Paul doesn't state that the Christian life will be one of ease. He never promises that living a life in which we strive "to do the right thing" will be without consequence. In fact, he promises just the opposite. Difficult days are coming. Because we have been warned, doesn't it make sense to prepare our hearts? Let's talk for a moment about the difficult times that are coming... what will such moments resemble? Surely there will be a rise in selfishness. Humankind will become increasingly self-centered and much less concerned for the needs of others. People will buy into a situational ethic in which love of self becomes the rule of the day. People will continue to have little regard for the things of faith. The Sabbath day will become anything but a day of rest. Greed will win out over grace. Hatred will increase. Personal pleasure will win out over meeting the common good. To paraphrase Paul, "It's going to get worse." But understand the triumphant of evil will be short lived. For those living in the midst of the last days, there will be a distant horizon whose brilliant light will quickly eclipse the darkest hour. Faith will prevail. Christ will triumph. The glory of God will be revealed. So don't be discouraged if the world seems more hostile, more desolate, and more cruel. Christ is coming and we will share the victory of that day.

Prayer

Dear Father, guard us during the darkest days so that we may know the joy of coming victory. Keep our heart pure and our faith strong. Amen.

"Preach the word; be ready in season and out of season; reprove, rebuke, exhort, with great patience and instruction." 2 Timothy 4:2 NASB

Observation

Paul is down to his last few words of instruction to Timothy as he writes this final chapter. His life will soon end and so these words are among his last. With almost his final breath he challenges young Timothy to "preach the word." Timothy is exhorted to be ready at all times. His preaching is to reprove, rebuke, challenge, inspire, and correct. But don't miss the phrase that follows... he is to offer such words with "great patience and instruction." In a very real way, Paul challenges Timothy to "speak the truth in love." Though his words of truth might confront and even be difficult for his listeners to hear, he is to preach with a sense of patience and grace. It would be his task to lovingly invite others to walk more closely with Christ.

Application

Sometimes those of us who are called to proclaim God's truth, are called to speak difficult words that call our hearers into accountability and repentance. We confront people with changes that need to be made and new life directions that need to be plotted. Whether you are a pastor, a Sunday School teacher, or even a friend who is attempting to offer a word of counsel to a brother or sister who has lost their way, please understand that the gospel message might offer sharp rebuke and painful self-examination. The message of Christ will both confront and comfort. What is at times just as important as the words we say are the ways in which we say them. Paul's challenge is to offer our words with patience and careful instruction. Our attitude should never be one of angry condescension, but instead our words should be of loving hope. We will build the Kingdom best when we learn to season our words with grace and patience. I challenge you this morning to "do the work of an evangelist." Go and tell others about the hope of the gospel. Challenge them to turn from the wrong pursuits and discover the life that Christ wills for them to live. But do so with patience and love and consistency.

Prayer

Father, as we dare to proclaim and teach to others the claims of the Christian faith, may we do so with grace, with love, and with patience. Amen.

Day 201 Titus 1: Walking the Walk

"An elder must live a blameless life. He must be faithful to his wife, and his children must be believers who don't have a reputation for being wild or rebellious." Titus 1:6 NLT

Observation

The book of Titus is named for a co-worker of Paul, whom Paul left in Crete to help establish churches in each city on the Island. Part of Titus' work was that of appointing elders, or pastors, who would shepherd each congregation. These elders were to be held to a high standard. There were certain expectations for those who would lead in such a way. High standards are not just for the paid clergy. Surely God expects much from each of us.

Application

Who or what sets the standards for your life? Who sets the standards of morality, ethical behavior, or decency? Who sets the standards for conduct or for words spoken? To whom do you look to serve as your mentor, your example, and your leader? Don't we tend to look for guidance in a lot of places? Sometimes the standards are set by political leaders. Sometimes it's the movers and shakers of Hollywood that shape our character. Sometimes our peer groups help set the standards in our lives. And yes, sometimes we look to our ministers to be the role models. We surely need standard bearers in our world. We need someone to draw the boundaries, set the limits, and model the right behavior. And sometimes, "those people" need to be us. Scary, isn't it, to think that each of us may be pressed into service as someone's role model? Every Christian believer bears responsibility for ethical behavior and moral decision-making. The non-believing world is always looking to us, to see if we are real and to note whether or not our faith is authentic. Though you may not want to bear the scrutiny of someone else's watchful eye, surely you are the object of someone's vision. So how do you shape up? Are you a blameless man or woman? Do you consistently model Christ-like behavior? Do you seek to honor God each day that you live? It's a high calling and heavy responsibility. But if not us, then who will bear the image of Christ to a non-believing world? So watch your step... be mindful of your example... carefully guard your witness. People are watching.

Prayer

Father, remind us that we are as your ambassadors to the world. Remind us that your image will only be displayed to the world, when it is display in each of us. Amen.

Day 202 — Titus 2: Help the Old Lady Cross the Street

"Jesus gave His life to free us from every kind of sin, to cleanse us, and to make us His very own people, totally committed to doing good deeds." Titus 2:14 NLT

Observation

Paul writes to remind Titus of the grace and demand of knowing Jesus. In Christ, we have great freedom from the oppression of sin. We are cleansed from our sins and called into a special relationship with him. We are also called to live out our faith by being committed to doing good deeds. In other words, there should be a practical expression of our faith. Changed people should live changed lives.

Application

Are you committed to doing good deeds? Is the desire to help others in your DNA? When I was just a young boy my parents got me involved in Scouting. I still remember the first pin I ever received as a Cub Scout. It was my Bobcat pin. It was given to all beginning scouts when they first learned the essentials of being a Cub Scout. The pin was placed on each scout's uniform upside down and could only be turned right side up after he had done a good deed. There had never been a group of boys more eager to clean a room or walk the dog! An early lesson in service was instilled. There is something of the joy of being a Christian that should motivate us to such a spirit of benevolence. Paul indicates that we are to be "totally committed" to doing good deeds. We should seek opportunities to invest ourselves in ways that meet the needs of others. It is my belief that every Christian should discover a place of service. Every Christian should be actively engaged in a ministry that provides healing, encouragement, assistance, or teaching. We must move outside the simple world of self-need and self-gratification. We must look to the needs of others and ask how our investment could make a difference. We should be committed to this idea of daily service. So where do you serve? Where do you "give yourself away?" What corner of the world is brighter because you have made an investment? When we do "good deeds" we may not have a pin on our uniform that we get to invert, but we will know the smile of our Father who calls us to a life of service and grace. So don't just sit there. Go do something good.

Prayer

Father, thank you for calling us into a life of service. May we invest well, the gifts and talents you have placed in our lives. May our commitment to service not only change the lives of those we serve, but our lives as well. Amen.

"But—'When God our Savior revealed His kindness and love, He saved us, not because of the righteous things we had done, but because of His mercy. He washed away our sins, giving us a new birth and new life through the Holy Spirit.'" Titus 3:4-5 NLT

Observation

Paul is careful to remind his readers that the genesis of our salvation is always found in God's kindness and love. Salvation is never a result of what we have done or have not done. We don't earn salvation and we can't buy it. There is nothing we can do to obtain it. It comes to us through the kindness and love of God. Because of mercy, patience, and affection for us, God grants us new life by removing our sins and giving us new birth into the eternal Kingdom.

Application

You may have heard the expression, "It's not about you." Life certainly presents those moments when it really isn't about us. More often than not, the spotlight doesn't shine on our accomplishments or great qualities. It is rare than any of us can take credit for any particular good thing. Though we may contribute toward a group effort that does some important work, it is unusual that we are the catalyst for any great deed. This is especially true in terms of faith and salvation. When it comes to our inclusion into God's eternal Kingdom, it really isn't about us. It's not what we have done that makes us righteous in the eyes of God. It's about God's merciful attention that is directed our way. To couch it in another context, salvation is always a "top-down" gift, never a "bottom-up" earned payoff. We simply don't have the means to obtain that which is not ours to grasp. It is the work of God and through God's intervention that we are given the hope of new birth. Does that mean that our actions don't matter? Does that mean our destinies have all been pre-determined? Not at all. Actions do matter. We do good things, not in order to be saved, but as proof of our surrender to God's Lordship. We do good things to demonstrate our love for God, not to somehow gain God's attention. In terms of our salvation, what God pre-determines is the method by which it is offered. Salvation comes through faith in Christ alone. Though is it a gift of grace, we have the ability to choose whether or not we will accept the gift. So don't long for the world's spotlight... just be grateful that God's grace is what will truly illumine your life.

Prayer

Father, thank you for loving us when we yet unlovable. Thank you for offering grace when we were far from deserving it. Amen.

Day 204 — Philemon 1: Be Known as a Grace-Giver

"Your love has given me much joy and comfort, my brother, for your kindness has often refreshed the hearts of God's people."
Philemon 1:7 NLT

Observation

The book of Philemon contains only one chapter comprised of 25 verses. It is the shortest of Paul's letters. Paul writes to Philemon, a proven and generous co-laborer in the gospel, with a very deep request. He asks that Philemon forgive and take back a runaway slave who has accepted Christ under Paul's teaching. This slave, Onesimus, has been a great source of help to Paul and so Paul asks that he be received, forgiven, and accepted as a brother. Obviously, the theme of forgiveness is at the heart of this short book.

Application

Notice the descriptive words said about Philemon. His "kindness has often refreshed the hearts of God's people." We need people like that in our lives. We need those friends who will offer us help when needed, encouragement when required, and grace when undeserved. We need people, who while living the faith authentically will refresh our very hearts. I can't know all the needs faced by each of you who will read this devotional thought. But I'm pretty sure that some of you have a heart that needs a little refreshment. You need a little joy... a little strength... a little hope... a little calmness... maybe a little sanity. I desperately pray that you have the people in your life who will provide you with such gifts. I hope that through prayers and conversations with others that you will feel renewed hope and will find in those friends the presence of Christ. In the past week alone, I have had several friends speak to me of their prayerful support and encouraging thoughts as we approach another busy holiday season. It always means a lot. Now let's play the flip side of this thought. Have you refreshed the heart of someone lately with your kindness? I know that you have some friends in your life who could use a little refreshment. Why not give them a call, or send them an email? Why not look for a way to do something tangible to show them your support? Love is always a two-way street. We need to receive it and we need to offer it. I hope your day is encouraging as you both give and receive a little refreshment.

Prayer

Father, thank you for placing in each of us the capacity to extend grace and offer ministry in the lives of others. Show us a way before this day ends, to offer someone a little refreshment. Amen.

Day 205 Hebrews 1: Image Bearer

"The Son reflects the glory of God and shows exactly what God is like. He holds everything together with His powerful word. When the Son made people clean from their sins, He sat down at the right side of God, the Great One in heaven." Hebrews 1:3 NCV

Observation

The writer of Hebrews is careful to equate the nature of Christ with the nature of God. Not only does the writer say that Jesus reflects the glory of God, but check out the next part of that verse... "and (He) shows exactly what God is like." Some translations state, "He is the exact representation of His being." Christ came to reveal the Father to each of us. When we read the words of Christ, see the compassion of his heart, and watch how he transforms the lame, crippled, and blind, we are able to see a very real and tangible image of God. We know what God is like because Christ has revealed God to us.

Application

Here in the South, we might say that, "someone is the spitting image of their father." Look up the origins of the phrase and you will find a couple of ideas. One idea is that the phrase is a derivation of the phrase, "splitting image," which refers to the splitting of a plank of wood into two separate pieces whose grain patterns match exactly. (You can sometimes see this decorative mirroring technique used on a tabletop or on the back of a violin.) The other suggestion is that the phrase refers to the idea that someone looks so much like their father that the father could have "spit him out of his own mouth." Choose whichever origin you like. Both work as an explanation for what the writer of Hebrews is describing. Jesus was an exact image or representation of the Father. Most of us understand that thought without much trouble. Here's the more difficult question this morning, "Do WE, who are called to be the image bearers of God before the world, reflect Him accurately?" In other words, are we the "spitting image of God?" Do we reflect God's grace, love, compassion, and forgiveness? We should. We need to be conscious of the fact that some people will get their entire impression of God by looking only at our lives. Does that scare you? It should. Let's resolve this day to at least attempt to see ourselves as those who will in some way reflect the Glory of our Father.

Prayer

Father, challenge us this day to speak with your grace, act with your mercy, and love with your heart. Amen.

"We must pay the most careful attention, therefore, to what we have heard, so that we do not drift away." Hebrews 2:1 NIV

Observation

The writer of Hebrews opens the second chapter with a very important word of counsel. Because there is always a danger in drifting away from core beliefs, important doctrine, and moral guidelines, the Christian is advised to pay very careful attention to what has been taught by the disciples and what has been written in God's word. In the second verse, the writer says, "How shall we escape if we neglect so great a salvation?" In other words, if believers are not careful to guard the words of truth shared with them, they are in danger of losing both distinctiveness and assurances because they have not treated the words of the gospel as if they matter. (I do not think that we can lose salvation once we have fully embraced the claims of our faith. I do think however, that we can certainly drift away from our faith positions and spiritual virtues if we are not careful to guard them.)

Application

More to the point... "We must pay careful attention to what we have heard." It's always possible to hear someone, without really listening to that person. Ever listen to your spouse without really hearing what he/she says? You may give the appearance of listening, but your thoughts are a million miles away and thus you haven't really heard a thing. Sometimes we treat God's word the same way. We might read it, or even listen as it is taught or proclaimed, but we do so without really hearing what the text has to offer. It's like the words go in one ear and out the other, without ever grabbing our attention. James warns us "to be doers of the Word and not merely hearers only." In the context of our focus verse, let me advise us all to "be listeners of the Word and not merely hearers only." Do you get the point? We need to give the word of God time to "stew" for a while in our minds. We need to hear it, ponder its meaning, meditate on its message, and find a point of application. The challenge is to "pay careful attention." The words of Christ matter. The message of the Kingdom matters. The gospel can never impact our lives, if we do not provide a fertile ground into which it might be planted. So take the word... hear it carefully and apply it accurately. Let it transform your life. Let it keep you from a dangerous drift.

Prayer

Father, may we guard carefully the words of truth, knowing that in them we find life. Amen.

"But encourage one another daily, as long as it is called "Today," so that none of you may be hardened by sin's deceitfulness." Hebrews 3:13 NIV

Observation

The writer of Hebrews was concerned that the deceitfulness of sin could pull people away from their pursuit of God. He was fearful that temptation and the constant pull of culture and peer pressure would cause some to lose focus and actually turn to false gods and unimportant matters. And so his admonition in our focus verse is that of encouraging each other "daily." The writer knew that constant encouragement was needed in the life of every believer in order to keep each person pursuing the things of God.

Application

What kind of encourager are you? How well do you push, prod, and pray others to keep walking in the faith? Most of us, if we have any sense of goodness in our hearts, know how to encourage the people around us. We say kind words. We write a little note. We stand and applaud when some recognition is given. We offer a pat on the back when some person has done a good job. We understand the concept. But how are we doing as "spiritual encouragers?" Are we pushing people along in their pursuit of Holy God? Knowing that every person on the planet can use a little encouragement, how do we offer spiritual cheerleading? Here are a few thoughts. First, be willing to talk about matters of faith. Because our spirituality is such a private part of our lives, we are reluctant at times to bring up such things with family and friends. We feel awkward about such conversations. But spiritual conversations are important and we must be willing to have them. Second, encourage Christian behavior. Prod your friends to do the right thing... worship attendance, scripture reading, moral and ethical living. I am convinced that many live morally ambivalent lives because no one is coaching them to do otherwise. Third, encourage others through your prayers. If you are not praying daily for your family and friends, you are not offering them spiritual encouragement. Prayer connects the needs of others with the power of Holy God. It is important that you pray for their needs. Pursuing the Christian faith is not an easy thing... so let's encourage each other, even this day.

Prayer

Father, forge us into being faithful encouragers who push both family and friends into a deeper, more courageous life of faith. Amen.

Day 208 Hebrews 4: Guarding the Thought Life

"Nothing in all creation is hidden from God's sight. Everything is uncovered and laid bare before the eyes of him to whom we must give account." Hebrews 4:13 NIV

Observation

In the verse that precedes our focus verse, the writer of Hebrews describes the way in which the word of God is active and alive and able to judge the thoughts and the intentions of the heart. Then comes the reminder of our focus verse that nothing is hidden from God's sight. Again, not our thoughts, nor the intentions of our hearts, nor even our actions are hidden from God. The scrutiny of God sees it all. We are therefore accountable unto God for the totality of our lives, both what we think and what we do. And notice that it is to our God that we are to give an account. In other words, we are responsible for how we live and what we think.

Application

The "thought life" can really get us into trouble. Most of us tend to do a pretty good job with our actions. For the most part, the world sees consistency from most of us. Our words are usually well controlled and our actions decent. Our outward lives seem consistent and godly. But the thought life can be very different. Most of us harbor a few attitudes and thoughts that we would be shocked for our family and friends to discover. There are impure thoughts that include everything from lust, to hatred, to greed, to ridicule, etc. Though others may never know what we are thinking, still the thoughts are there, rumbling around in our heads. One real danger is the fact that thoughts can lead to action. Every action that we commit was first crafted by a thought in our minds. James writes about this progression... "But each one is tempted when he is carried away and enticed by his own lust. Then when lust has conceived, it gives birth to sin; and when sin is accomplished, it brings forth death" (James 1:14-15). You see the problem. Thoughts lead to action. Impure thoughts can lead to impure action. And so we must guard our thought life. If we know that God sees the heart and knows even the thoughts that roll around in our heads, shouldn't we be embarrassed? Shouldn't we be ashamed? Shouldn't we beg for God's forgiveness? Shouldn't we try to consciously purge such thoughts away? Let's strive for Godliness, both inside and out.

Prayer

Teach us, O God, to guard what we harbor on the inside. May even our thoughts bring you glory. Amen.

"In fact, though by this time you ought to be teachers, you need someone to teach you the elementary truths of God's word all over again. You need milk, not solid food!" Hebrews 5:12 NIV

Observation

Obviously, the writer of Hebrews is offering a very strong rebuke to his hearers in our focus verse. Earlier in the chapter, he offered some important teaching about the role of Christ as a high priest who offers prayers and sacrifices for us. It is apparent that many of these early Christians had failed to pay careful attention to the teaching of God's word. Though they should have grown in both their maturity and in their understanding of the scriptures, they failed to do so. They were not even knowledgeable about the elementary truths of God's word.

Application

Someone once told me that "there are no resting places in your spiritual life. Either you are growing closer to God, or you are drawing further away from God." Such a statement speaks to the question of spiritual maturity. Either we continue to mature in our faith or we tend to atrophy in our relationship with God. There is no "plateau of satisfaction" on which we can afford to stand. These early Christians were being challenged because they had failed to mature in their faith. As we read these words we must consider our own faith development and ask whether or not we are growing or have become stagnant in our Christian walk. What causes us to stagnant and fail to mature? For some, it's a simple case of laziness. There are many who are just not willing to commit the time and effort it takes to develop spiritual disciplines that lead to growth. They want to be claimed by Christ, but not to the extent it causes much effort. Others fail to mature because of a lack of accountability. Not being plugged into a church family, a Bible study, or a discipleship group, there is no one to encourage and challenge growth. It's like the patient who thinks if he/she never goes to a doctor then nothing must be wrong. Others fail to mature because they choose immaturity. They choose not to embrace the demands of faith. They treat faith as "fire insurance," but not as a roadmap to living the life God intends. Call it apathy or stupidity, but many like to wallow as preschoolers in a grown-up world of faith. Let's do better. Let's step out in courage and expend the effort it takes to mature. It is the immature life that rarely influences others.

Prayer

Give us a passion, O God, to grow in our faith. Amen.

"For in the case of those who have once been enlightened and have tasted of the heavenly gift and have been made partakers of the Holy Spirit, and have tasted the good word of God and the powers of the age to come, and then have fallen away, it is impossible to renew them again to repentance, since they again crucify to themselves the Son of God and put Him to open shame." Hebrews 6:4-6 NASB

Observation

In the entire book of Hebrews, these verses have probably caused more discussion and led to more pages of commentary than any others. In fact, while I was in Seminary, one of the great professors of Theology lost his job because of his position on this passage. The subject matter is that of apostasy. Simply stated, apostasy means, "to fall away from the faith." The question that this passage raises is whether or not a true believer can leave the faith and renounce the things of Christ, and if he/she does, can he/she ever reclaim a faith in Christ or has that person lost the hope of the gospel forever? The passage offers some troubling thoughts. The writer does seem to describe a person who has fully embraced the faith. The real difficulty of interpretation lies in the phrase, "it is impossible to renew them again to repentance." Is it possible to lose your salvation if you renounce your faith and deny the Lordship of Christ? It is certainly a theological argument that has raged through the ages and we won't solve it completely this morning. There are certainly a number of other texts in the New Testament that speak of a true believer's eternal security. Romans 8:35-39 for example, "What can separate us from the love of God in Christ Jesus?" But again, there are also numerous passages that warn against false teachers who might deceive and lead the faithful from their belief.

Application

The author of Hebrews has given us a strong warning not to renounce Christ or ignore his offer of salvation. Only those who believe in Jesus Christ will be saved. On that point there is no "wiggle room." Salvation comes through our faith in Christ alone. Knowing that such a statement is absolute truth, isn't it important to embrace the gift of salvation that is offered to each of us? If you are reading this devotion as a non-believer, I urge you to embrace the love of Christ and to accept the salvation that he offers.

Prayer

We thank you that in Christ we are held secure, loved, and forgiven. Amen.

"Therefore he is able to save completely those who come to God through him, because he always lives to intercede for them."
Hebrews 7:25 NIV

Observation

In our focus verse, the writer of Hebrews reminds us of the superiority of Christ to those high priests who came before him. In earlier times, the high priest would serve for a time and then, at the moment of his death, would be replaced by a successor. Christ is superior to those who came before him because he is always alive. As an "eternal" high priest, Jesus is able to continually and completely intercede for us. There is never a moment when Christ does not stand on our behalf at the right hand of the Throne of God. Consistently, faithfully, and lovingly, Christ pleads our case before God, causing us to stand justified in the presence of God.

Application

It is important for our high priest to constantly intercede for us because we constantly make mistakes. How many times a day or week do we find ourselves in need of forgiveness? How many times do we practice disobedience, yield to temptation, and step outside God's boundaries for us? Because we need constant grace, a vigil is kept for all of us. Christ matches every moment of our sins with a word of grace before the Father. As soon as we sin, Christ pleads our case before God. Our story and our need for pardon are not buried way down some long docket that will eventually get attention. Christ is not comfortable for even a moment to pass with a broken relationship between ourselves and The Father. Though we might be slow to confess our sins or slow to repent of our mistakes, Christ is not slow about his intercession for us. What comfort and hope are found in knowing that Christ stands ready to resolve the iniquity of our hearts.

Need an image of this process? Try this. Next time it rains while you are driving your car, pay attention to what the wipers do when the raindrops hit your windshield. Within seconds, the water is wiped away and the windshield is clear again. With more raindrops will come more swipes of the wiper blades. As long as the moisture is present, the wipers stand ready to clear away the vision-distorting rain. Likewise, as long as you sin, Christ stands ready to intercede quickly on your behalf. So confess your sins this morning and rejoice that as soon as you do, Christ moves into action.

Prayer

We thank you for our great high priest who constantly intercedes for us. Amen.

"For I will forgive their wickedness and will remember their sins no more." Hebrews 8:12 NIV

Observation

In this chapter of Hebrews readers are reminded of the New Covenant with God. The writer goes to great lengths to illustrate the ways in which it is superior to the old. The Old Covenant, based on the Law, is "outdated and will soon disappear." The New Covenant, based on faith in Christ, provides a new way of relating to God and a new way of being made righteous in God's sight. Through Christ, we enter into a binding agreement with God. We promise to believe, he promises to save. God promises to "forgive our wickedness and to remember our sins no more."

Application

Forgiveness is a conscious choice. When God promises to "remember our sins no more," it is not that God lacks the capacity to remember... but God chooses to forget. God chooses to wipe away even the memory of our sinful event. What a glorious gift for each of us! God chooses to "wipe the slate clean" and remember our sins no longer. That's the essence of true grace and forgiveness. The offense is forgiven and the memory is erased. How we should revel in the joy of such complete grace! But here's the hard part... we are called to be like our Father, and forgive with the same spirit of grace and forgetfulness. Have we really forgiven if we offer temporary pardon while clinging to the memory of the infraction? The longer we cling to the memory, the more often we have to forgive. Keeping a record of wrongs committed only leads to continued anger, long-term bitterness, and a festering hatred. We are called to better living in Christ. Maybe today, there are people you need to forgive... but even more importantly maybe there are memories that you need to forget. Can you restore a relationship today by not only offering grace, but also by ripping even the memory of the infraction from your mind? Like God, we have to choose to forget. It's part of the journey of faith required from each of us. And… this verse also applies to the topic of self-forgiveness. If God chooses to forget our sins, why is it important for us to labor under the guilt of our iniquity as though God's grace is not sufficient?

Prayer

Father, we acknowledge that in our own strength it is hard to forgive and forget. Yet we know that in Christ we can do all things. Create in us a clean heart, a forgiving spirit, and a forgetful mind. Amen.

"For Christ did not enter a sanctuary made with human hands that was only a copy of the true one; He entered heaven itself, now to appear for us in God's presence." Hebrews 9:24 NIV

Observation

To fully appreciate this verse, it is important to understand a little Jewish history and theology. For hundreds of years, the faithful worshipped in the Tabernacle—a portable, canvas tent that the Hebrews moved to various places. Later, during the reign of King Solomon, the Temple was built. Both the Tabernacle and the Temple were rectangular and had a curtain or veil that divided the interior area into two parts. The front area contained an altar and places for the priests to make sacrifices. The inner room was called the Holy of Holies, where the Ark of the Covenant was placed. The high priest would enter the Holy of Holies once a year to atone for the sins of the people. (This day was Yom Kippur, or Day of Atonement.) The writer of Hebrews compares the superior work of Christ to that of the high priest whom he superseded. Rather than enter a place made by human hands, Christ has entered the realms of heaven. And rather than offer a yearly sacrifice for sins, Christ continually appears in the presence of God having offered himself as a perfect sacrifice for each of us.

Application

So why does all of that matter? It is important for us to know that in Christ, God has provided away of forgiveness and a way of escape from our past mistakes. Christ, who acts as our high priest, continually enters the presence of God to atone for our sins. Because of his sacrifice, our "sin price" has been paid and we are set free. Add it up and you will discover that we have a perfect high priest, who stands in a perfect place, making a perfect sacrifice for each of us. We need not worry that our sins or fears have gone unreported. Just as Christ reveals God to us, he also reveals us fully before God. In that Holy Place, he speaks of our sins, pleads for our forgiveness, and offers the payment required for our transgressions. That's why we call him Savior. He saves us from punishment and rescues us from the unpayable price of our sins. As you start this day, why not take a moment to express your thankfulness to God for gifting you with a perfect high priest.

Prayer

Father, this morning we thank you for Jesus Christ, who is our hope, our victory, and our comfort. Amen.

> "And let us consider how we may spur one another on toward love and good deeds, not giving up meeting together, as some are in the habit of doing, but encouraging one another—and all the more as you see the Day approaching." Hebrews 10:24-25 NIV

Observation

The writer is challenging Christians of all the ages to become encouragers. With conscious and deliberate effort, we are to push each other towards loving and compassionate acts. That encouragement should come each time that we join together to worship and study God's word. Our assembly should provide courage, strength, and insight. We are always better at living a faith-filled life when we are accountable to each other. Because the day of Christ's return is drawing ever closer, we must help every believer become prepared for that day.

Application

From a practical standpoint, how do we "spur one another on toward love and good deeds?" What steps can we take to prod others in giving full expression to the Christian faith? First, it is vitally important to pray for one another, especially those who are in a struggle or crisis. We encourage them by lifting their needs before the Throne of Grace. Second, it is important to maintain a connection to fellow believers. On Sunday mornings as we leave worship at my church, we ask for everyone in attendance to join hands with the person seated next to them. We want to emphasize the ministry of touch. But more than a few seconds of handholding on Sunday, we must discover ways to touch our fellow believers in a consistent way. It may be an invitation to dinner, a telephone call each week, or a simple text message during the day. It is vital for all of us to feel a sense of connection. Third, we need to role model Godly behavior if we want to encourage others to do the same. It is one thing to tell someone how to live, but quite another to show them how to live. Others can be encouraged by our walk of faith and by our commitment to the church. It's a tough world. There are many forces and factors that can easily derail someone's consistent walk of faith. Let's take the words of these verses to heart. Let us encourage all the members of the Body of Christ to live bold, consistent, and obedient lives.

Prayer

Father, remind us this morning of the important role that we can play in the life of a fellow believer. Use our faith to encourage someone else's faith. Amen.

"And without faith it is impossible to please God, because anyone who comes to Him must believe that He exists and that He rewards those who earnestly seek Him." Hebrews 11:6 NIV

Observation

Sometimes called "The Roll Call of Faith," chapter 11 of Hebrews lists a number of men and women of faith from the Old Testament who were strengthened, protected, encouraged, and rewarded because of their faith. This list is a virtual who's who of the Old Testament. As he writes about each character, the writer begins with the words, "By faith..." It becomes clear that faith is the echoing refrain that builds a relationship with Holy God. We are asked to believe in One we cannot see, and trust in Him whom we cannot touch. As our focus verse states, "without faith it is impossible to please God."

Application

It's a journey that we are called to take... a journey of faith. The journey begins with a pivotal first step, that of believing that God exists. For some the journey stops before it even begins. There are some who choose not to believe in an all-powerful, all-knowing, and all-loving Creator God. Such folks live without hope, without purpose, and without lasting joy. But for others, this first step causes the world to come alive. It is this "first step" of belief that opens the door to a life of faith and reward. Go back and read the stories of the ancients… the greater the level of faith and trust, the greater the level of reward. As our focus verse reminds us, "God rewards those who earnestly seek Him." Faith is a journey that requires multiple steps. Step one: Believe that God exists. Step two: believe that God is interested in establishing a personal relationship with you. Step three: believe that God longs to bless your life. Step four: believe that God sent Jesus to forgive your sins and cause you to stand righteous in God's presence. Step five: believe in the reality of heaven. Step six... the list goes on and on… The greater our faith, the greater our reward. God has called each of us to an exciting, passionate, eternally rewarding life. The journey all begins with the first step. Believe that God exists. Be careful... that first step can change your life forever.

Prayer

Father, forgive us when our faith is uncertain and our belief a bit too shaky. Give us a faith that will move mountains, cause the blind to see, and even save our very souls. Amen.

"Therefore, since we are surrounded by such a great cloud of witnesses, let us throw off everything that hinders and the sin that so easily entangles. And let us run with perseverance the race marked out for us, fixing our eyes on Jesus, the pioneer and perfecter of faith. For the joy set before Him He endured the cross, scorning its shame, and sat down at the right hand of the throne of God." Hebrews 12:1-2 NIV

Observation

After naming all the great heroes of faith who have come before us, knowing that they testify to us from their experience and from their eternal vantage point, the writer reminds us to cast aside all that slows us down in our journey of faith and all that entangles us, so that our life-focus is clearly on Christ. We are to run with perseverance the race marked out for us. In other words, we are to walk deliberately, courageously, and consistently this life of faith. Be careful to notice that Christ, who authors our faith, is the One who will bring it to completion. We don't run the race in vain... there is victory at the end of life.

Application

Ever notice how all of us tend to behave better and act more responsibly when others are watching? The scrutiny of witnesses tends to push us toward better living. For example, how many of us slow down when we see the State Trooper on the side of the road? How many of us are conscious of the supporting crowd when we are leading a group? How many of us work more deliberately when someone is looking over our shoulder? We tend to perform better in the presence of witnesses. It's the same in our spiritual journey. Knowing that the saints of the ages are present, not only to scrutinize our actions, but to also cheer us on to victory, shouldn't we be encouraged to live a greater life of faith? Because we know that we are accountable to the greater Body of Christ, shouldn't we be more dedicated? Let's be conscious of the "great cloud of witnesses" that surrounds us. Let's use the energy of their encouragement to help us live with great devotion and passion. Let's cast aside those things that hinder us so that we can march triumphantly into the Kingdom. Let's be accountable with the faith invested in us. As "they" cheer, let's run. Let's strive to honor Christ this day in all that we do.

Prayer

Father, we thank you that we are not alone on this journey of faith. How grateful we are for those who surround us and encourage us. May the support of the greater body of Christ spur us on to a victorious faith. Amen.

"Keep on loving one another as brothers and sisters." Hebrews 13:1 NIV

Observation

In this final chapter of the book of Hebrews, the writer offers several important words of admonition and counsel. He speaks of offering hospitality to strangers, remembering those imprisoned and mistreated, as well as giving advice about marriage and money. This opening verse however offers a word of counsel about how we are to treat each other in the body of Christ. The challenge is to love each other as though they were our actual flesh and blood. Such a response indicates a compassionate love, a forgiving spirit, and a hope for helping that person become his/her best.

Application

Years ago, while growing up in the First Baptist Church of Rome, GA, there was an older gentleman in our church named Walter Andrews, who loved to stand and share a word of testimony when such opportunities were presented. He always began his testimony with the words, "Every man is my brother and every woman is my sister." As teenagers we used to always laugh at his quirky and predictable speech. Funny thing though, 30-40 years later we still remember his words. The attitude of loving everyone as though they are indeed our brothers and sisters is an important concept to embrace. First, it takes away the impure thought. To see others as though they were our own family takes away the temptation to look lustfully or to think impurely. Second, it forces a sense of forgiveness and inclusion. You can occasionally be angered by a family member, but that person will still be in the family. There is no option of forever disassociating from such a person. Third, it leads to great compassion. We take care of our own, right? We don't let a family member go in need for very long. We consider how to help and give aid. Part of what it means to be in a church family is to adopt this attitude towards all those who are joined to us through the bonds of faith. We belong to each other. We forgive. We help. We pray. We love. That's the way Christ intends for the church to be. Every man is my brother. Every woman is my sister. Welcome to the family.

Prayer

Father, we thank you for what it means to belong to a church family. For those yet searching for such a place of belonging, we pray for your guidance. Amen.

"But don't just listen to God's word. You must do what it says. Otherwise, you are only fooling yourselves." James 1:22 NLT

Observation

James, believed to be a brother of Jesus, writes about practical Christianity. He speaks of putting faith into action. He believes that faith without resulting works proves worthless. If our faith is genuine, active, and real, there will always be evidence. In this first chapter he writes about seeking wisdom, the testing of faith, the source of temptation, bridling the tongue, and pure religion. James' writing is a mine filled with many gems to unearth. It needs to be read slowly and carefully in order to glean all of its truth.

Application

In our focus verse, James writes about the importance of applying God's word in practical ways to every day life. For James, it is never enough to simply listen to God's word. We must make it come alive in our hearing. We must hear it, mull it over, and think of the ways its teaching should be reflected in our lives. It is amazing to me how many voices we allow to speak to our hearts and minds. There is the radio on the morning commute. There is the daily newspaper. We talk to friends at work and listen to music on our IPhones. We sit mindlessly in front of the television and read countless articles on the web. Slowly but surely, a thousand voices make their way into our psyche and slowly but surely, they shape and mold our thinking. Perhaps we would do well to become a little more selective in the allowed input into our lives. Among all those competing voices must be the word of God. We need to hear from God daily. We really do need to seek God's input for each moment we live. But notice again what James writes... it is not enough to simply hear the word... obedience comes through action. In other words, we must take the revealed word and pray for the courage to apply it. To hear the word and be unaffected by it, is to be non-Christian. Believers must be controlled, pushed, prodded, and corrected by God's word. With our hearing of the word must come a willingness to respond to it. So how pliable are you? Will you let the word govern your thoughts and actions this day? Any one of the competing voices can grab your attention. Just make sure as you sort it all out that God's word is the one that shapes your life.

Prayer

Father, thank you for providing your word as a lamp unto our feet and a light unto our path. May we set the course of our lives by the guidance it provides. Amen.

"Suppose you see a brother or sister who has no food or clothing, and you say, 'Good-bye and have a good day; stay warm and eat well' —but then you don't give that person any food or clothing. What good does that do?" James 2:15-16 NLT

Observation

These two verses are at the core of James' ethical teaching about faith and works. James makes the argument that faith and works always go hand in hand. To separate the two is to miss the intention of faith. Faith should motivate us to DO things. Our faith should leave a trail of good deeds and sacrificial acts. As I often say, "The world is not impressed by our private devotion. It is our lived-out faith that makes the difference."

Application

Interesting, is it not, that when James speaks on this subject of faith and works that he chooses to address two of humankind's most urgent and basic needs... food and clothing. How can we see such need in the life of another human being and not raise a finger to offer any help? Is there not a Christian ethic that should drive us to meet needs as we offer the hope of the gospel? Part of what should drive our sense of compassion is how broadly we interpret the meaning of the words, "brother and sister." Is James describing only fellow Christians who need our help, or is he describing a more inclusive definition that sees all people as those whom we are obligated to help? I think it is safe to assume that yes, we are always obligated to help those who are part of our faith communities. But real faith must extend itself beyond the walls of our churches. To show compassion and attempt to meet needs wherever we discover them is at the heart of the Christian message. It is not enough to simply pray for the needs of the world. Faith should drive us to greater involvement and action with that world. James is all about "practical Christianity." So consider for a moment what practical Christianity should require of you. What ministry needs your volunteerism? What problem can you help to solve? Into what great need will you pour your life? Don't just talk with lofty words and pray with empty expressions. Go and live the faith. Be "as Christ" to the world around you.

Prayer

Father, may our faith make a difference... not only in our lives, but in the lives of others. Amen.

"And so blessing and cursing come pouring out of the same mouth. Surely, my brothers and sisters, this is not right!" James 3:10 NLT

Observation

James devotes a lot of his writing to the idea of learning to tame the tongue. He suggests that our mouths have the potential to bless or curse. With our words we can heal or we can wound. James states that it makes no sense that "blessing and cursing" should come from the same source. True Christian character cannot support such inconsistency. What do our words reveal about our true nature?

Application

There is an old story, written by someone else long ago that goes like this... a certain woman goes to a minister and confesses to him all the damage that she has done with her words. She has spoken deceitfully about a friend. She has slandered a neighbor. She has treated a store owner with harsh and unkind words. She comes to the minister to seek forgiveness. She longs to feel good about herself again. "What can I do?" she asks. The minister gives her a shoebox filled with a thousand small feathers. He directs her to climb to the top of the steeple and release the feathers from the window of the belfry. She does as she is told. She watches as the wind scatters the feathers in a hundred different directions. She then returns to the minister. The minister then instructs her to go and gather each feather. "That's impossible!" she cries. "They have been released into the world and scattered by the wind. There is no way to collect them all again." He simply replied, "So it is with your words. Once released, they cannot be collected again." Her only hope was to choose better words as her life moved forward.

How much regret do we harbor over things we wish we had never said? How many times have we longed to retract our words as soon as they have left our mouths? How many times have we praised God on Sunday and cursed those made in God's image on Monday? Our Christian witness is often destroyed by the careless use of our words. So mind your words. Choose them carefully. Let them be seasoned with grace and compassion, not bitterness and anger. Remember that sometimes the best choice is simply not to speak at all.

Prayer

Father, give us discernment with our words. May we become those whose words and lives reflect an authenticity and consistency of character. Amen.

"Remember, it is sin to know what you ought to do and then not do it."
James 4:17 NLT

Observation

Our focus verse is one of the defining verses in the Book of James. It is a reminder that we sin, not only in the evil acts we commit, but also in the noble acts we fail to do. Whenever there is a clear understanding of what God intends for us to do and we fail to act upon that word of wisdom, surely we sin. As God calls and equips, we are expected to go and do. To ignore God's call is to sin.

Application

A lot of us struggle with knowing God's will and purpose for our lives. Sure, we can speak of the big picture... God wants to be glorified in all that we do. But it's the smaller stuff of life that gives us angst. We struggle to know the day-to-day purposes to which we are called. What is God's will for my life this day? What is God's purpose in this decision, or in this conversation? And so we struggle and we pray and we attempt to discern the voice of God. And sometimes the message is crystal clear. Sometimes we really do feel the prompting of God to speak, or act, or pray on someone's behalf. It is in those moments that we are called to absolute obedience. If we fail to respond to the prodding of God, then we have sinned. Disobedience to God's prompting is just as bad as disobedience to scripture. Whether God speaks through written words or through the soft whisper of the Spirit, our place is still that of absolute obedience. So do this... go deeper with God. Ask God to be revealed to you in specific ways. Ask God to direct your path this day, to reveal a person in need, to prompt you to a conversation, or to stop and pray for someone. Determine to be obedient. If God points you in a direction, don't hesitate for a second, but chase after God's will with wild abandon. Remember, it's not always in the bad things you have done that cause you to sin... sometimes it's in the good you have failed to do.

Prayer

Father, forgive us of our many sins, both those we have committed in defiance of your word and those we have committed when we have failed to act as faithful Christians. Amen.

"Confess your sins to each other and pray for each other so that you may be healed. The earnest prayer of a righteous person has great power and produces wonderful results." James 5:16 NLT

Observation

James speaks about the healing that comes through confession. Whenever our hearts are unburdened through honest confession, we find a joy and wellness that transcends our physical lives and extends to our spiritual and emotional lives as well. In other words, confession can relieve much of our suffering. The admonition is to confess to, and pray for, each other. Notice that our confession is not for the purpose of giving others fodder for the rumor mill. It is so that the sincere among us can pray for us as we attempt to find wholeness and forgiveness. Having the right person pray earnestly for us has the power to bring great results.

Application

I'm just not sure that confession is a discipline that is widely practiced. Maybe our Catholic friends who insist on a more rigid schedule of confession have a better angle on this discipline. Confession really is good for the soul. The problem with confession is that it demands something from us. It demands that we do a little soul-searching and offer an admission that we have not always behaved in ways that we should. Confession demands that we view our sinfulness in the same way that God does. It forces us to admit failure and reveal the imperfections. Most of us would rather sweep such things under the carpet. We would much rather offer God a blanket "one-size-fits-all" kind of statement in which we simply say to God, "Forgive me of my sins." The problem with such praying is that we rarely come to terms with our sinfulness. By not specifically naming our sins, we find it easy to never deal with the root causes of our sinfulness. James reminds us that we are never fully healed until we at least "get it out in the open" with God. Please understand that I am not asking you to call me today and confess all of your sins. I'm not the one who can grant forgiveness and pardon. But God can. So do this. Take a moment to name a few of your sins. Confess them as honestly and specifically as you can, both to God and to yourself. You will find healing for your heart and strength as you take on the challenge of better living.

Prayer

Father, may we know the joy of honest confession. Remind us that the first step in finding redemption is acknowledging where we have failed. Amen.

Day 223 1 Peter 1: Some Things Never Change. Amen.

"All praise to God, the Father of our Lord Jesus Christ. It is by His great mercy that we have been born again, because God raised Jesus Christ from the dead. Now we live with great expectation, and we have a priceless inheritance—an inheritance that is kept in heaven for you, pure and undefiled, beyond the reach of change and decay."
1 Peter 1:3-4 NLT

Observation

As the early church grew, the persecution of the Roman Empire intensified. Peter writes to Christians living in the Roman provinces in Asia Minor to assure these early believers that God is still in control. In fact, Peter will instruct them to even rejoice in the midst of their suffering. Suffering will remind them that they are partakers of Christ's suffering and as such, they will also be partakers of his glory.

Application

We throw around the expression, "Some things never change," but in reality they do. Everything has a lifespan, an ebb and flow, a beginning and an end. Times change. Styles change. Health changes. Seasons change. Friends change. Relationships change. Nothing in life seems to be immune from the inevitable forces of change. And as things change, they might lose their value and worth. So we long for those things that don't change. We like a sense of permanence, and would love to count on something to stay just the way it is. In his writing, Peter promises an inheritance, one that is kept in heaven for each of us, pure and undefiled, beyond the reach of change and decay. No wonder that he states, "Now we live with great expectation." Because of our faith in Christ, we claim an inheritance that cannot be taken from us. It will never lose its value. It will never change. The inheritance is just as glorious now as it was the day we first claimed it. Not to worry... it will still be there when the time comes to receive it. In Peter's words, "It is not subject to change and decay." Most of our possessions tend to depreciate over time. Our homes age, our cars wear out, our clothes go out of style... but not what we possess through faith. Our inheritance is secure. Our reward of faith will never lose its value. So, live with a sense of anticipation. When this life is over it will be waiting.

Prayer

Father, we thank you for the inheritance that we share in Christ. We praise you for the joy that just the promise brings... let alone, the joy that will come when we claim it in its fullness. Amen.

"Respect everyone, and love your Christian brothers and sisters. Fear God, and respect the king." 1 Peter 2:17 NLT

Observation

Twice in this verse Peter throws out the concept of respect. According to Webster's dictionary respect means "to take notice of; to regard with special attention; to regard as worthy of special consideration; hence, to care for." Peter challenges us to "to take notice of everyone." To respect is to give care. It is to see in others the image of Christ and to treat others with dignity, value, and human decency. It is perhaps to live by a Golden Rule ethic in which we view others, not as objects of disdain, but as people made in the image of God.

Application

Long before Aretha Franklin belted out the words to her hit song calling for a little respect, God's word challenged us to do the same. I believe that to offer respect is one of the basic and fundamental distinguishing characteristics of the Christian faith. To respect is to value the lives of others—to treat others with common decency, civility, and grace. I wonder how well we "take notice of everyone." Do we really see the people around us, or look beyond them to see those whom we deem to have greater worth? Do we see the needs of others? Do we treat others as human beings who have quality and worth in the eyes of God? To respect is to acknowledge others and to extend consideration and courtesy in their direction. To respect others is to see them through the eyes of Christ and not through our jaded and prejudicial eyes of human nature. It takes a special maturity of faith, but I challenge you to look at others differently, especially those who have been marginalized by society and quickly cast aside. Look at them, not through the lens of your experience, your biases, or even your politic. Look at those in need as opportunities God has placed in your journey to teach you about grace, acceptance, and respect. What if the homeless man, or the poor, single Hispanic mother, or the immigrant who can't speak the language is more than someone for you to hate? What if they are tests of faith that challenge the depth of your Christian maturity? Will your response in any way match the response of Christ in the life of that person? Can we use the title "Christian" if we refuse to offer simple respect?

Prayer

Father, remind us that until we learn to respect all those created in your image, that we still have a long way to grow in our faith. Amen.

"Instead, you must worship Christ as Lord of your life. And if someone asks about your Christian hope, always be ready to explain it."
1 Peter 3:15 NLT

Observation

In the passage where our focus verse is found, Peter writes about suffering as a believer in Christ. He challenges us to worship Christ as the Lord of our lives even if doing so puts us in a place of potential suffering or ridicule. Our faith should be so important that we should be ready and willing to share about it anytime a moment presents itself. Our boldness of faith should be evident even when a moment might be awkward or embarrassing. We must live an "out-loud" faith.

Application

How ready are you to share your faith? If called upon to do so, could you share something of your salvation experience in an exciting, challenging, and convincing way? My guess is that most of us don't do a good job of faith sharing because we never think through the ways in which our testimony could be offered. We feel woefully inadequate either because of our lack of scripture knowledge or because of our lack of thought-organization. First, there is no wrong way to share your faith. God will honor any attempt you make to tell the story of Jesus. Second, there is no testimony more powerful than that of first-hand experience. As you share how you became a Christian and what difference Christ now makes in your life, you will plant important faith-seeds in the lives of others. Third, the old adage that "practice makes perfect," can apply. There are some things that you can do to prepare for when a faith-sharing moment arises. Why not take the time to organize a few thoughts? Nothing too complicated and no, you don't have to memorize the entire New Testament. Speak from your experience and from your heart. Try to respond to the statements, "This is why I became a Christian," and, "This is how I became a Christian." If you can memorize a verse or two, it will only strengthen your testimony and fortify your confidence. Every Christian needs to assume that God will place him/her in a position to share their faith. Prepare for the moment by assuring God of your willingness to speak when called upon to do so. God will honor both your willing spirit and your simple words.

Prayer

Father, thank you for the salvation that we have in Jesus Christ. Prepare our hearts to tell his story when opportunities for doing so come our way. Amen.

"God has given each of you a gift from His great variety of spiritual gifts. Use them well to serve one another." 1 Peter 4:10 NLT

Observation

Peter reminds his readers of their "giftedness" by God. God equips all believers with spiritual gifts to be used in serving one another. In other words, in whichever ways God has wired all of us, equipped us, and impassioned us, we are to use those gifts to God's glory and for the glory of the body of Christ. We have a role to play, a purpose to fulfill. The measure of our true spirituality is not in which gift we possess, but in how faithful we share that which we do have.

Application

Every one of us has a spiritual gift. Everyone. God has uniquely placed the Spirit within us by giving us an ability to in someway serve the Kingdom. Spiritual gifts can vary greatly from preaching and teaching, to hospitality and administration, to leadership and wisdom, to discernment and giving. Our gift is our "sweet spot." It is where we function best. It is where we find fulfillment and joy. It is not a question of "if" you have a spiritual gift; it is only a question of which one you possess. The value in knowing your gift is that of finding your place in ministry in the life of your church. Let me illustrate it this way... I spent a lot of time growing up playing the sport of football. I was an offensive right end. I had some speed and could catch a pass and so that is where I best "fit" on the team. I had friends who did other things well. Mike could kick. Joey could throw the ball. Pat could block. Brian could snap the ball. You get the point. When each of us did our particular task well, the task for which we were best equipped, the team had success. The Kingdom of God functions in the same way. When each of us willingly offers our gift in serving each other, God's work is done efficiently and effectively. In fact, the miracle of it all is that in each local church, God has placed the right people with the right gifts in order for that church to do what God intends for it to accomplish. So if you are a part of a local church and you are not plugged in, using your particular gift, you are hamstringing your church. Your "good" church could be doing even greater things. Let me challenge you to consider your spiritual gift. Ask the Lord, "What is it that you have equipped me to do?" And as you discover your gift, resolve to use it faithfully.

Prayer

Father, may we use that which you have given to each of us, to your glory. Amen.

Day 227 — 1 Peter 5: Simple Truth... Hard to Do

"Give all your worries and cares to God, for He cares about you."
1 Peter 5:7 NLT

Observation

In the closing verses of his first letter, Peter reminds his hearers of the suffering they will face as believers in Christ. He reminds them, however, that the suffering will only last for a brief time and then, as a result of their faith, they will know the eternal glory and honor of God's Kingdom. In our focus verse, Peter challenges us to place all our worries, fears, and anxiety on God, knowing that God cares for us.

Application

Peter's words are similar to the words of Paul recorded in Philippians 4:6: "Be anxious for nothing, but in everything by prayer and supplication with thanksgiving let your requests be made known to God." Two of the strongest leaders of the early church, two that knew well the pain of persecution, remind us to give our worries and cares to God. They both teach a Biblical principle that we hear and understand, yet seldom put into place. Notice the second part of Peter's verse... "for He cares about you." We need to be reminded that the one upon whom we cast our worries is not a disinterested third party, but the Father who loves us; the One who is intimately acquainted with all our ways. God certainly knows our fears and worries, even before we do. And, we are certainly the objects of God's good grace. By giving our worries to God, we acknowledge that life is too overwhelming for us to manage alone. We need the support, the power, and the wisdom that only God can provide. By giving our worries and cares to God, we make the journey from self-sufficiency to God-dependency. What comfort there is in knowing that we can replace worry with a simple trust in God! So why don't we do it? Why do we harbor our fears and wring our hands when God stands at the ready, waiting to help? It's a matter of trust. If we trust God enough, we can hang our worries on God's broad shoulders. God has never intended for us to walk through this life alone. Already within you as a believer is the Holy Spirit, to guide, teach, and yes, to comfort you. When we learn to trust more, we will worry less.

Prayer

Father, remind us again this day of the simple lesson of trusting you with the great and small needs of our lives. Remind us that you care for us and will provide for us in ways we can't even begin to imagine. Amen.

"So, dear brothers and sisters, work hard to prove that you really are among those God has called and chosen. Do these things, and you will never fall away." 2 Peter 1:10 NLT

Observation

Peter writes this second letter with a slightly greater sense of urgency. As he indicates in verse 14, he knows that his death is imminent and so he longs to impart some final words of teaching. Included is a challenge to remain faithful in doing the things of Christ. In our focus verse, he reminds us to work hard in proving that we really are people of faith.

Application

Words are easy. The proof of our profession is in our actions. One can claim to be a great parent or spouse, but the daily commitment, devotion, and acts of sacrificial, and unselfish love prove it. In like fashion, it is also always easy to claim the Christian faith. It is easy to say that we believe in Jesus. It is quite another to live out that confession. Being a Christian requires discipline, patience, love, obedience, and devotion to Christ. Peter's challenge is to work hard to prove to the world that we really are in the household of faith. Often, the greatest proof we can offer about our faith is not when we stand, sing, preach, and pray each Sunday during the Worship hour. Most often, the greatest proof can be found in how we live the rest of the days of our week. Real faith and real discipleship should be apparent in all that we do. We should "work hard" to insure that our words are seasoned with grace, that our actions display the Spirit of Christ, and that even our thoughts reflect surrender unto his Lordship. We must work hard at consistency. We have to demonstrate a devotion to all that Christianity demands. The proof of our faith is not that our names are recorded on the church roll as being members. The proof is found in how apparent it is to the rest of the world that we belong to Christ. I challenge you to "work hard" at your faith. Be disciplined. Be authentic. Be civil. Be respectful. Be generous. Be joy-filled. Be forgiving. Be consistent. Be courageous.

Prayer

Father, may we offer more than mere words of religious affiliation. May our lives reflect our daily commitment to our faith. Amen.

"Yes, Lot was a righteous man who was tormented in his soul by the wickedness he saw and heard day after day." 2 Peter 2:8 NLT

Observation

Peter writes in this second chapter about those who live faithfully in a very worldly culture. He offers several examples of those who continued to do right while all those around them chased after evil and vain idols. Lot lived an exemplary life in the midst of a very dark society. God was able to rescue Lot while the others of his city perished when God brought forth fire and brimstone.

Application

Peter writes of Lot that, "he was tormented in his soul by the wickedness he saw and heard day after day." Obviously, Lot was disturbed and concerned about all that he observed around him. Surely he wished for better things from his culture. Surely he dreamed of greater morality and a higher ethical standard. It begs the question, "Are we tormented in our souls by the wickedness we see and hear in the culture in which we live?" Are we bothered by the level of immorality and idolatry that surrounds us? Do we worry over the brokenness of our world? Do we weep over the lostness of so many who live in the midst of our culture? Once, when Jesus looked out over Jerusalem, he wept. He was grieved over the disobedience and lack of regard for the things of God that he saw in the actions of society. I wonder if we can muster up such sympathy over ours? One of the real dangers of 21st century Christianity is that of our inward focus. We tend to become pretty good at closing out the outside world in order to focus on our own needs and problems. If we are not careful, we will dismiss the greater world to her evil ways, forgetting that we have been called to offer redemption and hope to the planet. Until we begin to truly share a concern for the ways in which things are trending, we will never become the change agents that will make a difference. Ministry is always messy. It costs... it requires our involvement, our time, our energy, our patience, and even some risk. Though we often seek a peaceful calm in our lives, perhaps we should ask that God would occasionally torment our souls. We really do need to feel a sense of burden to take on the ills of our society. We need to see and hear what is being said in the hearts of a troubled world and then we must pray for the courage to begin our assault on such evil.

Prayer

Father, grant us wisdom and courage that we fail not man nor Thee. Amen.

"But do not let this one fact, escape your notice, beloved, that with the Lord one day is as a thousand years, and a thousand years as one day."
2 Peter 3:9 NASB

Observation

In this closing chapter, Peter writes about the coming Day of the Lord. Some were apparently concerned about its delay, thinking that the Lord's Second Coming was slow to come about. Peter reminded them that God's timetable is vastly different from that of man's and that the delay in bringing forth the redemption of humankind was a result of God's patience that would allow many additional people to come to faith (v. 10).

Application

Time is relative. At moments it seems too slow, while at other moments it seems to race by far too quickly. A young teenager can't wait to get his drivers license. An excited bride can't wait for her wedding day. The college student longs for graduation. The pregnant wife awaits the birth of her child. For such people, time tends to creep along. And then for others time races far too quickly. The dying man longs for another day. The father of two daughters watches his young girls become brides way too quickly. For a family on vacation time passes in the blink of an eye. You get the point. Time is both fast and slow; both a welcomed friend and a relentless foe. But what is time to God? A thousand days are but a moment and in each moment a thousand days are lived. God doesn't worry over time because time is God's to control. It is God's to speed up and slow down. It belongs to God, who makes everything appropriate in its time. Because we are such slaves to time, we are seldom patient with its progression. When God's timing doesn't make sense to us, we question God and wonder about God's ability to be sovereign. Sometimes we need the perspective of hindsight to see all the ways in which God works in our world. It is sometimes as we look back that we begin to understand God's arrangement of people and time to create life-changing moments. So remember this... whether you want your life to speed up or slow down, be patient. There is a plan in place. And God's timing is always precise. You may not understand the "moment in time" (*kairos*) in which you are currently living, but God does. And in God's time, all things are made right.

Prayer

Father, thank you for the gift of time. May we use it wisely, carefully, and efficiently. May we learn to value our time as a gift from you. Amen.

"If we confess our sins, He is faithful and righteous to forgive us our sins and to cleanse us from all unrighteousness." 1 John 1:9 NASB

Observation

First John, believed to have been written by the Apostle John, includes none of the usual features of a Bible letter. Written with compassion and warmth, the letter speaks of the life that we have in Christ and the marvelous grace that is ours when our confession leads to forgiveness.

Application

There is an important Biblical principle contained in this verse. It's the relationship between confession and forgiveness. In Christ's faithfulness and righteousness, He is able to forgive us of our sins as we are willing to confess those sins. There is a direct correlation between the specificity of our confession and the extent to which our guilt and shame are removed. When we go to the effort to confess honestly, openly, and specifically, we find the greatest sense of forgiveness and grace. Conversely, the more vague our confession, the less "cleansed" we feel. We tend to rush through confession without taking time to articulate our transgressions. We offer a catch-all phrase like, "God, forgive me of my sins." Real confession takes time, it takes soul-searching, and it takes a sense of regret. Confession means that we agree with God about our sins. It means that we view our sinfulness through the lens of God's righteousness and not our own sub-par standards. But notice what happens when we really take the time and effort to confess. We are cleansed from all unrighteousness. What does that mean? It means that when we claim the forgiveness of God through confession, as far as God is concerned, the matter is closed. Our sins are forgiven and remembered no longer. Honestly, most of us can't really fathom that fact. We tend to hang on to our guilt long after God has offered complete absolution. So do this... if you are struggling with a horrific sin and a deep sense of regret, pray through the matter as fervently and as long as it takes. Confess the brokenness and ask God to forgive. Then go out and buy an Etch-A-Sketch. Twist the knobs and write out your sin on the screen. Then flip it, shake it, and turn it over again. Notice the clean screen. It's like that with God... you get to begin again. So learn the value of confession and find the joy of being made whole.

Prayer

Father, thank you for the grace we discover through confession. Amen.

Day 232 1 John 2: Did You Hear the One About the Lawyer?

"My dear children, I am writing this to you so that you will not sin. But if anyone does sin, we have an advocate who pleads our case before the Father. He is Jesus Christ, the One who is truly righteous."
1 John 2:1 NLT

Observation

Our focus verse speaks of Christ's ability to forgive our sins and to intercede on our behalf before the Father. In this chapter he also writes about loving our brother, ignoring the lusts of the world, the antichrists who deny the truth of God, and the promise of eternal life. John very much wants us to grow so deeply in our faith that we walk fully in the "light of Christ" in the midst of the world's darkness.

Application

Need some good news this morning? How about the knowledge that Jesus Christ is currently pleading your case before Almighty God? John writes his letter to offer encouragement to believers. It is his hope, and that of Christ, that we would not sin. He sets a high standard of moral and ethical behavior. But in case we do, we have an advocate who pleads our case. An advocate is someone who represents us in court, defending who we are and pleading for our release. Imagine the scene... in some celestial courtroom God opens a book and begins reading the record of your life. God reads of disobedience, poorly chosen words, inappropriate thoughts, lies, deception, and a thousand other offenses. And then your Advocate steps in. Jesus acknowledges that it's all true… every word. Then he says to the Father, "But I have claimed this life. I died to redeem it. I have already paid the price of all his/her sins." God dismisses the case against you and welcomes you home. Christ has claimed our lives. He has died to redeem us. He has already paid the price for our sins. So as Jesus declares, "Truly, truly I say to you, he who hears My word, and believes Him who sent Me, has eternal life, and does not come into judgment, but has passed out of death into life." So take heart. Right now, at this very moment, you have an advocate pleading your case before God. And because of his love and sacrifice, the verdict will be, "not guilty." Stunning, isn't it?

Prayer

Father, we thank you that even when we sin, and we will... that Jesus Christ stands as our advocate in your presence. Amen.

"If someone has enough money to live well and sees a brother or sister in need but shows no compassion—how can God's love be in that person?"
1 John 3:17 NLT

Observation

In many ways, the book of 1 John reminds me of the book of James. Both call for a practical expression of faith. If we have truly been transformed by the love of Christ, then certainly there will be resultant actions. John writes much about the love of Christ that should be evident in each of us. In our focus verse, the love of Christ demands that we share out of our abundance with those who have great need. It is through sharing that our Christian faith will become evident.

Application

There is a great contrast drawn in this verse between "to live well" and to be "in need." One represents those who have gained success and some sense of prosperity, while the other phrase represents those who struggle for the basic necessities of life. How can we enjoy and justify living a life of affluence while others struggle with such need? The verse is not intended to impose guilt upon those who are financially secure, but to instill a sense of benevolence within them in order that they may claim a spirit of sharing. Having wealth in and of itself is not a bad thing... it is when our wealth builds greed and forces us to ignore the plight of others that it is problematic. John insists that the love of God within us will forge us into compassionate people. If we have no compassion for the poor among us, then we must question whether or not the love of Christ truly dwells within us. Specifically, John is writing about fellow Christians... fellow believers who are struggling to survive. Do we not bear some responsibility for those who share this life of faith with us? I've noticed that those who are truly "rich in the faith," are those who have learned the value of sharing. Some of the happiest and most content people are those who freely give of their wealth, their time, and their passion to those who have needs. Those who "give out of the abundance" seem to always have an abundance from which to give. So how gracious are you? Or, how reluctant are you to share your things? Benevolence is a distinctive mark of a Spirit-filled Christian. It is one of the ways we show our dedication to Christ.

Prayer

Father, teach us to become more like you. May our hearts be filled with compassion that will drive us to help those who are in need. Amen.

"If someone says, 'I love God,' but hates a Christian brother or sister, that person is a liar; for if we don't love people we can see, how can we love God, whom we cannot see? 1 John 4:20 NLT

Observation

In this chapter John writes extensively about the love of God and how that love is to be expressed through each of us. God's love within us becomes a catalyst for expressing love towards others. In fact, John commands us to love one another as a proof of our relationship with God. "The one who does not love does not know God, for God is love" (v. 8).

Application

Who wants to be called a liar? Not me. A liar is a person whose ways and words can't be trusted. A liar deceives. A liar thinks nothing of telling a falsehood if it helps his/her cause. Who wants to have that kind of reputation? And yet, John insists that we will all earn that name if our love for one another fails to be genuine. I know a lot of people who enjoy saying the words, "I love you," to the people around them. They glad-hand, hug necks, and say those words as casually as saying "hello." But is such love real? Real love always finds expression through our actions, deeds, and devotion. Love is consistent over time. It forces us to really care, really listen, and really get involved. It's an investment of life. In this passage, John warns about claiming to have such devotion and dedication to God while treating our brothers and sisters with disdain. Such a practice doesn't make sense. How can we claim to love God and not love the people made in God's image? In fact, it is in our expression of love to others that our love for God is truly demonstrated. God hears the words we say about others and certainly observes our conduct towards them. God even knows the thoughts and the intentions of our hearts. So what if we could only use the words we say about each other as our expressive words about God? What if our vocabulary of praise was limited to the words we say when we think of those folks we really don't like? Would we dare say, "God is such a pest, I really can't stand Him?" Or, "God's just an idiot. I wish He would just go away." We would never say such things, would we? But then again, if we say them about our brothers and sisters, then maybe that's exactly what God hears us saying to Him. Scary stuff, right?

Prayer

Father, teach us a greater love for you as we learn to love our fellow man. Amen.

"And this is what God has testified: He has given us eternal life, and this life is in His Son. Whoever has the Son has life; whoever does not have God's Son does not have life." 1 John 5:11-12 NLT

Observation

John writes reminding us of the promise of eternal life. He is very clear and concise, teaching us that the eternal life we all long to have is found in only one source, Jesus Christ. He also reminds us that those who have claimed a faith relationship with Christ are those who will overcome the world. These things are written, John writes, so that we can know that we have eternal life (v. 13).

Application

Sometimes we tend to overcomplicate things. We take a hundred words to explain something that could be said in ten. Ask a simple question like, "How can a person become a Christian?" and before long, there is talk of substitutionary atonement, justification, sanctification, sin nature, etc. We use words and phrases that over spiritualize and complicate our thoughts and soon those asking the question get so lost and frustrated that the answer is ineffective. Look at John's words this morning... "Whoever has the Son, has the life; whoever does not have God's Son does not have life." Pretty simple, right? Boil it all down and the truth of scripture is this... eternal life is extended to us only through Jesus Christ. There is no other path, no other Savior, no other methodology, no other plan. It's a simple litmus test... Do you believe in Jesus Christ as the only Son of God and do you trust him to take away your sins? It's a "yes or no" kind of thing. Either we believe or we don't. Either we are saved or we are not. It all comes down to the simplicity of a relationship with Christ. He who has the Son has the life. So why complicate it or make it hard to understand? Do you believe? Is your trust in him? God doesn't place a lot of qualifiers or complicated jargon to the process. He just asks us to believe and trust. It's that simple.

Prayer

Father, thank you for giving us eternal life through our Lord and Savior Jesus Christ. Teach us to trust that promise and to make it known. Amen.

Day 236 — 2 John 1: Flesh and Blood Friends

"I have much more to say to you, but I don't want to do it with paper and ink. For I hope to visit you soon and talk with you face to face. Then our joy will be complete." 2 John 1:12 NLT

Observation

The letter of 2 John is written to a church and attempts to take on the heretical idea that Jesus had not been physically present on the earth. The letter may be a reaction to the "Gnostics" who taught that Jesus was spirit only and that he just appeared to suffer and die on the cross. John warns that this teaching, which is of a "deceiver and an antichrist," should be avoided at all costs.

Application

John expresses a strong desire to speak with these fellow believers, face to face. He recognizes that time and distance sometimes require a written letter, but his real desire is to stand in their presence and talk face to face, eye to eye, and heart to heart. We like to boast that with the advent of modern technology that we are more "connected" than ever before. And to some extent that is true. We can send a text around the world in a matter of seconds. Facebook keeps us connected with old friends on any continent. We can Zoom our image to family and friends on the other side of the country. And yet, all of us would agree that there is still nothing like "being there." There is something important about standing in someone's presence. We have been "wired" to live in community with one another. We are social beings. We need to have interaction with other faces, voices, and hearts. We can boast all the Facebook friends we want to claim or have thousands of followers on Twitter, but the real relationships are those that we can touch, feel, and see. In fact, that's the way the church has been established. We can broadcast our services, maybe podcast them on the Web, but until we become flesh and blood representatives of Christ, we really won't change lives. It still takes a personal, one-to-one touch. Let me challenge you to be the presence of Christ in someone's life this week. Go and be physically present with them. Hold their hand. Hug their neck. Listen to their words. Speak a prayer. Make a difference by being more than a face on a screen or a voice on a phone. Stand in their presence and offer yourself fully to that moment of grace.

Prayer

Father, teach us the important ministry of presence. Give us the time and the resolve to spend some moments in the company of someone who needs our care. Amen.

Day 237

3 John 1: Faithful Parenting

"I could have no greater joy than to hear that my children are following the truth." 3 John 1:4 NLT

Observation

In his third letter, John writes about giving care to traveling teachers who pass through the region in order to support their ministry. He explains that to do so, will allow the church to participate with them in spreading the Good News. It's a reminder to all of us who faithfully support church budgets that when we give to the various ministries of the church, we help push the Kingdom forward. Sometimes, we pray for the work and sometimes we give to the work. Both are essential.

Application

A close pastor friend of mine recently turned my attention to our focus verse. He claims it as his favorite verse. In fact, when his children were young, he would tuck them in at night, touch them on the forehead as if bestowing a blessing, and then he would quote, "I could have no greater joy than to hear that my children are following the truth." Great thought, right? What could give a parent any greater joy than that of knowing that their children were following the truth? Let me remind you that children learn most of what they know from their parents. They watch the example. They listen to the words. They imitate the actions. If you want your children to follow in the truth, then you have to role model truth for them. Your faith... your fidelity to Christ... your commitment to the church and its ministrics, will all be clearly communicated to your children. If you want them to care about matters of faith, then you must care about matters of faith. Why would they develop a passion for things in which you have no interest? Faith matters. Truth is important. The promise of the gospel needs to be told. If you want to have the joy of knowing that your children care about such things, then pour out your life doing the things that matter most. Live with consistency, devotion, and authenticity. What if your child one day turned the phrase and said of you, "I could have no greater joy than to know that my parents are following the truth." Remember, you can't leave a legacy if you don't live a legacy.

Prayer

Father, burden us with the responsibility of carefully role-modeling the faith for the next generation. May we never mar the image of Christ in the eyes of our children. Amen.

"Be merciful to those who doubt; save others by snatching them from the fire; to others show mercy, mixed with fear—hating even the clothing stained by corrupted flesh." Jude 1:22-23 NIV

Observation

Jude is a very short book (only 1 chapter) written by a man whom many believe was the half-brother of Jesus. It is primarily a word of warning to the early believers to beware of heretical teachers in their midst who offer false doctrine. The fear was that these false teachers could lead many away from the faith. Our focus verses serve more as a general word of encouragement to the church. His challenge is three-fold... show mercy to those who doubt (be patient with those who have yet to come to faith), save the unbelievers (notice the strong image of snatching them from the fire of destruction), and third, be careful as you show mercy to sinners making sure that their influence does not corrupt your walk with God.

Application

Let's focus our thoughts for a moment on this image of "snatching (non-believers) from the fire." We must remember the "destruction" from which we save those who have yet to believe in Christ. I am afraid that in our "live-and-let-live" mentality, we have watered-down the threat of eternal punishment. Many are not comfortable with the idea that someone they know and maybe even love could be destined for an eternity of separation from God in which they will suffer agonizing pain and anguish. The "fires of hell" are seldom mentioned in our conversations. To soothe our minds and ease our troubled sleep, we acquiesce into a God-won't-really-punish-folks-forever kind of mentality. Some modern day theologians even offer the idea that maybe hell doesn't last forever. Read the Book! The Bible clearly states that hell is real, punishment will be severe, and that the only way of escape is through faith in Jesus Christ. As believers who know Christ and who affirm the unalterable truth of God's word, we have to be about this task of "snatching folks from the fire." If we really believe the word of God how can we be so flippant about the task of evangelizing the lost? There are people we all know who are in very real danger. How long will we let them live in peril when the hope of salvation is ours to share? Rescue a life. Go share your faith.

Prayer

Father, may we live this day with the burden of sharing hope with those who are lost. May we be faithful to the task of sharing the story of Jesus. Amen.

Day 239 Revelation 1: The Transcendent God

"'I am the Alpha and the Omega—the beginning and the end,' says the Lord God. 'I am the one Who is, Who always was, and Who is still to come—the Almighty One.'" Revelation 1:8 NLT

Observation

The book of Revelation is filled with many images, symbols, numbers, and words of prophecy. Although many of us struggle to understand its meaning, even a casual reading of the text will allow certain key themes to emerge. One of those themes is the power and greatness of Almighty God. As God is revealed through the angel's revelation to John, the reader quickly gains a sense of God's authority, judgment, and ultimate victory. Our focus verse this morning speaks of the eternal nature of God. God is described as the "beginning and the end, the first and the last, the One who has always existed and who will always be." Such a concept is a little difficult for the human mind to comprehend. We think in terms of measurable time—lifespans, days, and years. God, Creator of time and space, is clearly not bound by such parameters.

Application

Why is it important for us to know the eternal nature of God? First, it is a reminder that God sees beyond the day-to-day stuff. Although God is certainly aware of the daily needs, pressures, and worries of our lives, God is also able to see beyond them to the greater things He is seeking to accomplish. God sees the bigger picture and arranges the people and places of our lives to accomplish God's will and purpose. Second, God's love is eternal in nature. The One who called us into being one day will not abandon us on the next. From the moment we draw our first breath, until the moment God calls us to the eternal Kingdom, we will always be under the shelter of Gods love. Third, the presence of God always surrounds us. We will never live a moment apart from the knowledge and protection of God. Because God is eternal in nature, God's presence doesn't fade in and out. God is always with us. Fourth, God will finish the battle. Because God is Lord of heaven and earth, and Creator of all things, God's ultimate will and purpose will be accomplished. What God says, God will do. What God plans, God will complete. God is a promise keeper whose word will never fail. Rejoice, we serve a mighty God.

Prayer

Father, we praise you and thank you for your mighty power, your eternal love, and your unending Kindness towards each of us. Amen.

"Look how far you have fallen! Turn back to me and do the works you did at first. If you don't repent, I will come and remove your lampstand from its place among the churches." Revelation 2:5 NLT

Observation

In the second chapter of Revelation, Jesus speaks through John to the seven churches of Asia Minor. He offers both praise for their faithfulness and rebukes for areas that need improvement. In our focus verse, Jesus offers a strong word of challenge to the Church at Ephesus. His complaint against them is that they have abandoned their first love. They have forgotten how to love God devotedly and how to love each other sacrificially. His promise is that of removing the church if they don't pull it together.

Application

As you may know, there are a number of churches that close their doors each year. There are all kinds of factors that lead to such an occurrence. Some close because of transitions in the neighborhood. Some close because of financial collapse or lack of vision. Some close due to conflict. Some close because of a lack of relevancy. But notice this... some close because God wants them to close. Churches that do not represent God well can do great harm to the Kingdom's work. The church at Ephesus was in danger because they had forgotten how to love genuinely, authentically, and graciously. God called them to repentance so that the mission of the church would reflect the heart of God. So here's my observation... Churches that fail to represent God fully and completely are always in danger of closing their doors. We maintain our vibrancy and place in the Kingdom, not with budgets, strategies, nor committee meetings. We maintain our mission and value as we keep the purposes of God ever before us. We are to love with deep devotion, share Christ with purpose, and worship with passion. At the end of the day our legacy will not be built on the size of our sanctuary, the beauty of our building, nor the programs we implemented. We will be remembered for one thing... how carefully we demonstrated the love of God and the hope of the gospel. Let's keep the lampstand burning.

Prayer

Father, create in our churches the kind of spirit that glorifies you and attracts others to the gospel story. Amen.

"Look! I stand at the door and knock. If you hear My voice and open the door, I will come in, and we will share a meal together as friends."
Revelation 3:20 NLT

Observation

Again in chapter 3, John's revelation points to the problems of the early churches in Asia Minor. His words to the church at Laodicea are well known. Jesus speaks about their need for repentance and change. They have become "lukewarm" and in so doing have lost their effectiveness. But rising up from those words of challenge comes this great word of hope as Christ promised to enjoy fellowship with those who will open their lives to him. Notice that Jesus stands at the door, knocking. It is his desire to dwell within every human heart.

Application

Notice three things about this verse, Jesus' willingness, our response, and the resulting relationship. One of the most enduring paintings of Jesus is that portrait of Jesus standing before a large wooden door, lantern in hand, knocking. The artist intentionally paints no handle on the door, meaning it must be opened from the inside. You've seen the picture a hundred times. Let me play off that image for a moment. We need to understand that Jesus desires to be fully present in each of our lives. He is ready, willing, and able to come into any human life. We don't have to beg, plead, or cajole Christ to come in. He stands ready at our invitation. The struggle for us becomes our willingness to swing the door open completely and fully. There are many who want a little gospel in their lives, but not a lot. Many want to be saved by Christ, but not controlled by Christ. Many want a friend, but not a Lord. Jesus' desire is to come and abide fully within all of us. Lordship implies that we allow him to enter into every facet, every relationship, and every conversation. And notice the result when we "open" our lives to him. He dines with us as a friend. Catch that image... joy, laughter, compassion, grace, no pretense, and no hurry. The relationship becomes one, not of rebuke, but of friendship. We are welcomed in his presence. It's the kind of relationship that each of us would love to have. So why not have it? Take the time to listen today... you may hear a gentle tap at your door.

Prayer

Father, how we thank you for the willingness of Christ to enter our lives and dwell with us. May we open our lives fully before him, knowing that the greater the openness, the greater the joy. Amen.

"You are worthy, O Lord our God,
to receive glory and honor and power.
For You created all things,
and they exist because You created what You pleased."
Revelation 4:11 NLT

Observation

In this opening scene describing the throne of heaven, Jesus sits enthroned, surrounded by a circle of 24 elders. Who these elders are is a bit unclear. Some suggest Church Fathers who have guided the church through various periods of church history. Others suggest that these represent some inner circle of angels. But whoever they are, they offer continual praise to Christ. They express Christ's worthiness to receive praise, honor, and glory. They remind us as readers that all things exist because Christ has created all things, and is therefore worthy to receive praise.

Application

Let's talk for a moment about offering praise to Christ. Obviously he is worthy to receive any and all expressions of praise that we can offer. We would do well to consciously and consistently speak words of praise to Christ each day, maybe even sing a praise song in the car during the morning commute. (Warning... Your fellow commuters may give you very strange looks!) You get the point. We should express our praise each day through the words that leave our mouths. But shouldn't our praise go beyond simple words? Surely we can be more creative than that. Praise should erupt from our attitudes, our outlook, our passions, and our thoughts. Praise should erupt from the simple things we do each day. Everything in word or deed is to be done to his glory, right? So maybe it's important to stop every once in awhile, in the midst of the mundane and ordinary tasks, and ask, "Am I offering praise by what I am doing right this moment?" Try doing this... Get out your calendar for today. Make a little mark every two hours during the day. Then at those intervals, stop for a moment and consider what you are doing and with whom you are interacting. Offering praise? You should be. All of life should reflect the glory of Christ. Be intentional. Be passionate. Be like the angels.

Prayer

Father, may we know the joy this day of offering continual praise. Remind us that all of life should reflect your glory. Amen.

"Then I looked again, and I heard the voices of thousands and millions of angels around the throne and of the living beings and the elders."
Revelation 5:11 NLT

Observation

In this scene, God, who sits enthroned in heaven, holds a scroll, on which is written the names of all those who have been and will be redeemed through the sacrifice of Jesus. The scroll contains seven seals. No one in heaven or on earth is found worthy to break the seals and open the scroll. The Lamb appears, a symbol of the Risen Lord Jesus. At his appearance all of the universe erupts in praise because he is found worthy to open the scroll. The praise that echoes through all the heavens is comprised of the voices of millions of men and angels. Millions...

Application

As I read that passage, I was struck by the mention of the sheer number of those who will be present at that moment to offer praises before God and Jesus. It is no small number. In fact, the word of God states that there will be "thousands and millions." Apparently, some who offer their praises will be in the form of earthly beings, while others will have taken on the form of angels. Though I am uncertain as to how or when or if we become "angelic" in the forever Kingdom of God, I am very certain of one thing... there will be room for all of us who have claimed the name of Jesus as Savior and Lord. Because of his sacrificial death, we will be redeemed, claimed, and welcomed. And yes, we will raise our voices in praise. Here on earth we always struggle with acceptance and inclusion. We try to get in this club or into that organization and get our feelings hurt when we are excluded. Not to worry. In God's Kingdom there is always room for more. There is always room for us. The only requirement is our faith in Christ. He remains the way, and the truth, and the life. We come to the Father through him. So rejoice. You're included. Guaranteed.

Prayer

Father, we thank you that we have already been included in your Kingdom. We praise you for the joy that is ours as we consider that our place is reserved and our destinies are secure. Amen.

"Then a white robe was given to each of them. And they were told to rest a little longer until the full number of their brothers and sisters—their fellow servants of Jesus who were to be martyred—had joined them." Revelation 6:11 NLT

Observation

This chapter describes both the joy and terror that the Day of Judgment will bring upon the earth. In the early verses of the passage, the "Four Horsemen of the Apocalypse" are called forth by the four Creatures who sit around the throne. (Thought by many to be the four gospel writers.) Each horseman is described, along with his duty and power. Our focus verse points to a number of souls who have been kept just beneath the altar of Heaven. These are the souls of those who have been martyred and tortured for their faith. A white robe is given to each and they are told to "rest" a little longer until all those who are yet to be martyred join them.

Application

Two things become evident as we read this passage. First, there is a special place of honor reserved for those who have died for their faith. Those who have perished as a result of defending the faith will be recognized and celebrated by the Father. Their deaths are not in vain. Their reward will be great. Second, there are others who will yet join them. Here in America, we are pretty far removed from religious persecution. We have the freedom to Worship in peace and express our faith openly. Such is not the case for many in our world. For millions, religious persecution is a very real threat. There are many who live in very grave danger because they claim the name of Christ. Many lose their lives because they dare to proclaim their faith in Jesus. Sometimes boldness and obedience results in death. How ashamed should we be when we dumb-down our religious fervor or affiliations just to fit in or find acceptance? This morning, as we sit in the peace and safety that our situation affords us, let us be mindful of those who are suffering for the faith and pray fervently for their deliverance.

Prayer

Father, we thank you that we are part of a global community of faith in Christ. We recognize that many will suffer and perhaps even die before this day is over. We are inspired by their dedication and pray for their deliverance. May they know an inextinguishable joy that is afforded to all the saints who refuse to compromise. Amen.

Day 245 — Revelation 7: A Bigger Gospel

"After this I saw a vast crowd, too great to count, from every nation and tribe and people and language, standing in front of the throne and before the Lamb. They were clothed in white robes and held palm branches in their hands." Revelation 7:9 NLT

Observation

In this passage, John describes another scene in heaven, where a vast throng of people, too great to count, stand before the throne of Heaven. When John asks one of the elders who these people are, the answer is that they are those who have been claimed by Christ in the day of "tribulation" or suffering. Their garments are washed clean by the blood of Christ and they offer praises before him. Like those who once stood on the roadway that led into Jerusalem, they wave palm branches to honor the King of Kings.

Application

As I read this verse, I am once again struck by the universality of the gospel. Notice this vast array of people before the throne of God includes people from every nation, every tribe, every people, and every language. In other words, Christ will claim followers from every ethnicity, race, and culture. The gospel is inclusive enough to reach to all and claim the souls of many. And so, if the gospel embraces such a diversity of people, then shouldn't our worldview become inclusive of many races and faces? Our definition of Christian "brother" has to be radically widened. The gospel includes more than English-speaking, white Americans. The gospel will reach to every nation and people. The question becomes whether or not we become obedient and bold enough to be part of that worldwide reach. Being an inclusive-Christian may demand much of us. It may force us to learn another language, embrace another culture, gain an acceptance of diversity, and learn tolerance for other nationalities. To love Christ is to love all those created in his image. It's a big world and it needs our witness. Go. Pray. Give.

Prayer

Our Father we thank you that you are indeed "our" Father. Remind us that no one has an exclusive claim on your love, or on the gospel story. Teach us to see the world through your eyes and not the limited vision of our own perceptions. Amen.

"Then I looked, and I heard a single eagle crying loudly as it flew through the air, 'Terror, terror, terror to all who belong to this world because of what will happen when the last three angels blow their trumpets.'" Revelation 8:13 NLT

Observation

This chapter describes the terror and destruction on earth that will occur when the seventh seal is broken on the Scroll held in the hands of God. The Lamb breaks open the scroll and when he does, there are seven angels that blow a trumpet blast. With each blast, things seem to get increasingly worse. The earth quakes, the seas and rivers are partially destroyed, and the stars, moon, and sun are partially darkened. Our focus verse describes what will happen just before the last three trumpets are sounded. There will be the cry of a single eagle saying, "Terror, terror, terror, to all who belong to this world."

Application

The imagery of this passage may get increasingly unclear to us as readers, but the message becomes poignantly clear... those who "belong to this world" will receive the full brunt of God's wrath on the great Day of Judgment. Consistently told throughout the pages of the New Testament is the message of salvation through Christ. The Biblical record is clear… those who have put their faith and trust in him, "will not perish but have everlasting life." The "terror" of the Day of Judgment belongs to those who have chosen not to belong to Christ, but who have given their allegiance to the things of this world. For those who have placed their trust in property, possessions, power, and people, there is no hope and no defense in that great and terrible day. The world would do well to hear the warning that this passage offers. And if the love of Christ truly abides in us, we are forced to care for the unsaved, unclaimed world. And so our zeal to tell the story must increase and our passion for the lost must grow. There is an urgency we must embrace. Knowing the time grows ever closer, we must ask, "Have we done enough? Prayed enough? Given enough? Shared enough?" Lives hang in the balance. Let's be faithful witnesses to the things of God.

Prayer

Father, we thank you for the security we have as we approach the Day of Judgment. We thank you that in Christ, we pass out of death and into life. We pray this morning for those yet unreached, unclaimed, and unsaved. May we never tire in telling the gospel story. Amen.

"In those days men will seek death and will not find it: and they will long to die and death flees from them." Revelation 9:6 NASB

Observation

Again in this chapter, John speaks about the destruction that will come on the earth as the various seals are opened on the scroll that is in the hands of God. After the fifth trumpet blast, more calamity will fall on the earth, including an attack by locust-like creatures who will torment the men of earth for months. So great will be the torture that men will "seek death and will not find it." Again, it will be the faithful who will be spared of such tribulation.

Application

It's been said that there is nothing sure "except death and taxes." And such a statement is nearly always correct. Many of us will fear both for as long as we live. Though I can't do much about your taxes, I can offer you a little hope when talking about death. One of the Biblical views of death is to speak of it in terms of a time of transition. We move from this life to the next, from one reality to the other, from one existence to a more glorious one. Death is what will take us from the "troubles of the world" in order to live an eternal life of peace with God. But what if death were not an option? What if death never comes as a welcomed guest to move us to our eternal home? What if we longed to die, but could never make it happen? In other words, what if we have to live forever with the torment of physical aches and pains, sorrows and sadness, regrets and remorse? For those living outside of the gospel, something of such an existence becomes real. There will be those who would love to transition to a better life, but will never have the opportunity. The problem is that many put their absolute trust in things that can't provide eternal life. Christ alone becomes the guardian of our days and the One who will usher us into the life to come. In him, we will have life... abundant and everlasting. So maybe the greater fear is not that we will die, but that we will NOT die. For believers, death brings us into the glorious Kingdom. We prepare for that moment each day that we live on earth, seeking to follow Christ more closely.

Prayer

Father, remind us again, that though we may fear the unknown of death, that we never have to fear its uncertainty. We thank you that whether we live or die, we are claimed by your Grace. Amen.

"So I went to the angel and told him to give me the small scroll. 'Yes, take it and eat it,' he said. 'It will be sweet as honey in your mouth, but it will turn sour in your stomach!'" Revelation 10:9 NLT

Observation

As the tenth Chapter of Revelation unfolds, a mighty angel descends from heaven with a small scroll in his hand. John is instructed to take the scroll and eat it. Such a word of instruction, though seemingly strange to us, was a scenario depicted in the Old Testament among the prophets, particularly Ezekiel. The idea of eating a scroll would represent the fact that God's words had been placed in the mouth of the prophet as he spoke. And so, John is instructed to eat the scroll in order that he might have a word from God to share with the nations. It will be a sweet taste to him, but will become a very difficult word "to stomach" as he shares it with those needing to be told of God's impending wrath.

Application

Chances are that you are not going to eat any sacred writings this morning along with your bacon and eggs. I doubt that you will tear out a few pages of scripture and swallow them down. So maybe the instruction is not a literal one to us as it was to the prophets of old. But the message is clear and the image is poignant. We are to "internalize" the word of God. We are to take it, read it, chew on it, digest it, and live it. We are to do more than simply "bump up" against it from time to time. It is to be that which sustains us and gives us life. It is to be as our daily bread and our life-sustaining breath. Far from being a casual word, it is to be the daily guide, the map for the journey, the word of encouragement, correction, and conviction. God is revealed through scripture. And so it is vital that this day and every day, that you take the time to digest what it says to you. Don't just quickly race through a chapter. Read. Think. Reflect. Pray. Wrestle with the word until you receive the blessing. Getting hungry? Go chew on a few good words.

Prayer

Father, we praise you and thank you that you have chosen to share with us, your divine word. Give us the encouragement this day to read and meditate on what you would choose to reveal to us. Amen.

"And I will give power to My two witnesses, and they will be clothed in burlap and will prophesy during those 1,260 days."
Revelation 11:3 NLT

Observation

In this chapter of Revelation, God gives two witnesses the power to prophesy over Jerusalem for a period of 3½ years, or 1260 days. These two witnesses, who bear truth about God's impending wrath upon the disobedient, are given the ability to do extraordinary things. They can cause the rain to cease, turn water into blood, and cast plagues upon the nations. The imagery leads many to connect these two witnesses with the work of Elijah and Moses. Elijah represents the work of the prophets of God who attempted to bring the nation back to repentance during the time of the demise of the Northern and Southern Kingdoms. Moses represented the Law and sought to bring the nation into compliance by the keeping of God's statutes. These two are also mentioned as appearing to Jesus during the story of the Transfiguration. The overall impression is that these faithful witnesses, though ignored and slain, will rise and their testimony will prove true.

Application

These words of Revelation contain testimony to the enduring truth of God's word. Biblical truth, because it is revealed by God, remains steadfast, accurate, and authoritative. The people of John's revelation attempted to ignore the truth presented by the "two witnesses." They even gloated when the two were slain. But when the time of judgment was revealed, the two witnesses stood victorious and the words of God came to full fruition. Even though culture, popular opinion, and modern thought seek to manipulate truth and water down the message of scripture, God's word is faithful and true. Obedience to the will of God is not an optional or casual pursuit. God demands fidelity to it. We do not have the right to manipulate scripture and Biblical truth to bend to our liking. We don't change the Bible; the Bible changes us. Those who ignore the teachings of God or twist the teachings of scripture to fit personal agenda have underestimated the importance of God's word. Our goal is not to see how we can bend the rules, but to see how the rules need to bend our behavior. My challenge for you is to seek compliance with the word of God, with thought, action, and attitude.

Prayer

Father, forgive us when we foolishly think that we have the freedom to live anyway we would choose. Make us captive unto the word of God. Amen.

Day 250 — Revelation 12: Good News, Bad News

"Then there was war in heaven. Michael and his angels fought against the dragon and his angels. And the dragon lost the battle, and he and his angels were forced out of heaven." Revelation 12:7-8 NLT

Observation

It is in this chapter of Revelation that the imagery and mystery of the book seem to kick into high gear. There are many interpretations that derive from this chapter. For example, the woman who gives birth to a male child... is this a reference to Mary or to the church? What does it mean when the dragon hurls a third of the stars to the earth? Is the wilderness place where the woman is protected by God a reference to the wilderness experience of ancient Israel? What is meant by the serpent spewing "water like a great flood?" It's a lot to unpack and certainly a short devotional thought doesn't allow for much interpretation. The one image that does become rather clear is the image of the "dragon" that battles the Angel Michael and all his forces. The image is clearly one of victory in which Satan is cast out of heaven and forced to dwell on earth.

Application

I find a little good news, bad news in this chapter. The really, really good news is that Satan is ultimately and permanently defeated in Glory. In the Kingdom of Heaven, evil will have no place, no power, and no threat. That's the good news. The bad news is, according to John's vision, that Satan was cast to the earth where he will continue to bring evil until his ultimate and final defeat. Most of us are quite aware of the fact that evil is alive and well on the planet on which we live. The by-products of evil are continually evident... greed, hatred, lust, war, perversion, abuse, and prejudice, just to name a few. We live in the midst of a place where the darkness is strong. Yet, we are not without hope. In fact, we are more than conquerors. Let me remind you of a verse, "You are from God, little children, and have overcome them; because greater is He who is in you than he who is in the world" (1 John 4:4). So yes, the bad news is that we will face evil as long as we live here on earth. But the really good news is that it will not defeat us. The God of Grace is greater than the prince of evil. We walk as "children of the light." We belong to Christ. In him we will claim victory both now and forever more.

Prayer

Father, we thank you that we serve a victorious, risen Lord. In him, may we find our strength, our hope, and our joy. Amen.

"And all the people who belong to this world worshiped the beast. They are the ones whose names were not written in the Book of Life before the world was made—the Book that belongs to the Lamb who was slaughtered." Revelation 13:8 NLT

Observation

In this chapter we read about a beast from the sea and a beast from the land. The beast from the sea has seven heads, ten horns, and ten crowns. Most Bible scholars believe that these reference the world powers of the day that persecuted Christians and offered false worship against God. The final verse speaks of the name of the beast that is given as a number, 666. Again, many scholars who do much with Biblical numerology interpret the number as the name of Nero, one of the worst torturers of the early Christians. More than likely, the chapter is describing the evil power of the Roman Empire, given by Satan, which although very strong, will be very limited. The hopeful word is that the beast will ultimately become defeated.

Application

For me, this chapter speaks to us about choice. Ultimately, we must choose in whom will we place our allegiance. We may choose to follow Christ with great devotion, passion, and absolute allegiance. Or we may choose to put our trust in the power, pleasures, and possessions of this world. More than a few have sold their souls here on earth for the fleeting thrill of power and fame. So, the choice becomes one of a lasting joy or a temporary thrill. Is our vision long-term, or is it shortsighted? Notice our focus verse... "all the people who belong to this world worship the beast." Those folks are headed for ultimate ruin. Others have their names carefully recorded in the Lamb's Book of Life. They will know the joy of dwelling securely and eternally with God. Though persecuted and tortured here on earth, they will find places of prominence and glory in the life that is to come. So the choice remains. Choose to give your loyalty to the temporary powers of this world and you will inherit destruction. Choose to give your loyalty to King of Kings and you will inherit life. Which Kingdom holds your heart?

Prayer

Father, we thank you that we are part of the glorious, victorious, forever, Kingdom of God. Teach us, while here on earth, to serve you faithfully and proclaim your Kingdom boldly. Amen.

"They have told no lies; they are without blame." Revelation 14:5 NLT

Observation

Chapter 14 begins with a description of 144,000 who stand at the throne of God, singing praises, and who have the mark of God and the Lamb on their foreheads. This large group seems to represent a special group of people who are described as being pure and unstained followers of God. They are further described as being the "first fruits" presented to God as an offering of praise and worship. Our focus verse offers a descriptive word, bearing testimony to their purity and lack of deceit... "They have told no lies; they are without blame." The impression is that there is a special place reserved in heaven for those who have loved God with pure hearts and dedicated lives.

Application

I wonder if it is said of any of us that "we are without blame... that we have told no lies." Learning to tell the truth is certainly a discipline that should be associated with every Christian believer. From the time we first became "self-aware," we were taught that it is wrong to tell a lie and distort the truth. As children, we had to learn, sometimes painfully, that telling the truth was always required of us. It was impressed upon us that we should never lie to a teacher, a parent, or any grown-up. At first our struggles with deception centered around simple things... "Did you break Mommy's vase? Did you hit your brother? Did you clean you room?" There was always the temptation to speak deceitfully. As we grow older, the temptation to lie seems to grow worse and the results for doing so, seem to have greater consequences. Maybe we are tempted to lie about a business practice, or about a flirtation, or even about a broken promise. We often try to play the "blame game" and shift the blame for some wrong doing to someone else's shoulders. Truthfully, there are not many of us about which it will be said, "They have told no lies; they are without blame." But let's at least make that the standard... the goal toward which we strive. Because we seek to honor Christ in all things, let's strive to be honest, authentic, pure-hearted, and consistent. Let's strive to live a life that will require fewer apologies when we stand before the presence of Christ.

Prayer

Father, remind us this day, that we always represent you. Remind us that a lack of faithfulness and purity on our part, can damage the reputation of the Kingdom. Make us pure. Make us honest. Make us holy. Amen.

"I saw before me what seemed to be a glass sea mixed with fire. And on it stood all the people who had been victorious over the beast and his statue and the number representing his name. They were all holding harps that God had given them." Revelation 15:2 NLT

Observation

This chapter describes the work of seven angels that come forth from the Temple in heaven to pour out on the earth the seven plagues that will complete God's wrath. Before they depart, John sees in his vision, a vast group of saints who had been victorious over the beast and his statue while on earth. (Probably a reference to those who had stood strong in the midst of Caesar's persecution.) Notice in our focus verse, that they are all holding harps, with which they will sing a great and new song of worship and praise in the verses that follow. The harps on which they will play, have been given to them by God.

Application

Many of the keepsakes that we hold as being "most important" to us, have great significance because of the person who gave us that gift. The object itself may or may not have much value. But because it has been given by someone of significance in our lives, the object becomes quite a treasure. Maybe you own a clock that once belonged to your grandfather. Maybe you possess a piece of furniture that your mother gave to you years ago. Maybe you guard with care, an old Bible that your father once placed in your hands. We all have such treasures... gifts that are important to us because of the giver. Notice in our focus verse that God gives this group of saints a harp on which to play God's praises. That's quite a thing to own, is it not? "Where did you get that lovely harp?" "Oh, God gave it to me one day." Here's the deal... most of us are not going to get a harp from God. But what we do receive from God are the gifts, talents, and abilities that we need to bring God glory and praise. God places in our hands the tools needed to build the Kingdom and offer Him praise. Rather than belittle our gifts, or let them atrophy by a lack of use, we should rejoice in our blessings and actively seek ways of using them for the Kingdom's glory. In other words, don't treat the treasures of God in your life as though they are of little value. Remember who placed those qualities and talents in your life and use them as though they matter most.

Prayer

Father, thank you for giving us those qualities that are meant to bring you praise. May we be faithful stewards of what you entrust to us. Amen.

"Then I heard a mighty voice from the Temple say to the seven angels, 'Go your ways and pour out on the earth the seven bowls containing God's wrath.'" Revelation 16:1 NLT

Observation

Read carefully, this chapter should strike fear in the hearts of all those who have rejected the salvation that Christ offers. In this powerful chapter, the seven angels are sent to pour out God's wrath over all the earth. The results are devastating. The seven demonstrations of God's wrath include: sores, the sea turning to blood, the rivers and streams turning to blood, the sun scorching the earth with heat, darkness covering the land, the Euphrates river drying up, and a horrific earthquake destroying most of the cities of earth. The destruction is relentless and the judgment is severe. The message is clear... those who have chosen to chase after the beast and all his temptations will surely bear the wrath of God.

Application

The choices we make always determine the destinies of our lives. The better the choices, the better the outcome. In the course of our lifetimes, we make billions of choices. Some are simple... what to wear today, what to eat, which route to take to work. Other decisions carry greater importance... where to attend school, what career to choose, what person to choose as a spouse. And then there are destiny-determining decisions... what God to pursue, what faith to embrace, which path to take. Both great and small, the decisions made will define who we are and whom we will become. The problem is that most of us make very poor decisions. We don't always weigh out the consequences. We don't always seek wise counsel. We don't always take the time needed to think rationally. So how can we make the choices that offer life? Simple... we pray for wisdom. Doesn't it make sense to include in all of our choices the Sovereign Lord who has created heaven and earth? Doesn't it make sense to seek the counsel of God, who is all-knowing, all-powerful and who has the ability to judge the hearts of all men? In the book of James, God promises to give wisdom to all those who seek it. We are simply told to "ask God who gives to all men generously and without reproach" (James 1:5). In other words, if we will ask, God will provide. I bet you have a few decisions to make today. How will you choose to make those decisions? Rely on your own intellect, or seek the wisdom of God? Ask, seek, knock. God longs to help.

Prayer

Father, may we have the sense required to seek your wisdom in all our choices. Amen.

Day 255 Revelation 17: Victory Has Already Been Claimed

"Together they will go to war against the Lamb, but the Lamb will defeat them because He is Lord of all lords and King of all kings. And His called and chosen and faithful ones will be with Him."
Revelation 17:14 NLT

Observation

This chapter of Revelation describes in detail a great prostitute that will gather the nations and rulers to do battle against the Lamb. The image is clearly a reference to the city of Rome and to the far-reaching Roman Empire. As John describes his vision, there are references to the various leaders of the Roman Empire and to the persecutions that are inflicted upon the righteous followers of Christ. The vision goes on to reveal how the various kings of the earth will go to battle against the Christian faith. But just as the reader might begin to feel a sense of fear and defeat, this triumphant verse is given, "but the Lamb will defeat them because He is Lord of all lords and King of all kings."

Application

This verse represents the dominant theme of the book of Revelation. John consistently reminds his hearers that there is great hope, promise, and victory even in the midst of overwhelming persecution, because the Lamb wins. The power of Christ will be victorious over sin, death, and evil. Those joined to the Lamb through faith will experience that victory with him. As I read these verses, I am reminded of the experience I sometimes have as I watch a football game replay, one in which I know that my team has won. As I watch the game, there is no stress, no anxiety, and no fear because I know the ultimate outcome. When there is a fumble, an interception, or maybe the quarterback is thrown for a loss, again, there is no worry, because I know the final score even before I watch the game. There is always great confidence in knowing the final outcome. So it is in matters of life and death and faith. Because we know the ultimate outcome is victory, because we know that Jesus Christ is the King of all kings and Lord of all lords, we walk through this life with the assurance and hope of the gospel. Sure, there will be setbacks, heartaches, and difficulties, but the life we live will be one of ultimate triumph and joy. In whatever defeats you may suffer, take hope. The Lamb wins.

Prayer

Father, we thank you that as believers in Jesus Christ, we have the promise of ultimate victory and hope. Amen.

"For her sins are piled as high as heaven,
and God remembers her evil deeds." Revelation 18:5 NLT

Observation

This entire chapter of Revelation is devoted to a description of the destruction of Babylon, the great and wicked city. (Again, the reference is to Rome and the far-reaching influence, power, and domination of the Roman Empire.) In this chapter, John recounts the words of the angels sent to earth to proclaim judgment on all those who have been included in the selfish prosperity and rampant immorality that have been a part of the culture of the empire. The angel reminds the reader that all those who have embraced such a culture will be caught up in the wrath of God.

Application

There is an important word in this chapter for all of us who live in the midst of a prosperous and immoral culture and who are unwilling to speak out against her sins. Let's be honest in our interpretation... I don't think the pages of Revelation were written specifically as an indictment against the American culture. However, I do think the warnings have great relevance for our day and our situation. The problem is that most Christian believers in America have refused to accept the responsibility of being "salt and light." Rather than speak up, we shut up. Rather than calling our culture to change, we compromise with it. Not wanting to "ruffle feathers," and not wanting to cause friction, we have slowly allowed immorality, greed, and insensitivity to slowly infiltrate our society. We have allowed tolerance to give way to acceptance. We refuse to proclaim the standards that are acceptable to God. Do we possibly think that our lack of zeal for the Christian faith, our silence, and our compromise are pleasing to God? Do we think we hold no responsibility for teaching and living out the faith? Notice that in the destruction described in the Revelation all those who participated in the immorality of Rome, along with all those who let it happen, were caught up in the day of wrath. So what about our generation of believers... are we seeking to usher in the Kingdom of God or are we content to let our culture become shaped by popular opinion and individual ethic? Let's be bold. Let's be vocal. Let's be inspired. Let's be faithful.

Prayer

Father, burden us with the responsibility for our nation. With love and grace, along with boldness, may we proclaim your ways and speak your truths. Amen.

"'She has been given the finest of pure white linen to wear.'
For the fine linen represents the good deeds of God's holy people."
Revelation 19:8 NLT

Observation

These words describe the wedding feast of the Lamb. Consistent throughout scripture is the image of church as the "Bride of Christ." In this passage, John writes about the moment when the church will be presented in all splendor and glory. The bride will be adorned in the finest white linen. The explanation given is that the fine linen represents the good deeds of the church. All of the noble causes, victories claimed, lives rescued, and ministry offered will be part of the celebration on the day when Christ shall come.

Application

The local church is not always the glorious bride of Christ that it was intended to be. Churches have a way of getting it all wrong. Churches can be cantankerous, judgmental, and exclusive, filled with people who fuss and fight, who have selfish motivations, and judgmental attitudes. Rather than share the love of Christ, churches can be mean-spirited and even offensive to the outside world. That happens because the church is made up of people... flawed, broken, and stubborn. But the good news is that within those flawed, broken, and stubborn people, the Spirit of Christ dwells. And because of that Spirit, sometimes the church gets it right. There are moments when the church acts compassionately, gives unselfishly, and ministers effectively. There are days when the Bride is adorned with grace and love and gladness. When the body of Christ gathers, a wonderful thing sometimes happens. The worst of our attitudes, opinions, and thoughts are transformed into more noble, more glorious, and more loving deeds. We become better as we serve together. The truth is simply this... the more we give ourselves over to the Spirit of Christ as individuals, the more the church becomes the radiant Bride. The good deeds that we will accomplish, the lives touched through ministry, and the servant-initiatives that we pursue will all bring honor and glory to Christ. May God help each of us to be Spirit-led so that the churches of which we are a part will be Kingdom focused.

Prayer

Father, bless the Church. May it forever represent your desires and offer your compassion. Amen.

"And anyone whose name was not found recorded in the Book of Life was thrown into the lake of fire." Revelation 20:15 NLT

Observation

This chapter of Revelation reveals the final judgment of the earth and the ultimate defeat of Satan. (Within this chapter is the mention of a 1000 year period in which Satan is bound and in which Christ will reign, prior to the ultimate defeat of Satan, whom after being released from the "pit" is cast into the lake of fire for ultimate destruction. The interpretation of this 1000-year period has been the subject of much controversy in theological circles. Even the discussion of whether or not the time period is literal or figurative has been widely contested.) The greater "take-away" from this passage is to see the ultimate victory of Christ and the assurance of salvation for those who are joined to him through faith.

Application

There are always a few "lists" on which you want to find your name. For example, if you go to a fine restaurant and the crowds are large, it's good to have your name on the reservation list. You also want your name to appear on the will-call list at the big game, or on the list for those getting a tax refund. Maybe you have had the experience of waiting to see if your name appears in the right column following a try-out of some kind. Sometimes having your name on the right list makes all the difference. This is the message of Revelation 20. In the midst of great upheaval, destruction, and judgment, those whose names appear on the right list, have nothing to fear. That list of course, is the Lamb's Book of Life in which all the names of faithful believers have been written. The list determines who enters into the splendor of heaven and, conversely, those who do not. So how do you get your name on the list? By doing good deeds? By giving faithfully to noble causes? By knowing the right people? No. It's a faith list. Your name is written in that place according to one single criterion... whether or not your faith and trust have been placed in Jesus Christ. The Biblical record is clear, "He who has the Son has the life. He who has not the Son of God does not have the life" (1 John 5:12). Your confession of Jesus as Lord makes all the difference. It's what inscribes your name on the list that matters most.

Prayer

Father, we thank you for the inclusion we have because of our faith and trust in the Lord Jesus Christ. May our gratitude find expression in our evangelism. Amen.

"He will wipe every tear from their eyes, and there will be no more death or sorrow or crying or pain. All these things are gone forever."
Revelation 21:4 NLT

Observation

This chapter of Revelation reveals an amazing look at the New Jerusalem and the new world order. If you are looking for a description of the "streets of gold" then this is the chapter to read. The angel reveals to John all of the glorious splendor of the New Jerusalem, which will descend from the heavens. The city is all but indescribable both in size and splendor. It is built as a perfect square, 1400 miles on each side! Yes, the streets are gold, as are the buildings and dwelling places. In that place, there will be no need for day and night for the glory of God will continually illumine the city.

Application

One of the images that is so vital to the description of the New Jerusalem is of God dwelling with God's people. There is no Temple, or designated place of worship in the city, because the presence of God permeates every single facet and corner. In other words, the entire city will become the dwelling place of God. But more than all the gold and precious stones that are described, notice the promise of our focus verse... no more tears, no more death, sorrow, crying, or pain. When the saints of God dwell secure in the city of God, with God's very presence surrounding them continually, there is no longer cause for grief, or sorrow, or pain. The emotions and troubles of this world will quickly fade in the presence of God's fully revealed glory. Imagine the day when all is well and when our tears are forever erased. Such a hope is the promise of God's word for those who claim the Lordship of Christ. So if you are struggling today with sorrow, grief, and pain, please know that "weeping lasts only for the night..." A day is coming when victory will be claimed and joy will win out over grief.

Prayer

Father, we thank you today for the promise of an endless life of joy. How thankful we are as we live this day in the abiding hope of your forever Kingdom. Amen.

"Blessed are those who wash their robes. They will be permitted to enter through the gates of the city and eat the fruit from the tree of life."
Revelation 22:14 NLT

Observation

The final chapter of the Book of Revelation ends on a triumphant note. The reader is reminded again of the splendor of God's glory. Much like the account in Genesis, the final chapter speaks of a tree of life that will stand beside the river of life that flows through the middle of heaven. The promise of God's word is that those who "wash their robes," meaning those who repent of their sins and seek the forgiveness of God, will be permitted to enter through the gates of the new Jerusalem and eat from the tree of life. The message is very clear... those who seek the grace of God through faith in Christ will enjoy the bliss of knowing eternal life.

Application

Driving home from church last night, I hit something in the road that punctured my tire. And so the first order of the day was to remove the tire, plug the hole, and put it back in place. No matter how careful I attempted to be, it was still a very dirty job. My hands were filled with grime and my clothes were covered in dust and dirt. At the end of the job, I obviously was not "presentable" for work. It was necessary for me to wash-up and change my clothing so that I could take on the tasks of another busy day at church. The parallel is obvious. It's the same situation in which we find ourselves as we think about our eternal destiny. No matter how careful we are we are still going to find ourselves covered with the dirt and grime of life here on earth. Our sins, both great and small, both unintentional and carefully committed, have a way of making us unfit for heaven. As the writer of Revelation suggests, we have to "wash our robes." It's called repentance. We must begin to see our sins through the eyes of God. We must see our mistakes, our shame, and our soiled lives. Such conduct is not received well in glory. But if we will "confess our sins, He is faithful and just to forgive us our sins, and CLEANSE us from all unrighteousness" (1 John 1:9). Before you go any further into this bright new day, why not wash your robe? Confess your sins to your Loving Father and let grace wash you clean.

Prayer

Father, we thank you this day for your grace that washes us clean. Forgive us, again. And give us the strength to please you this day in action, word, and attitude. Amen.

Donate to Support GOODFAITHMEDIA

Good Faith Media, publishing under the Nurturing Faith imprint, is a registered 501(c)3 nonprofit organization. For Good Faith Media to remain competitive in the marketplace as a small nonprofit, we depend on the generosity of donors to support personnel and overhead costs. We are incredibly grateful for the support and generosity of our donors. Please consider donating today by scanning on the QR Code on this page with your phone or visiting goodfaithmedia.org/donate.

In Good Faith,
Rev. Dr. R. Mitch Randall
CEO

www.ingramcontent.com/pod-product-compliance
Lightning Source LLC
LaVergne TN
LVHW010607100826
845148LV00014B/2886

* 9 7 8 1 6 3 5 2 8 2 4 0 5 *